Against the Tide

_____

Against the Tide

AN INTELLECTUAL HISTORY OF
FREE TRADE

Douglas A. Irwin

PRINCETON UNIVERSITY PRESS

PRINCETON, NEW JERSEY

Library of Congress Cataloging-in-Publication Data

Irwin, Douglas A., 1962–
Against the tide : an intellectual history of
free trade / Douglas A. Irwin.
p.   cm.
Includes bibliographical references and index.
ISBN 0-691-01138-9 (alk. paper)
1. Free trade.   I. Title.
HF1713.I78   1996
382′.71—dc20   95-25447   CIP

This book has been composed in Times Roman

Princeton University Press books are printed
on acid-free paper and meet the guidelines
for permanence and durability of the Committee
on Production Guidelines for Book Longevity
of the Council on Library Resources

Printed in the United States of America
by Princeton Academic Press

1   3   5   7   9   10   8   6   4   2

For my parents

———————————

CONTENTS

ILLUSTRATIONS

Following Page 98

ACKNOWLEDGMENTS

ECONOMISTS and other intellectuals have debated for centuries the merits of free trade as an economic policy. The purpose of this book is to provide a history of the free trade doctrine, first tracing the idea up to Adam Smith and the classical economists, and then examining the leading controversies about theoretical objections to free trade since that time. I have been guided by George Stigler's plea for the history of economic thought to concentrate more on ideas and concepts than on individuals and personalities, as well as by a desire to write a book that is both relatively short (considering the tremendous time span covered herein) and relatively accessible to non-economists (despite the sole focus on theoretical considerations in the second half).

In this effort I have been aided by numerous friends and colleagues, and I am pleased to record my appreciation to them. I am indebted to Jagdish Bhagwati, not only for his comments on part of this manuscript, but for several years of encouragement and discussion about the subject matter of this book. John Chipman provided generous assistance in the form of several careful readings of manuscript drafts. I also wish to thank others who graciously took the time to comment upon various sections of the book: Max Corden, Donald Dewey, Barry Eichengreen, Ronald Findlay, Gene Grossman, Adam Klug, Anne Krueger, and Arvind Panagariya. Their advice is greatly appreciated. Claire Friedland also gets my thanks for helping track down prints and photographs of various economists.

I gratefully acknowledge the financial support of the Lynde and Harry Bradley Foundation through a grant to the Center for the Study of the Economy and the State (with a tip of the hat to its director, Sam Peltzman). Financial support has also been provided by the University of Chicago's Graduate School of Business. Among other things, this funding enabled me to partake of Herbert Somerton Foxwell's priceless bequest to subsequent generations of scholars, the Goldsmiths's Library of Economic Literature at the University of London.

Finally, I thank my wife Marjorie for her exemplary patience during the long gestation of this book and my daughter Ellen for not accidentally deleting any of my files in the search for computer games, and my daughter Katie for being a welcome addition as this book was being completed.

Against the Tide

_____

INTRODUCTION

> . . . the doctrine of free trade, however widely
> rejected in the world of politics,
> holds its own in the sphere of the intellect.
> —Frank Taussig (1905, 65)

"THE PROPOSITION that freedom of [international] trade is on the whole economically more beneficial than protection," Harry Johnson (1977, 187) once wrote, "is one of the most fundamental propositions economic theory has to offer for the guidance of economic policy." This proposition has survived repeated scrutiny from economists ever since Adam Smith made his celebrated case for free trade in the *Wealth of Nations* and continues to receive overwhelming support from professional economists today.[1] The aim of this book is to describe how free trade came to occupy such a commanding position in economics and how free trade has maintained its intellectual strength as a doctrine despite the numerous arguments that have arisen against it over the past two centuries.

To address these distinct but related themes, this book is divided into two parts. The first discusses the reasons for the widespread presumption in economic thought prior to Adam Smith that an appropriate use of import tariffs and other government trade restrictions was likely to constitute a better economic policy than free trade. Such a view reached an apex in the mercantilist literature of the seventeenth century. The general presumption in favor of trade restrictions was gradually tempered by criticisms from within the mercantilist camp, as well as by a quite different form of reasoning from moral philosophers and others in favor of economic freedom. Eventually, the presumption was undermined by the more theoretical analyses of Adam Smith and the classical economists. Smith and the classicals firmly established among economic thinkers the proposition that free trade is superior to import protection in producing a greater amount of aggregate economic wealth. From this point on, the burden of proof in economic debates has been with those advocating restrictions on trade to demonstrate how such policies would contribute to a country's economic wealth.

---

[1] One survey reports that 95 percent of economists questioned in the United States (and 88 percent of economists surveyed in the United States, Austria, France, Germany, and Switzerland) support or support with qualification the proposition that "tariffs and import quotas reduce general economic welfare." See Bruno Frey et al. (1984).

"Defeated as a general theory," John Stuart Mill ([1848] 1909, 920) once observed, "the protectionist doctrine finds support in some particular cases"—or, perhaps more accurately, *seeks* to find support in some particular cases. The book's second part examines how the economic analysis behind the case for free trade has remained compelling or has been compromised by the various criticisms and counterarguments that have arisen since the time of Adam Smith. With uncanny regularity, a major theoretical argument for protection surfaces every few decades and sparks a controversy among economists about the strengths and weaknesses of the case for free trade. The infant industry argument for protection has achieved the widest popular recognition, for example, but many other cases exist, most recently the theory of strategic trade policy in the 1980s.

Although each and every theoretical claim made against free trade is not addressed, the book concentrates on what I believe to have been the most important and contentious debates over the economic merits of free trade. After describing the economic arguments against free trade and for protection, the ensuing debate over the validity and generality of these theoretical cases among their proponents and those defending the free trade doctrine is examined. I conclude by assessing the extent to which the theoretical argument has been accepted as a legitimate and important qualification to the case for free trade, dismissed as a *curiosum* with little relevance to economic policy in practice, or simply rejected on grounds of logic. I emphasize the historical aspects of these debates and, while I attempt to impart a sense for where things stand today, I also seek to avoid delving into the often voluminous current literature on many of these topics.

Although the first part of the book on the intellectual origins of free trade is necessarily more eclectic in considering a broad array of arguments for and against free trade, this second part focuses more narrowly on the *economic* arguments against free trade and for protection. By economic arguments I mean those that address the economist's stringent standard of whether a particular policy will increase aggregate economic wealth, where wealth is suitably defined as, for example, real national income.[2] Debates surrounding the economics of free trade and protection all revolve around the question of efficiency: how does a particular trade policy affect a country's ability to use its limited resources (in terms of primary factors of production, such as land, labor, and capital) to produce the greatest possible real income, which in turn enables it to procure a larger set of all goods.

Critics of the economic approach frequently contend that the criterion of wealth is too narrowly materialistic and excludes other more important

---

[2] Chapter 12 takes up in greater detail the thorny distributional issues that arise in taking economic welfare rather than economic wealth as the criterion for economic policy.

societal considerations. Hence, there are a multitude of noneconomic arguments for protection that are a perennial feature of trade policy debates.[3] These include political arguments (e.g., protection of an industry for national defense) or others broadly geared toward achieving some vaguely national or social objective (e.g., greater self-sufficiency in certain goods). Such considerations may or may not be important, but they will not be considered here. Economic analysis can contribute little in determining whether or not such policy objectives are advisable in themselves, although it can say something about the relative costs of various means (i.e., the policy instruments) by which noneconomic objectives can be achieved.[4]

Before proceeding further, I should briefly discuss what is meant by free trade, a term that has no unique definition. In theoretical terms, free trade generally means that there are no artificial impediments to the exchange of goods across national markets and that therefore the prices faced by domestic producers and consumers are the same as those determined by the world market (allowing for transportation and other transactions costs). These prices reflect the relative scarcity and abundance of goods around the world and constitute a relevant opportunity cost to domestic firms and households (and hence to the country as a whole) because the world market is always available for trades at those prices. In practical terms, free trade describes a policy of the nation-state toward international commerce in which trade barriers are absent, implying no restrictions on the import of goods from other countries or restraints on the export of domestic goods to other markets.[5] Under a policy of protection, by contrast, government policies discriminate against imported goods in favor of those produced within the country, usually with the aim of sheltering domestic producers from foreign competition through tariffs, quantitative restrictions, or other import barriers. These trade interventions distort the prices faced by domestic producers and consumers away from those arising in the world market.

In his monumental *History of Economic Analysis*, Joseph Schumpeter (1954, 370) emphasized the importance of "distinguish[ing] sharply the development of free-trade *policies* and free-trade *doctrines* from the development of *analysis* that was associated with both." This book is on intel-

---

[3] This criticism of the economic approach is fine so far as it goes, but proponents of noneconomic arguments for protection often assert that such a policy will benefit the nation without stating exactly the criteria being used to reach such a conclusion. Invariably, their application of any consistent standard for assessing the costs and benefits of various policies is weak or nonexistent.

[4] See, for example, Jagdish Bhagwati and T. N. Srinivasan (1969).

[5] A somewhat more limited, nineteenth-century definition holds that under free trade the government does not discriminate between domestic and foreign goods in its tax or regulatory policies. In this case, free trade does not necessarily mean that tariffs are zero if equivalent direct taxes on domestic production ensure that no preference is given to domestic over foreign goods.

lectual history and attempts to relate how economic analysis has supported or invalidated the free trade doctrine; that is, it is on the economic *analysis* that was associated with the free trade *doctrine*. This book is not an economic history of commercial policy and will neither address the particular trade policies of a given country at any given time nor explain what accounts for those policies, whether they be free trade or protectionist. This book will also not consider the fascinating but quite distinct question of whether economic analysis (or those toiling away on such ideas, often in obscurity) had any influence on economic policy.

By concentrating almost exclusively on the realm of economic analysis, intellectual thought will often be divorced from the political and economic circumstances of the period in which it takes place. While this is sometimes a questionable procedure, for such a context is often useful to gain a greater appreciation of historical writings, I defend it here on two grounds.[6] The first justification is simply a matter of convenience: the agenda of this book had to be limited to prevent it from growing to unmanageable proportions. Perhaps more to my specific purposes, understanding the political, social, and economic background of intellectual thought may enrich one's knowledge of the development and propagation of ideas, but this context is generally not required to assess the quality and durability of economic thought and analysis as logical propositions. One need not understand the intricacies of the late seventeenth-century competition in the textile trade to appreciate the brilliance and originality of Henry Martyn's defense of free trade in 1701. One need not know about the political debates surrounding U.S. trade policy in the 1980s to understand the economic reasoning behind the theory of strategic trade policy.

Circumstances may give rise to a body of work—new theories and fresh analysis, for example—and circumstances are needed to determine whether such work is applicable or not in terms of actual policy. But without a conceptual framework, awareness of such circumstances cannot assist in understanding the challenges that seek to refute an existing theory. There is really no way of evaluating a substantive economic argument that purports to have some generality as a proposition except by exploring its underlying logic. Economic analysis is simply a principled conceptual framework for understanding various economic phenomena and evaluating the effects of various economic policies; it has the advantage of imposing certain standards of thought and logic, although admittedly these standards can change with time. Perhaps an undercurrent running through this book

---

[6] Although I propose this as my general approach, I feel free to deviate from it where appropriate, such as in chapter 13 where circumstances help us to understand the nuances of (and appreciate the limits to) John Maynard Keynes's argument for protection.

is how the conceptual framework for evaluating commercial policy has evolved over time.

This approach to the history of economic science is quite Schumpeterian, even if Schumpeter himself often strayed from this objective. Schumpeter (1954, 10, 337n) also taught that the motive behind economic thought—whether political, ideological, or self-interested—is irrelevant in assessing the analytical merits of an economic argument: "The scientific character of a given piece of analysis is independent of the motive for the sake of which it is undertaken. . . . The most stubborn class interest may induce true and valuable analysis, the most disinterested motive may lead to nothing but error and triviality . . . motive has nothing to do with the objective nature of a proposition." This needs to be kept in mind when probing the advocacy of either free trade or protection, particularly in dealing with the mercantilist literature of the seventeenth century, since self-interested pleas on both sides are well represented in the economic literature. This book cares less about *who* was saying what and *why* they were saying it than it cares about *what* was said and whether it continued to make *sense* after undergoing the critical scrutiny of contemporary commentators and later scholars.

In relating economic analysis to doctrine, this book describes the evolution of ideas about free trade if for no other reason than sifting through historical writings gives us an acquaintance with how theoretical and conceptual knowledge about economic policy has evolved and has been accumulated over time. Acquaintance with this knowledge gives us a perspective in which we can understand where current insights about trade policy have come from and perhaps enables us to draw some tentative conclusions about the relationship between economic science and its implications for economic policy.

In describing the controversies of past decades and centuries, I will rely extensively on quotations from primary sources to provide a flavor of the reasoning and argumentation originally employed by the participants themselves. (I have taken the liberty of modernizing the spelling and capitalization in many instances.) This book focuses largely on the English language literature, partly because an overwhelming preponderance of economic inquiry and debate has taken place in Britain. In some periods, such as the mercantilist epoch, economic thought in places such as France, Spain, and elsewhere closely mirrored that in Britain (or vice versa), so little is lost in focusing on the English economics literature as representative of that prevailing elsewhere. In other periods, such as the nineteenth century, Britain has been unique as the home to the best and most innovative economic analysis in the world. While focus on the English language literature would produce a severely biased study of free trade *opinion* or *policies* in general, it does not so seriously affect a study of the economic *analysis* of free trade.

The major conclusion of this work can be anticipated at the outset. Adam Smith made a forceful case for free trade in 1776 against the tide of prevailing economic doctrines. His powerful arguments proved intellectually convincing. Since then the free trade doctrine has been subjected to close and searching scrutiny, and has sometimes come under serious doubt. Yet the idea of free trade, the conceptual case for free trade, has survived largely intact against the tide of repeated critical inquiry. This examination has, of course, shed light on the strengths and weaknesses of the free trade doctrine, and has sometimes resulted in valid theoretical qualifications to the doctrine. The case for free trade has endured, however, because the fundamental proposition that substantial benefits arise from the free exchange of goods between countries has not been overshadowed by the limited scope of various qualifications and exceptions. Free trade thus remains as sound as any proposition in economic theory which purports to have implications for economic policy is ever likely to be.

PART ONE

Origins of the
Free Trade Doctrine

Chapter One

EARLY FOREIGN TRADE DOCTRINES

ON WHAT GROUNDS was the case for free international trade rejected among intellectuals prior to the appearance of Adam Smith's *Wealth of Nations* in 1776? On what conceptual basis did the case for free trade finally emerge and come to be accepted by economic thinkers? Attention to these two questions will be the focus of the first half of this book. Economic thought in support of free trade arose and coalesced in reaction to the seventeenth- and eighteenth-century mercantilist literature, which frequently proposed government regulation of foreign trade (through tariffs and other trade interventions) to achieve various objectives. Before discussing this literature in chapter 2, early attitudes toward trade and descriptions of trade policy, especially those prevailing in the Graeco-Roman and Judeo-Christian traditions, will be briefly considered. The ideas generated over the course of these early centuries, despite the absence of any significant economic analysis, strongly influenced the intellectual basis of later considerations of commercial policy.

. . .

ANCIENT ATTITUDES TOWARD FOREIGN TRADE

Because land transportation was costly in antiquity and the sea provided easy access to the various regions in the eastern Mediterranean and beyond, ancient attitudes toward the sea lend insight into some of the earliest recorded thoughts about the nature and desirability of foreign commerce. Greek and Roman writers were ambivalent about whether location near the sea was a blessing or a curse. Some believed that God created the sea to promote interaction and to facilitate commerce between the various peoples of the earth. Around A.D. 100, for example, Plutarch (1927, 299) wrote of the sea's beneficence: "This element, therefore, when our life was savage and unsociable, linked it together and made it complete, redressing defects by mutual assistance and exchange and so bringing about cooperation and friendship . . . the sea brought the Greeks the vine from India, from Greece transmitted the use of grain across the sea, from Phoenicia imported letters as a memorial against forgetfulness, thus preventing the greater part of mankind from being wineless, grainless, and unlettered." Without the exchanges made possible by the sea, Plutarch maintained, man would be "savage and destitute."

Others writers and poets were more suspicious of the sea. Instead of charitable in its effect, the sea brought contact with strangers who could disrupt domestic life by exposing citizens to the bad manners and corrupt morals of barbarians. With this lament, Horace (1960, 27) saw the sea as being deliberately divisive: "In vain has God in his wisdom planned to divide the land by the sea's separations, if, for all that, ungodly ships are crossing the waters that he placed out of bounds." These contrasting views of the sea led naturally to dual views of trade, either that it presented an opportunity to enhance national prosperity or that it threatened the security of the nation and its economy. This dichotomy has continued throughout history to the present day, and popular preferences about free trade may hinge in part on which preconception about international commerce (as a threat or an opportunity) one adheres to.

Ancient attitudes toward those engaged in commercial activity also lend insight into early conceptions of trade. In the fourth and fifth centuries (B.C.), philosophers in ancient Greece looked down on traders and merchants, especially in retail trade, as occupations beneath the dignity of citizens. Plato, for example, suggested in the *Republic* that well-governed cities ensure that shopkeepers and laborers were chores reserved for inferior persons who were useless in other tasks. In *Politics*, Aristotle (1932, 51) maintained that the use of money in exchange arose from exporting and importing and condemned such nonbarter trade as "justly discredited (for it is not in accordance with nature, but involves men's taking things from one another)." Indeed, it was widely believed that citizens should not participate in commerce, but that it should be left entirely to resident aliens who were deprived of political rights and kept separate from the civic life of the Greek city-state. According to Johannes Hasebroek (1933, 39), this separation of commerce and citizens meant "not only was [Greek foreign commerce] not based upon national labour, but it was divorced from national life." Consequently, there was no real economic issue of imports displacing domestic production by citizens; indeed "the very notion of a protective tariff . . . was utterly unknown to the classical Greek world."

Philosophers and statesmen in ancient Rome generally shared this contempt and low regard for merchants and trade, as John D'Arms (1981) has described. To them, a trader or middleman, who bought goods at one price and retailed them at a higher one without changing the nature of the product, was engaged in a vulgar occupation. Such activity was beneath the dignity of elite citizens, and laws even prohibited senators from participating in commerce.

In *De Officiis*, Cicero concurred with this perspective in the context of international trade, but made an exception for commerce that either entailed great benefits or that improved the intelligence of the people. Despite acknowledging the great advantages arising from trade, Cicero (1913, 155) could not bring himself to endorse such commerce positively, but only to view it less negatively: "Trade, if it is on a small scale, is to be considered vulgar; but if wholesale and on a large scale, importing large quantities from all parts of the world and distributing to many without misrepresentation, it is not to be greatly disparaged." Pliny (1969, 2: 385–86) was more positive in his attitude toward overseas trade, praising the construction of public works, such as roads and especially harbors, which "linked far distant peoples by trade so that natural products in any place now seem to belong to all . . . and without harm to anyone."

The Greeks recognized that those party to a voluntary exchange of goods reaped a benefit from such transactions and appeared to acknowledge that this also applied to overseas trade. Certain writers also appreciated the public benefits that resulted from the arbitrage of goods prices undertaken by profit-seeking merchants. Xenephon (1918, 519–21) mocked the notion that merchants performed their jobs out of inherent love for the occupation:

> So deep is [the merchant's] love of corn that on receiving reports that it is abundant anywhere, merchants will voyage in quest of it: they will cross the Aegean, the Euxine, the Sicilian sea; and when they have got as much as possible, they carry it over the sea, and they actually stow it in the very ship in which they sail themselves. And when they want money, they don't throw the corn away anywhere at haphazard, but they carry it to the place where they hear that corn is most valued and the people prize it most highly, and deliver it to them there . . . all men naturally love whatever they think will bring them profit.

As it was to develop centuries later, the case for free trade was based in large part on the gains arising from the division of labor. If individuals or regions or countries specialized in the production of goods for which they are most suited and then exchanged those goods amongst each other, total output and consumption can be larger than in the absence of such specialization. Perhaps Plato's (1930, 153) greatest contribution to economics was his early discussion (dating from about 380 B.C.) of the advantages of the division of labor in the *Republic*: "The result [of such a division], then, is that more things are produced, and better and more easily when one man performs one task according to his nature, at the right moment, and at leisure from other occupations." In this discussion Plato also observes that "it is practically impossible to establish the city in a region where it will not need imports." To carry on trade, Plato realized that the state will need merchants and that domestic production of certain goods will exceed domestic requirements so the excess can be exchanged for imports.

Perhaps this constitutes an implicit extension of the benefits of the division of labor and specialization to trade between regions or countries, but

Plato was far from explicit in making the connection. About twenty years after Plato, Xenephon linked the extent of the division of labor to the size of the market. Xenephon (1914, 2: 333) noted that in small towns each individual was employed in multiple tasks, whereas in large cities each individual concentrated on a single task: "It follows, therefore, as a matter of course, that he who devotes himself to a very highly specialized line of work is bound to do it in the best possible manner." Close though he came, he never quite spelled out the notion that interregional trade effectively expands the size of the market, permits a more refined division of labor, and yields material economic benefits. Both Plato and Xenephon described the division of labor with reference to the individual but did not apply the notion to the different trading regions of the world.

The development of these concepts also did not translate into a favorable view of foreign commerce. Indeed, Greek philosophers advocated restrictions on trade because of the moral and civic danger associated with it. They believed that contact with foreign strangers would be detrimental to law and order and could undermine the moral fabric of society. Aristotle argued in *Politics*, for instance, that in choosing the ideal location for a city, preference should be given to territories that ensured maximum self-sufficiency because this would limit trade to "natural" domestic barter, promote national defense, and preserve domestic morals—all by reducing contact with foreigners. Self-sufficiency was deemed far better than dependence on overseas trade, although self-sufficiency did not imply complete autarky because Greek philosophers reluctantly conceded that at least some foreign trade was imperative.[1] If the exposure to undesirable foreigners could be avoided, then Aristotle (1932, 561–63) agreed that trade "is advantageous in respect of both security and the supply of necessary commodities . . . importation of commodities that they do not happen to have in their own country and the export of their surplus products are things indispensable." For example, a seaport active with trade could be adjacent to the city, but separated (perhaps by a wall) so that it could be closely monitored by the authorities. Aristotle stressed, however, that even under these conditions the import trade should stop at the provision of certain essential items, such as food for consumption and timber for shipbuilding, and not be carried beyond this point for the sake of profit. Thus, Aristotle (1926, 45) advised statesmen to know which exports and imports were "necessary" in order to obtain commercial agreements with other countries to furnish them with what they required and to ensure just conduct in trade. Plato (1914, 2: 185) was more explicit than Aristotle in stating the means for attaining self-sufficiency: no duties should be placed on exports and imports, but the government shall ban imports of "foreign imported mate-

---

[1] This point is discussed further in Marcus Wheeler (1955).

rials for a use that is not necessary" and should forbid exports of "any of the stuff which should of necessity remain in the country."

What accounts for this, at best, tepid approval of trade in ancient times? The economic gains from trade were clearly recognized by Greeks and Romans, but they were wary of trade for a number of noneconomic reasons. Each group thought itself superior to foreigners and had no desire to promote extensive contact with others. Early writers were suspicious of merchants and traders and raised questions about their activities and their loyalty as citizens. "It has been argued that the contempt of the Greeks for industry [and trade], as it is displayed in so much of their literature, is really an aristocratic prejudice," Hasebroek (1933, 39) suggests, "but it was really far more profound and widespread than that." Yet trade was far from unreservedly condemned and the goal of self-sufficiency was never thought to imply complete autarky. Early thinkers reluctantly admitted that some amount of trade was indispensable and, consequently, merchants and tradesmen had to be tolerated but not encouraged.

THE DOCTRINE OF UNIVERSAL ECONOMY

The doctrine of universal economy evolved from early favorable accounts of the sea to become the leading theory as to why trade between regions should be accepted as beneficial and even be permitted to run its course free from interference. The doctrine held that Providence deliberately scattered resources and goods around the world unequally to promote commerce between different regions.[2] According to Jacob Viner (1976, 27–54), in its best expressions the doctrine uniquely combines four distinct elements of thought. First, it embraces the stoic-cosmopolitan belief in the universal brotherhood of man. Second, it describes the benefits to mankind arising from the trade and exchange of goods. Third, it embodies the notion that economic resources are distributed unequally around the world. Finally, it attributes this entire arrangement to the divine intervention of a God who acted with the deliberate intention of promoting commerce and peaceful cooperation among men.

The doctrine was developed by philosophers and theologians in the first several centuries (A.D.). Seneca, the stoic philosopher writing sometime just before the year 65, came close to expounding the doctrine fully. Seneca (1972, 115) noted that Providence arranged the natural elements such that "the wind has made communication possible between all peoples and has joined nations which are separated geographically." However, his state-

---

[2] Jacob Viner (1991, 42) has gone so far as to say "the doctrine . . . has claims to be the oldest and longest-lived [economic] doctrine we know of" and suggests that it is a precursor to modern factor-endowments theory of international trade.

ment is not far in advance of Plutarch's quoted earlier. Philo (1929, 2: 73–74) of Alexandria presented the doctrine at greater length:

> He has made none of these particular things complete in itself, so that it should have no need at all of other things. Thus through the desire to obtain what it needs, it must perforce approach that which can supply its needs, and this approach must be mutual and reciprocal. Thus through reciprocity and combination. . . . God meant that they should come to fellowship and concord and form a single harmony, and that a universal give and take should govern them, and lead up to the consummation of the whole world.

Origen (1953, 245), an early Christian writer, wrote around the year 245: "Lack of the necessities of life has also made things, which originate in other places, to be transported to those men who do not possess by them the arts of sailing and navigation; so that for these reasons one might admire the providence."

Perhaps the finest early statement of the doctrine came from the fourth-century pagan Libanius, who declares in his *Orations* (III):

> God did not bestow all products upon all parts of the earth, but distributed His gifts over different regions, to the end that men might cultivate a social relationship because one would have need of the help of another. And so He called commerce into being, that all men might be able to have common enjoyment of the fruits of earth, no matter where produced.[3]

This succinct statement has all the four elements that Viner pointed to and was often cited centuries later as the epitome of the universal economy doctrine. Libanius taught several students at Antioch who helped propagate it further. St. Basil (1963, 65) wrote that the sea "becomes a patron of wealth to merchants, and it easily supplies the needs of life, providing for the exportation of superfluous articles by the prosperous and granting to the needy the remedy for their wants."[4] Another student of Libanius, the theologian St. John Chrysostom (1874, 124–25), echoed his teacher's words in writing that the sea connects various lands to prevent distance from discouraging friendships and to make the earth as if it were one home inhabited by all.

Theoderet (1988, 30), a theologian at Antioch and a student of Chrysostom's, was among the most able expositors of the doctrine, writing around 437 in his "Discourse on Providence":

> For the Creator, wishing to instill harmony into human beings, made them depend on one another for various needs. For this reason we make long voy-

---

[3] I am not aware of any modern English translation of this Oration. The quoted version is from Grotius ([1625] 1925, 2: 199).

[4] St. Ambrose (1961, 83), writing around the year 389, echoed Basil: "The sea is good . . . as a carrier of merchandise, thereby linking distant people together."

ages on sea, seek our needs from others, and bring back cargoes of what we want; nor has providence allocated to each section of the earth all the needs of mankind lest self-sufficiency should militate against friendship. Accordingly the sea lies in the center of the earth, divided into countless bays like the market place of a huge city, providing an abundance of every necessity, and receives many sellers and buyers and brings them from one place to another and back again.

In the centuries since these writings, the doctrine of universal economy has been a recurring theme in the case for free trade. The doctrine was embraced by both mercantilists and free traders alike, although in the case of the former it could become somewhat distorted to serve the particular purposes of its expounder. It became a part of natural law teaching and made its way into the cosmopolitan doctrines of philosophers that flourished during the enlightenment and thereafter.[5] If we consider this doctrine along with the earlier Greek and Roman doctrines, the economic gains arising from trade clearly appear to be appreciated at an early stage. A complete economic case for free trade could be constructed from the notion that resource endowments were apportioned differently across regions and the idea that the division of labor could take on a regional character. In many instances, however, concerns about the noneconomic effects of trade made free international commerce seem undesirable to writers during this period.

EARLY CHRISTIAN AND SCHOLASTIC ECONOMIC THOUGHT

The infiltration of the doctrine of universal economy into Christian theology notwithstanding, the early Christian Fathers treated economics as a branch of ethics and, somewhat like the Greeks and Romans before them, condemned commerce as abetting fraud, promoting avarice, and encouraging worldly gains.[6] Many early Christians took their cue from the biblical text in which the Lord had thrown merchants out of the temple. Employment in trade was therefore held to endanger seriously one's soul by risking temptation with the sins of covetousness, lying, cheating, and fraud, to name but a few. "Let Christians amend themselves, let them not trade," remonstrated St. Augustine (1888, 320) in the early fifth century. Although Augustine sympathetically entertains a hypothetical plea from a moral and honest trader engaged in foreign commerce, he ultimately rejects the plea: "For they that are active traders . . . they attain not to the grace of God." Rejecting the teaching of Libanius, St. Ambrose wrote that "God did not make the sea to be sailed over, but for the sake of the beauty of the element.

[5] An occasional reference to the role of providence in shaping trade by the classical economists can also be found in the work of James Mill, John Ramsay McCulloch, Nassau Senior, and Robert Torrens, but not John Stuart Mill.

[6] For a brief overview, see Jacob Viner (1978, 34–38).

The sea is tossed by storms; you ought, therefore, to fear it, not to use it . . . use it for purposes of food, not for purposes of commerce."[7] Ambrose believed that commerce exists because the covetous desires of merchants exceed the restlessness of the sea. So unreservedly is commerce condemned that his translator remarked that Ambrose "does not appear to recognize the possibility of honest trade."[8]

Although this broad condemnation of commerce appears similar to the Christian and the Graeco-Roman objection to foreign trade, there are several important differences. The Christian hostility was not based on an aristocratic bias and somewhat greater sympathy was had for the small, poor trader who was thought more likely to be virtuous. Unlike the Greeks and Romans before them, the Christian fathers were not interested in local self-sufficiency and did not advocate cultural autarky, wishing instead to spread their religious and other moral values around the world. However, they shared with the Greeks and Romans concerns about the moral aspects of trade, such as its role in promoting avarice and luxury, to which Christians added that trade diverted too much attention toward worldly concerns. They also shared the distinction between commercial activities which improved the nature of the good by adding to its value, and those in which the same good was merely sold at a higher price and were therefore worthy of condemnation.

Medieval scholastic thought continued with suspicions about commercial activity, but became decidedly more liberal as the centuries passed. The scholastics were learned clerics and academics (writing from roughly 800–1500) who drew upon both church teachings and the Greek philosophers (especially Aristotle) to investigate and extend all aspects of human knowledge. Scholastic doctrine was more apt to view commerce with moral indifference but with ultimate judgment hinging on the goals and circumstances of a particular line of business.[9] Emphasis was again placed on the distinction between using one's own labor in a productive economic activity and the lower profession of the mere trader or merchant. Reward for one's labor was justifiable in church teaching, whereas the temporal position of traders or merchants, those who produced nothing but merely exchanged goods for profit, was less certain. Traders tended to be associated with fraud, avarice, and other sins because the excessive pursuit of gain led to temptation and potentially endangered one's soul.

St. Thomas Aquinas, the leading medieval theologian, contributed to the reduction of doctrinal sanctions against trade and traders by subtly shifting the presumption in favor of merchants. In his *Summa Theologica*, written in the thirteenth century, Acquinas accepted three types of economic activ-

---

[7] Quoted in F. Homes Dudden (1935, 2: 549).

[8] See F. Homes Dudden (1935, 2: 548).

[9] See George O'Brien (1920, 144ff) and Raymond de Roover (1974).

ity as useful for society: the storing of goods, the importation of necessary goods, and the transport of goods from abundant to scarce regions. Although there was "a certain debasement" attached to trading, Aquinas (1947, 2: 1517) argued that pecuniary gain, "though not implying, by its nature, anything virtuous or necessary, does not, in itself, connote anything sinful or contrary to virtue." The motive and conduct of the trader was essential in ascertaining the moral worth of an economic activity.

Aquinas accepted the legitimacy of the trade, but he was more infused with an Aristotelian preference for domestic to foreign trade than influenced by the universal economy tradition. Aquinas (1945, 75ff) recognized that food could be provided either through local production or overseas trade, but believed local production superior because self-sufficiency was "more dignified." Also following Aristotle, Aquinas warned that contact with foreigners would disrupt civic life. Furthermore, "if the citizens themselves devote their life to matters of trade, the way will be opened to many vices," such as greed, corruption, and a failure of virtue. Yet Aquinas also conceded that "trade must not be entirely kept out of a city, since one cannot easily find any place so overflowing with the necessaries of life as not to need some commodities from other parts" and there being no reason why overabundance in one place should not be transported to another place. Aquinas therefore counseled the "moderate use" of merchants for the purposes of trade. In placing scholastic thought firmly within the Aristotelian framework, Aquinas moved scholastic thought in a pro-trade direction by accepting that some trade was necessary for every country while not slipping in derisive comments about traders and their occupation.

Aquinas's views formed the basis for later doctrine, and several of his contemporaries and followers presented commerce in an even more favorable light. In the early thirteenth century, Thomas of Chobham stated that "commerce is to buy something cheaper for the purpose of selling it dearer. And this is all right for laymen to do, even if they do not add any improvement of the goods which they bought earlier and sell later. For otherwise there would have been great need in many regions, since merchants carry that which is plentiful in one place to another place where the same thing is scarce."[10] This is similar to Xenephon's passage about the benefits of trade and points out the useful service that merchants provide in shipping goods between different markets.

Indeed, Richard of Middletown, writing in the late thirteenth century, set forth a clear statement of the causes and benefits of international trade:

> According to the right dictates of nature all men ought to come to one another's mutual assistance in their contracts, inasmuch as they are living under one sovereign, which sovereign is God. Now it is like this, that some parts of

[10] Quoted in Odd Langholm (1992, 54–55).

the world abound in some things of utility for human use, in which other countries are lacking, and vice versa. For example, this part of the world abounds in corn and is lacking in wine and another abounds in wine and is lacking in corn . . . and therefore the right judgment of natural reason is that a country which abounds in one thing suitable for human use should come to the aid of another part of the earth which is lacking in this (thing), so that that (country) which abounds in corn aids another country lacking in corn and also receives aid from that one which abounds in wine . . . the transaction is made according to the right judgment of reason, and the service rendered is as great as the one received and yet that transaction is profitable, for a measure of corn in the country which abounds in wine is worth more than a cask of wine in that country.[11]

Middletown's statement of trade was far in advance of its time and was apparently not explored by others. The subsequent scholastic literature elaborated very little on the point that trade is driven by the abundance and scarcity of different goods in different countries or that the prices of goods in different market would tend to equalize with trade. Furthermore, there was virtually no discussion of commercial policy.

By the fifteenth century scholastic doctrine had moved even beyond the "certain debasement" stigma of trade to viewing commerce as an ethically neutral activity, in which one had only the potential to be corrupted. As Carletus put it in his *Summa Angelica*: "Commerce in itself is neither bad nor illegal, but it may become bad on account of the circumstances and the motive with which it is undertaken."[12] Theologians of later centuries did not depart radically from the scholastic tradition. John Calvin (1953, 1: 115) weaved the universal economy doctrine with concerns about the morality of trade, thereby capturing the widespread, and by now age-old, ambivalence about commerce:

Navigation cannot, indeed, be condemned on its own account; for, by importing and exporting articles of merchandise, it is of great advantage to mankind. Nor can any fault be found with this mode of intercourse between nations; for it is the will of God that the whole human race should be joined together by mutual acts of kindness. But as it most frequently happens that abundance leads to pride and cruelty, Isaiah reproves this kind of merchandise, which was the chief source of the wealth of the land. Besides, in that merchandise which is carried on with distant and foreign nations, there is often a large amount of tricks and dishonesty, and no limit set on the desire of gain.

Indeed, not all later theological statements on trade were as liberal as those scholastic views cited above because not everyone would accept Aquinas's relatively positive view of commerce. Martin Luther, for exam-

---

[11] Quoted in Langholm (1992, 333–34).
[12] Quoted in George O'Brien (1920, 150).

ple, thought that a country should be more than content with its domestic trade, arguing that abundance at home would eliminate recourse to foreign trade as a means of overcoming domestic scarcity. Luther ([1520] 1966, 212–14) also objected to the importation of certain types of nonessential and ostentatious goods: "God has certainly given us, as he has to other countries, enough wool, flax, and everything else necessary for the seemly and honorable dress of every class. We do not need to waste fantastic sums for silk, velvet, gold ornaments, and foreign wares." Luther even advocated restraining imports of spices as well, a trade that aroused too much pride and envy. "I do not see that many good customs have ever come to a land through commerce," he concluded sourly.

Still, the scholastic tradition established by Aquinas evolved with time to consider trade and commerce much less objectionable than previously had been the case. Regardless of the skeptical pronouncements about trade by clerics and scholastics, countries were in fact engaging in a substantial amount of trade that necessarily raised important legal and policy issues. And Aquinas's concept of "natural law," using human reason to interpret the divine plan of what is right and just, later proved influential in establishing new grounds for allowing free commerce. Francisco de Vitoria, a Dominican theologian and international jurist, applied this concept to the relationships between nations and thereby became one of the founders of international law. In defending the sovereign rights of Indians against the Spanish explorers, Vitoria ([1557] 1917, 151–53) also asserted that "Spaniards have a right to travel into the lands" of the Indians, "provided they do no harm to the natives," and, indeed, the natives may not prevent them from doing so. This proposition, he argued, "is derived from the law of nations (*jus gentium*), which either is natural law or is derived from natural law." Furthermore, "it is an apparent rule of the *jus gentium* that foreigners may carry on trade, provided they do no hurt to citizens." For example, "neither may the native princes hinder their subjects from carrying on trade with the Spanish; nor, on the other hand, may the princes of Spain prevent commerce with the natives." Thus, "if the Spaniards kept off the French from trade with the Spaniards, and this not for the good of Spain, but in order to prevent the French from sharing in some advantage, that practice would offend against righteousness and charity."

Here we find it asserted that trade, regardless of its moral implications, is a right of nations. Of course, a Spanish insistence that free trade is a dictate of natural law in the sixteenth century when Spain was a great maritime power, like the same Dutch insistence in the seventeenth century when the Netherlands was a great maritime power, can be dismissed as reflecting pure national self-interest. But Vitoria's natural-law-of-nations approach spawned another intellectual program that, despite resolute free trade beginnings, eventually failed to have the necessary intellectual cohesion to make it a lasting case for free trade.

The Natural Law Philosophers

The natural law philosophers of the seventeenth and eighteenth centuries, the final strand of pre-mercantilist Western intellectual thought on trade considered here, drew heavily upon late scholastic thought. Like Vitoria, these thinkers applied Aquinas's idea of natural law to international relations. Their aim was to derive, from a moral and jurisprudential perspective, an objective code describing the proper and just conduct of the nation-state that is in accord with nature, just as the scholastics had for individuals. While there was scant economic reasoning in the natural law approach, this significant branch of intellectual thought made important prescriptions for the conduct of commercial policy.

Following Vitoria, early natural law thinkers established the principle of freedom to trade in rather sweeping terms admitting of few exceptions. Francisco Suarez ([1612] 1934, 2: 347) believed that all international commerce should be free, not as an obligation from natural law but from the law of nations (*jus gentium*), "which all the various peoples and nations ought to observe in their relations with each other." "A state might conceivably exist in isolation and refuse to enter into commercial relations with another state even if there were no unfriendly feeling involved," he asserted, "but it has been established by the *jus gentium* that commercial intercourse shall be free, and it would be a violation of that system of law if such intercourse were prohibited without reasonable cause." No state is ever so self-sufficient, Suarez held, that it can avoid foreign trade altogether.

Alberico Gentili ([1612] 1933, 86ff) even argued that war may be justified against countries refusing to trade: war is "natural, if it is undertaken because of some privilege of nature which is denied us by man. . . . For example, if right of way is refused, or if we are excluded from harbours or kept from provisions, commerce, or trade." At the same time, imports could rightfully be prevented if they were judged harmful by a country's moral code, exports of gold and silver could be forbidden, and foreign merchants could be denied access to the interior of a country. "Strangers have no right to argue about these matters, since they have no license to alter the customs and institutions of foreign peoples. . . . But if apart from these cases or other isolated ones there is interference with commerce, it is justifiable to make war."

Hugo Grotius ([1604] 1950, 1: 218ff), the most illustrious natural law thinker of the period, made a similar point in strongly denouncing the Portuguese exclusion of the Dutch from the East India trade: "Under the law of nations, the following principle was established: that all men should be privileged to trade freely with one another." No state can forbid access or trade of other subjects with its subjects as the "right to engage in commerce pertains equally to all peoples" and the right to traverse the sea without interference. Grotius also suggested that those "prevented from sharing in those things which are common property under the law of nations" have just grounds for war (255). Therefore, he ([1608] 1916, 63–64) concluded, "freedom of trade is based on a primitive right of nations which has a natural and a permanent cause; and that right cannot be destroyed, or at all events it may not be destroyed except by the consent of all nations."

In his magnum opus, *The Law of War and Peace*, Grotius ([1625] 1925, 2: 199ff) reiterated these points: "No one, in fact, has the right to hinder any nation from carrying on commerce with any other nation at a distance. That such permission be accorded is in the interest of human society and does not involve a loss to anyone." Grotius's point is that a state cannot deny the opportunity of other states to trade with one another. It is in this sense that there should be freedom to trade, not that a state's own trade cannot be restricted. But Grotius comes close to accepting even this interpretation of free trade: although he allows small taxes on trade to compensate for security and other expenses associated with foreign commerce (such as lighthouses), he rejects taxes that had nothing to do with the merchandise in question. "Surely equity does not permit the imposition of any burdens that have no relation to the merchandize actually in transit. . . . If, however, expenses are incurred in furnishing protection for the merchandize . . . then a tax may be levied upon the merchandize in order to make reimbursement."

Grotius played a major role in resurrecting the universal economy doctrine by documenting its early sources. Grotius ([1604] 1950, 218) endorsed the idea as follows: "For God has not willed that nature shall supply every region with all the necessities of life; and furthermore, He has granted preeminence in different arts to different nations." Consider, for instance, the ocean breeze: "Are these things not sufficient indications that nature has granted every nation access to every other nation?"

Despite serving as an authority for later scholars, Grotius failed to receive much support for his specific views on freedom to trade. For example, he greatly influenced the German legal scholar Samuel Pufendorf on many issues, but Pufendorf went on to make substantial and damaging exceptions to the natural law of nations case for free trade. Indeed, Pufendorf so severely weakened the previous tenets of the philosophy in its general admonition for open trade relations that a state could justify almost any commercial policy, however restrictive. Citing Grotius and Libanius, Pufendorf ([1660] 1934, 368ff) first presented a version of the universal economy doctrine: "A great advantage arises for all peoples from commerce, which makes compensation for the niggardliness, as it were, of the soil, which is not equally productive of everything everywhere, and causes the product of one place only to appear to have a habitat in every land. . . .

So it is highly inhuman to wish to deny a native of our world the use of those goods things which the common Father of all men has poured forth."

"Yet such an assertion," Pufendorf added, "allows many restrictions." A nation is not obliged to trade in goods not essential for human life, such as luxury goods, and may prohibit export of such essential goods if there is domestic scarcity or if "the commonwealth will prosper by forbidding them." A country can prevent trade "if our country thereby would lose a considerable profit, or in some indirect way suffer harm." According to Pufendorf, a country can justifiably restrict exports of a distinctive breed of horse to prevent its reproduction abroad and could favor its own citizens over foreigners in the case of taxation of goods. Imports could not just be taxed but should even be prohibited "either because the state may suffer some loss from its importation, or that our own citizens may be incited to greater industry, or that our wealth may not pass into the hands of foreigners."

In allowing so many exceptions, Pufendorf almost completely undermined the law of nations case for free trade. From this point on, the cosmopolitanism of the earlier natural law thinkers was largely abandoned in favor of rules that supported the independent sovereignty of the nation-state in its right to restrict trade. Two prominent natural law writers in the eighteenth century provided additional support for the view that state restrictions on trade and commerce would not violate natural law or the law of nations. Emmerich de Vattel ([1758] 1916, 43) stated: "When the rulers of a State wish to turn commerce into other channels without, however, forcibly controlling it, they subject the articles, which they intend to keep out of the country, to such import duties as will discourage their consumption. . . . Such a policy is perfectly wise and just . . . ; for every Nation may decide upon what conditions it will receive foreign goods, and may even refuse to receive them at all." And Christian Wolff ([1764] 1934, 38) argued that "since no nation has the right to sell its goods to another nation without its consent, if any nation is not willing that certain foreign goods be brought into its territory, it does no wrong to the nation from which they came, consequently if the bringing in of foreign goods and their sale is prohibited, there are no just complaints by foreigners concerning this prohibition."[13]

These statements are diametrically opposed to the early natural law doctrines set down by Grotius and others. The subtle change that had taken place was that the right of all countries to engage in trade had been trans-

---

[13] Wolff (1934, 107) apparently contradicts himself when he later writes: "Since nations are bound by nature to engage in commerce with each other, as far as it is in their power, and it is not possible for any nation to prohibit or prevent another nation from engaging in commerce with any other, by nature freedom of commerce between nations must be left untrammelled, as far as possible."

formed into the right of all countries to regulate their own trade. With such shifting standards, almost any protective measure could be interpreted as justifiable on some grounds. The cosmopolitan character of the universal economy doctrine as handed down by the early natural law philosophers became unrecognizable. Whatever the underlying causes of this marked intellectual shift (the rise of nationalism may be a factor), the law of nations proved to be a spineless doctrine, incapable of providing an intellectually consistent set of arguments for free trade.

· · ·

This sketch of pre-mercantilist doctrines on commercial policy has been perfunctory in part because little of note was written prior to the seventeenth century on the proper state policy toward international trade. Economic questions were considered peripheral to ethical and other related concerns. What writings there were on economics tended to address such issues as value, price, and usury rather than international trade. Greek and Roman writers have passages on the division of labor, but their attention was largely directed elsewhere; the scholastics were mainly interested in ethical aspects of economic activity and deriving codes of conduct in the marketplace from divine law; the natural law thinkers tried to create objective moral standards that were in accord with the law of nature. The use by Grotius and others of "natural right" to justify free trade as a general proposition is interesting, but from the standpoint of economic analysis it is, as Joseph Schumpeter (1954, 371) put it, "perfectly devoid of scientific meaning." Still, the cosmopolitan doctrines of some scholastics and natural law thinkers was an important intellectual bequest to those who later speculated about trade policy, and a clear intellectual thread links Aristotle to Aquinas to Vitoria to the natural law jurists and then to the Scottish moral philosophers, particularly Francis Hutcheson, one of Adam Smith's teachers. But before reaching this stage, the many mercantilist writers on trade whose published output accelerated over the course of the seventeenth century must be contended with.

Chapter Two

THE ENGLISH MERCANTILIST LITERATURE

AT THE SAME TIME that the natural law philosophers were composing their weighty tracts, a pamphlet literature on commercial topics was blossoming in England. Though offering a multitude of perspectives on trade and trade policy, these writings have acquired the label "mercantilist" because certain themes characterize this enormous and wide-ranging literature. Most authors encouraged state regulation of trade with any of several objectives in mind, such as "the accumulation of treasure or bullion; the promotion of national wealth or economic growth; the achievement of a favourable balance of trade; the maximization of employment; the protection of home industry; and the increase of state power."[1] In many respects, the conclusion that the state should oversee if not restrict international trade was not fundamentally different from that of earlier traditions. But the mercantilists' method of reasoning and their justifications for this conclusion were distinctive, and certainly more elaborate and refined than had previously been the case. Furthermore, mercantilist doctrines not only constitute a major epoch in economic thought, but provide the immediate backdrop for the emergence of free trade thought.

. . .

The seventeenth century saw the publication of numerous tracts on a range of economic subjects, particularly international trade, by English merchants, government officials, and other pamphleteers. The tremendous expansion of trade and overseas exploration during this period prompted many attempts, however incomplete and unsophisticated, to persuade the government to undertake a particular economic policy or simply to understand and explain the essential nature of trade and its relationship to such issues as employment, money and credit, immigration, shipping, and colonies. The exclusive focus here will be on how trade was described in general by seventeenth- and eighteenth-century writers and how this description influenced their conclusions about commercial policy, particularly import duties.[2] The focus will also be confined to the English litera-

---

[1] See A. W. Coats (1992, 46), who helps sort out the stereotypes and confusions that frequently afflict assessments of mercantilist thought.

[2] The seventeenth-century English economics literature on international trade is so vast that the brief discussion here cannot do it full justice. For general surveys on mercantilism, see

ture, although quite similar ideas were expressed elsewhere in Europe at this time.[3]

The stage was set for the early mercantilist writings in the emerging economics literature of sixteenth-century England. These pamphlets and tracts were penned by individuals interested in public affairs, not by theologians or legal philosophers, and consequently were amoral and practical, not ethical or legalistic, in their discussion of economic issues. For the first time, economic phenomena (and their implications for state policy) were considered worthy of study in themselves and not simply as a by-product of ethical, moral, and legal concerns. What few writings there were on economic issues in the sixteenth century focused primarily on such questions as usury, inflation, land allocation and enclosures, but commercial policy became increasingly important toward the end of the century.

The first notable tract of the period is *A Discourse of the Commonweal of this Realm of England*, attributed to Sir Thomas Smith, which was written around 1549 but originally published in 1581 and reprinted several times in the seventeenth century. Like others before him, Smith ([1581] 1969, 62ff) recognized that trade between nations was indispensable: "For although God is bountiful unto us and sends us many great commodities, yet we could not live without the commodities of others." The universal economy doctrine was reinterpreted as the hand of providence creating the conditions for trade to take place, not just to enable the consumption of a greater variety of commodities, but also to encourage trade in similar goods as a means of sharing risk: "God has ordained that no country should have all commodities, but that that one lacks, another brings forth, and that that one country lacks this year, another has plenty thereof commonly that same year, to the intent men may know that they have need one of another's help." Although Smith argued for a favorable balance of trade ("we must always take heed that we buy no more of strangers than we do sell them; for so we should impoverish ourselves and enrich them"), he also clearly recognized the interdependence of exports and imports: "If we keep within us much of our commodities, we must spare many other things that we have now from beyond the seas." There is also acknowledgment that world prices (at which international trade is conducted) constitute the relevant opportunity cost for a country: "But since we must have need of other[s] and they of us, we must frame our things not after our own fantasies but to follow the common market of all the world, and we may not set the price

---

Joyce Appleby (1978), Terence Hutchison (1988), and Lars Magnusson (1994). For particular surveys on trade, see Jacob Viner (1937, 1–118), Chi-Yuen Wu (1939, 13–74), and Joseph Schumpeter (1954, 335–76).

[3] On various aspects of European mercantilist thought, see Charles W. Cole (1931) on France, Lars Magnusson (1987) on Sweden, and Marjorie Grice-Hutchinson (1978) on Spain.

of things at our pleasure but follow the price of the universal market of the world."

Despite these benefits of trade, Smith advocated protecting domestic producers and taxing luxury imports. Smith particularly objected to exporting goods that would be processed abroad and imported once again: "They make of our own commodities and send it us again, whereby they set their people awork and do exhaust much treasure out of the realm." Smith thought it "better for us to pay more to our own people for these wares than less to strangers" and would either forbid imports or raise duties on them until domestic goods became cheaper. As a result, "our own men should be set awork at the charges of strangers; the customs should be borne all by strangers to the King, and the clear gains remain all within the realm." Smith also complained about "trifles . . . for which we either pay inestimable treasure every year or else exchange substantial wares and necessary for them, for the which we might receive great treasure." Such unnecessary imports "that come hither from beyond the seas that we might either clean spare or else make them within our realm."

Like the Smith of 1776 fame, the themes discussed and the conclusions reached by this Smith set the tone for the subsequent two centuries of economic literature. Maintaining a favorable balance of trade and manufacturing raw materials at home represented two key planks in the mercantilist platform. The criticism of imported luxury goods and the focus on employment in import competing sectors were also hallmarks of the mercantilist perspective. In some sense, the subsequent two centuries of mercantilist literature simply reiterates and elaborates on these themes expounded, though not necessarily originated, by Thomas Smith in the mid-sixteenth century.[4]

By the dawn of the seventeenth century, English writers were developing a broad perspective on trade that departed in several fundamental ways from the ideas of scholastics and natural law thinkers.[5] Two features of the contemporary international economic environment shaped mercantilist thought on trade: the vast expansion of world trade and overseas exploration, and the rise of nation-states as political entities. The first opened up tremendous opportunities that merchants as a class were positioned to exploit for themselves and their country. As a result, instead of viewing merchants with suspicion and commercial activity as disreputable, their role in society was no longer denigrated and their contribution to national wealth was no longer disparaged. The mercantilists praised traders for serving the well-being of the nation and lauded foreign trade as a means by which the

---

[4] W. H. Price (1906), for example, traces English concerns about the balance of trade back to the fourteenth century.

[5] For a comparison of scholastic and mercantilist thought, see Raymond de Roover (1955).

nation could achieve wealth and riches. The merchant was often glorified as a vanguard of the nation's prosperity and security. Thomas Mun (1664, 3) spoke of the "nobleness of this profession" in referring to merchants, and Thomas Milles (1599, [19]) wrote that "the merchant of all men is to be favored, cherished, and encouraged in all Commonwealths."

This more favorable attitude toward merchants arose not just because the authors themselves were often merchants arguing on self-interested grounds, but because the expansion of world trade and exploration promised to secure greater domestic wealth and prosperity.[6] Attention to wealth and prosperity was perhaps not the most laudable objective in the minds of clerics and other philosophers, but it naturally proved appealing to lay writers. Unlike earlier thinkers who wished to discourage participation in trade, mercantilists expressed enthusiasm for policies that would promote merchants and expand trade (or conversely prevent the decay of trade) in a direction shaped by the government. Early mercantilists were often so effusive in expressing their desire to see trade flourish that they seemed to exaggerate its importance for the country's well-being. International trade was believed to be "the only mean to enrich this kingdom," and "the very touchstone of a kingdom's prosperity."[7] "[T]he greatness of this kingdom depends on foreign trade," it was said, and exports were "the touchstone whereby the wealth of England is tried, and the pulse whereby the health of the kingdom may be discerned."[8]

By contrast, mercantilists often dismissed the contribution of domestic commerce to the country's prosperity. "If [we exchange] amongst ourselves, the commonwealth cannot be enriched thereby; for the gain of one subject is the loss of another," Mun (1664, 127) maintained. "And if we exchange with strangers, then our profit is the gain of the commonwealth." Josiah Child (1693, 29) agreed, stating that those involved in foreign trade (merchants, fishermen, and cattle breeders) "do principally, if not only, bring in wealth to a nation from abroad," whereas domestic traders (nobility, lawyers, physicians, and shopkeepers) "do only hand it from one to another at home." John Pollexfen (1697a, 40) argued similarly: "Buying, selling, and trading amongst ourselves, may occasion that one man may grow richer than the other, but hath no immediate influence upon the enriching or impoverishing of the nation." In addition, domestic commerce hinged on the course of foreign trade; according to William Petyt (1680, 11), "The home trade in every nation hath dependence on the foreign

---

[6] Of course, Jacob Viner (1937, 59) points out that "the great bulk of the mercantilist literature consisted of tracts which were partly or wholly, frankly or disguisedly, special pleas for special economic interests," but clearly such tracts should not be disqualified from reasoned consideration for analytical merit.

[7] See Roger Coke (1670, 4) and Thomas Mun (1621, 1).

[8] See Josiah Child (1693, 135) and William Petty (1690, 51).

trade." "For when trade flourishes, the King's revenue is augmented, lands and rents improved, navigation is increased, the poor employed," Edward Misselden (1622, 4) put it. "But if trade decay[s], all these decline with it." This belief persisted among mercantilists throughout the century and only a few writers held that the home trade was equivalent to or more advantageous than international trade.[9]

Mercantilists sometimes justified their zeal for foreign trade by invoking the doctrine of universal economy. The doctrine was employed to vindicate the activities of merchants and to emphasize the distinctive role of international trade among the various commercial occupations. Misselden (1622, 25) stated the doctrine in these words:

> And to the end there should be a commerce amongst men, it hath been pleased God to invite as it were, one country to traffic with another, by the variety of things which the one hath, and the other hath not: that so that which is wanting to the one, might be supplied by the other, that all might have sufficient. Which thing the very winds and seas proclaim, in guiding passage to all nations: the winds blowing sometimes toward one country, sometimes toward another; that so by this divine justice, every one might be supplied in things necessary for life and maintenance.[10]

Thus, the cosmopolitanism of the universal economy doctrine and the early natural law approach, which stressed the benefits to the world from international exchange, was not absent from mercantilist thought. It is surprising how frequent this glowing description of trade was invoked, but it is in keeping with their enthusiasm for commerce.

Still, the mercantilists never used this approach to advocate free and unrestricted trade for reasons that will be made clear below. Imaginative authors twisted the doctrine to reach the opposite conclusion. Viner (1937, 100–101) has noted how mercantilists "managed ingeniously to adapt the intent of Providence to their own particular views . . . [they] used the doctrine either to justify the restriction of certain products to Englishmen, on the ground that Providence had assigned them to this country, or appealed to the doctrine in support of that branch or type of trade which they wished to have fostered, while conveniently forgetting the doctrine when attacking other branches or types of trades." A classic example is the statement from the 1690s by Daniel Defoe (1895, 40) that Henry VII "justly inferred that Heaven having been so bountiful to England as to give them the wool, as it were, in a peculiar grant, exclusive of the whole world, it was a mere rebellion against His providence and particularly ungrateful to His bounty that the English nation should reject the offer, give away the blessing, and

---

[9] See, for example, [Carew Reynell] (1685, 7–8).

[10] For another early example, see Gerard Malynes (1601, 6).

by an unaccountable neglect send their wool abroad to be manufactured, and even buy their own clothing of the Flemings with ready money."

The second feature of the international economic environment, the emergence of the nation-state as the primary political entity on the world stage, set clear political boundaries to trade policies. Writing during a period fraught with political and religious conflict between states, early mercantilists took a strictly national economic perspective wherein the only relevant gains from trade were those that accrued to one's own country. The political and economic rivalries between states gave rise to the view, if not that the amount of trade in the world was fixed at any point in time, that an increase in one country's trade (and the gains from that trade) must come at the expense of other countries. John Graunt's (1676, 29) notion that "there is but a certain proportion of trade in the world" led easily to William Petty's (1690, 82) conclusion that "the wealth of every nation, consisting chiefly, in the share which they have in the foreign trade with the whole commercial world, rather than in the domestic trade." According to Josiah Child (1693, 160), trade should be managed to ensure "that other nations who are in competition with us for the same, may not wrest it from us, but that ours may continue and increase, to the diminution of theirs."

The proposition that the overall volume of trade is fixed, however, is quite distinct from a belief that such trade is a zero-sum game, wherein one country benefits and the other loses from an exchange. With qualification, mercantilists generally accepted the idea that trade was mutually beneficial, particularly as indicated by their broad acceptance of the universal economy doctrine. It was the amount of trade, or the gains to be had by trade, that some mercantilists perceived to be fixed and wanted to accrue to their own country. This perspective is one aspect of the seventeenth-century mercantilist literature, but not a dominant one. This aspect of mercantilist thought could still be found in the eighteenth century, though it had faded as a part of mercantilist doctrine by the end of the seventeenth century. Others even denied the argument, as when William Petyt (1680, 280) maintained that "it does not follow that everything which will prejudice the trade of one nation, shall better the trade of another."

The generic praise of merchants and trade was tempered by the proviso that merchants might pursue profitable commercial activities that could prove detrimental to the nation as a whole. Therefore, not all branches of trade equally served the national advantage. Malynes (1622, 3–4) complained that trade yields "benefit[s] to be procured for the general welfare, or for the particular profit of some few persons . . . yet it may fall out, that the general shall receive an intolerable prejudice and loss, by the particular and private benefit of some" because merchants trade in "that which yields them the most gain: and commonly without consideration had of the good of the Commonwealth." Similarly, Petyt (1680, 11ff) wrote that "private trade hath regard to the particular wealth of the trader, and doth so far differ in the scope and design of it from the national, that a private trade may be very beneficial to the private trader, but of hurtful, nay of very ruinous consequences to the whole nation . . . particular men may grow rich by a trade, whereby the nation is impoverished."[11] These beliefs were stated repeatedly in the seventeenth century and can be found well into the eighteenth century. Theodore Janssen (1713, 5) set down the maxim that "a trade may be of benefit to the merchant and injurious to the body of the nation."[12] The *British Merchant*, a set of anti-free trade essays written in 1713–14, followed Janssen by adopting this as the first of its "general maxims in trade which are assented to by everybody."[13]

The divergence between the private interests of the merchant and the broader interests of the nation formed the fundamental basis for the mercantilist advocacy of state regulation of trade. State oversight, guidance, and intervention was necessary to align the activities of merchants with the national interest, ensuring that trade was carried on for the enrichment of the country rather than for the merchants alone.[14] Many thought that national leaders were situated to see beyond the narrow interests of particular merchants and design such regulations. Because "private advantages are often impediments of public profit," Samuel Fortrey (1663, 3–4) argued, "how necessary it is that the public profits should be in a single power to direct, whose interest is only the benefit of the whole." Malynes (1622, 3–4) maintained that merchants commonly deal "without consideration had of the good of the Commonwealth, which is the cause that Princes and Governors are fit at the stern of the course of trade and commerce."

Because "not all trading advantages a nation," as Reynell (1685, 12) put it, the mercantilists developed criteria for determining the "good" and "bad" channels of trade, depending on how the trade contributed to the specific objectives of the author. The purpose of state policy, of course, was to regulate trade to the country's advantage by promoting the good channels and discouraging the bad channels. The most obvious distinction between good and bad channels of trade, indeed a central tenant of mer-

---

[11] John Pollexfen (1697*b*, 15ff) warned that "measures taken of trades by the gains made by traders will always prove erroneous . . . some traders for their private gain may be tempted to carry on, who may get by trade, and yet the nation may lose at the same time by such trades."

[12] Simon Smith (1736, 12) concurred: "There are many commodities advantageous to the importer, that at the same time bring poverty and ruin to a nation."

[13] See Charles King (1721, 1: 1).

[14] "Nothing can so effectually and certainly secure the peace of the nation, as the regulating of our trade," wrote Petyt (1680, 15–16). "A foreign trade managed to the best advantage, will make a nation vastly stronger than naturally it was." Carew Reynell (1685, 16) suggested forming a committee on trade composed of merchants to propose legislation "so should we have trade brought more to a general benefit."

cantilism that persisted up to the time of Adam Smith and is still not extinguished today, is that the principal benefit of trade arises from exports and not imports. A few statements amply illustrate this point. "Gain procured by our commodities outward, more than by foreign commodities inward."[15] "The national gain, by foreign trade, consisting either in vending home commodities to foreigners, or in trading from port to port."[16] "[T]hat trade is advantageous to the kingdom which exports our product and manufactures."[17] "Exportation is gain, but all commodities imported is loss."[18]

The appropriate policy regarding most exports was abundantly clear: remove all possible impediments. Mercantilists endorsed almost any measure that would encourage exports, from ensuring greater safety for merchants abroad to building trade-related domestic public works (such as navigable rivers, etc.). Mercantilists clearly favored reducing, if not abolishing, most export taxes and other "clogs" on exports: the "means to increase and nourish this country's trade is that whatever is fabricated in this nation, and exported to any foreign parts, may pay no custom, or if any a very little," argued John Bland (1659, 9).[19] Only in the case of grain and certain raw materials, as we shall see, were mercantilists more cautious about the benefits of an unrestricted export policy.

There were also calls for the establishment of free ports to allow the duty-free transshipment of goods for reexport and thereby promote the entrepôt trade. Although few writers actually advocated general export subsidies (bounties), their positive effects on exports did not pass unnoticed. Lewes Roberts (1641, 53) noted that "for the furtherance of the traffic of some kingdoms, it hath been observed, that great sums of monies have been lent *gratis*, or upon easy rates and security, to skilful merchants, out of the sovereign, or common treasury, which hath also found such good success, as that the customs of that Prince have been thereby much increased, the kingdom enriched, the poor set on work, and the native commodities thereof, vented to all parts of the world thereby."

Regarding imports, mercantilists frequently complained that they were predominantly luxury consumption goods (such as silks, jewelry, wines, etc.) and advocated restraint of these "superfluous and unnecessary" goods, particularly those that could be produced at home.[20] Misselden (1622, 12–13, 131) advocated shifting the tax burden from domestically produced goods to such unnecessary imported goods as wines, raisins, silk, sugar, and tobacco, precisely the types of consumption imports that Janssen (1713, 8) argued should be "very prudently charged with excessive

---

[15] Malynes (1623, 54).
[16] [Petyt] (1680, 23).
[17] Cary (1695, 48).
[18] [Reynell] (1685, 10).
[19] "The chiefest way of enriching a kingdom is the expence of its nature or home commodities (that can well be spared) in foreign parts" [Battie] (1644, 3).
[20] Misselden (1623, 134).

duties."[21] Such calls echoed the early Christian and scholastic view that spending on luxuries was essentially corrupting and wasteful, and that greater frugality was in order.

But the mercantilist concern was less a moral judgment than an argument that such goods were unproductive, that they would not increase the wealth and production of the nation. "A consumptive trade must render a nation weaker and weaker . . . because it must still exhaust more and more of the national riches, and sink the value of men's estates," argued Petyt (1680, 137). As Bruno Suviranta (1923, 147) observed: "Instead of expressly stating 'We do not want foreign commodities except those of real benefit for the progress of economic life,' they argued, 'We do not want foreign commodities' and the unstated reason was, 'Because they mostly consist of luxuries and such consumable commodities which tend to increase consumption without increasing production.'" Concerns about luxury imports and insufficient frugality abounded among seventeenth-century writers, and persisted in a less prevalent way among eighteenth-century writers. William Wood (1718, 225) concluded that "it is our business to keep out as much as conveniently we can . . . all sorts of goods for consumption and luxury: and that there is no other way of doing it, but high duties and impositions."[22] Even Adam Smith made disparaging remarks about certain imports for consumption, although he did not recommend taking action against them.[23]

This general view of exports (as productive) and imports (as wasteful) encompassed two specific criteria by which the profitability or advantage of a trade could be determined: first, a favorable balance of trade (to generate an inflow of specie); second, a favorable commodity composition of trade (to promote economic development and employment in manufacturing).

A Favorable Balance of Trade

For much of the seventeenth century, mercantilists argued that a key objective of trade should be to achieve or maintain a favorable balance of trade. Trade with a given country or region was judged profitable by the extent to

[21] Petyt (1680, 184) used vivid language to illustrate his complaint about the loss of specie due to what he felt were excessive imports of wine from France: "Everyone is an ambitious pretender to a critical palate in wine. . . . Thus do we swallow and piss out inestimable treasures."

[22] "'Tis certain, a disadvantageous trade can't be too much cramped, but to erect select companies is not the most effectual way; this is to be done by the legislature's laying great duties and impositions upon goods imported, or prohibiting the importation of them" (Wood [1718, 270]).

[23] Adam Smith wrote that "purchase such goods as are likely to be consumed by idle people who produce nothing, such as foreign wines, foreign silks, &c., . . . So far as it is employed

which the value of exports exceeded the value of imports, thereby resulting in a balance of trade surplus which added precious metals and treasure to the country's stock. In the classic statement of the period, Mun (1664, 11) wrote: "The ordinary means therefore to increase our wealth and treasure is by foreign trade, wherein we must ever observe this rule; to sell more to strangers yearly than we consume of theirs in value." In these early debates, a favorable balance of trade was considered desirable on several grounds, some political (an accumulated stockpile of specie could be used as security in times of national emergency, such as war) and others economic (the inflow of specie and precious metals would increase domestic liquidity and relieve credit shortages).[24] This stress on the monetary aspects of the balance of payments was most pronounced in the early and mid-seventeenth century, but the notion of the favorable balance as a criterion for judging trade survived in general terms up to the time of Adam Smith.

There has been extensive debate in the secondary literature on mercantilism about whether economic conditions in the seventeenth century provided an economic justification for concerns over the balance of trade.[25] For our purposes, the relevant question is: did mercantilist writers advocate using commercial policy to achieve a favorable balance of trade? The answer is: not very much. There was actually little direct discussion of commercial policy during this early period of mercantilist thought. Indeed, most early seventeenth-century writings on commerce were dominated by controversies over monetary issues, such as the international flow of specie, the balance of trade, and exchange rates and foreign exchange markets. Because the early balance of trade controversies tended to have a monetary focus, the proposed solutions were also monetary in nature, as in the exchange-rate adjustment debate between Malynes and Misselden in the 1620s. But as a balance of trade surplus was almost universally acknowledged to be a desirable objective, mercantilists like Mun (1664, 14) did pay some attention to trade policy as one of "those ways and means which will increase our exportation and diminish our importation of wares." At this point, however, they ran into some difficulties.

Increasing a country's exports did not lend itself to easy and obvious

---

in the first way, it promotes prodigality, increases expence and consumption without increasing production, . . . and is in every respect hurtful to the society" *WN*, II.ii.33–34.

[24] This monetary mechanism would reduce interest rates, allow merchants to borrow and finance projects at more profitable rates, and thereby stimulate economic growth and produce greater employment. Viner (1937, 15–51) describes other reasons stated for favoring an inflow of bullion.

[25] In the early seventeenth century, specie was an important means of international payment and was used to settle external account balances. Later in the century increasing use of bills of exchange gave rise to a multilateral payments mechanism which obviated the need to have specie to conduct international transactions. See J. Sperling (1962).

legislative remedies, aside from the removal of existing impediments to exports. Therefore, trade policy–related methods to improve the balance of trade turned to commercial policies toward imports, such as prohibitions or high duties. Mercantilists generally preferred import duties to prohibitions, which either restricted trade too harshly or would be evaded by smuggling. Roger Coke (1675, 48) opined that "if my opinion were worthy to be admitted, no goods of any sort should be prohibited: but if any be imported which are luxuriously consumed, with little or no employment of the people, . . . they should pay the King the full value" of import duties. Francis Brewster (1695, 41) argued that prohibitions should never be employed except under "extraordinary circumstances" and undesirable or excessive imports should instead be charged with high duties.

Did this mean that import duties could improve the balance of trade? In one passage, Mun (1664, 30) considered higher import duties potentially useful: "The consumption of such foreign wares in the realm may be the more charged [with customs duties], which will turn to the profit of the kingdom in the balance of trade." But he did not discuss tariffs at length and other writers did not elaborate on this particular mechanism, concentrating instead on monetary determinants of the trade balance. Most recommendations to improve the balance took the form of improving the quality of coinage, encouraging greater domestic production for export, and fostering improvement in quality of those goods, not the use of trade barriers.

Indeed, concern about the balance of trade did not automatically imply support for import restrictions, and mercantilists did not always believe that higher import duties could improve the trade balance. Several mercantilists recognized the barter nature of trade, that trade was a two-way process of exchanging exports for imports. With this interdependence of exports and imports in mind, many mercantilists found it difficult to believe that import restrictions could lead to a favorable balance of trade. In advocating a shift in the burden of taxation from exports to imports, Henry Robinson (1641, 8) cautioned that "here is it worth remembrance that a great part of foreign commodities brought for England are taken in barter of ours, and we should not have vented ours in so great quantity without taking them." Petyt (1680, 61–62) took this point to its logical conclusion: "For the opening of a sufficient foreign vent and market for our home commodities, it is not only necessary to remove all unequal clogs on mere exportation, but also those on imported goods; because . . . the value of our English exportation must be in a manner confined to the value of the goods imported. . . . Whereas were the clogs on our imported goods taken off, we might yearly vend of our own home commodities to the value of all foreign goods we should then import and re-export . . . whereby our exported home commodities would then amount to much more." Thomas Tryon (1698, 23) made this uncommon point: "It is most clear that the consumption of [imported] things at home is as profitable to the nation, as those that are exported again: for if we can neither consume them at home nor export them abroad, how should our neighbors be able to pay for our manufactures, for which we have those commodities in exchange." Paxton (1704, 61ff) concurred, arguing that high duties are "only an expedient, but no cure" to the problem of excessive imports, and that "duties are a violence upon trade" which "must, in the course of trade, lessen our own exportations."

Recognition of the interdependence of exports and imports put mercantilists in a bind because import tariffs appeared to be the obvious instrument for improving the balance of trade. Deeming that ineffective, mercantilists exhorted their readers to reduce the import bill through greater frugality and restraint, thereby moderating the demand for luxuries and other superfluous trifles.[26] Mun (1621, 56) cautioned that "we ought not to avoid the importation of foreign wares, but rather willingly to bridle our own affections, to the moderate consuming of the same." According to Mun (1664, 16), England should simply "soberly refrain from excessive consumption of foreign wares in our diet and rayment." Pollexfen (1697a, 58) argued for duties and prohibitions only if moral suasion failed: "When the balance of trade is against us, if we cannot alter it by increasing the expense of our goods there, or by spending in the room of theirs the like goods taken from another country, from when we may have them on better terms, then the safest way (if we can be without such goods) is to discourage the use and expense of them by example: if that be not likely to have any effect, then high customs or prohibitions may be used; but prohibitions should always be the last remedy, when no other way can be found out." Yet, just like import duties, moral suasion could not be taken to extremes. Mun (1664, 148–49) cautioned that "all kinds of bounty and pomp is not to be availed, for if we should become so frugal, that we would use few or no foreign wares, how shall we then vent our own commodities? . . . do we hope that other countries will afford no money for all our wares, without buying or bartering for some of theirs?" Thus, voluntary efforts to reduce expenditures on imports would reduce exports just like an import tariff.

Toward the end of the seventeenth century, doubts arose about whether the trade balance was a useful indicator of a winning or losing trade. Although the balance continued to be used as a short-hand guide of a gainful trade, either less emphasis was put upon it or that emphasis was subject to greater qualification. Instead, mercantilists increasingly considered trade as an effectual means of promoting the economic development of the country

---

[26] Samuel Fortrey (1663, 26ff), among others, believed that the nobility should set a proper example for society by consuming only English clothing, thereby reducing imports that would otherwise "impoverish" the country.

and creating greater employment opportunities by expanding the manufacturing sector. In this context, the issue of commercial policy, in the
sense of free trade versus protection, finally came to the forefront of economic discussion.

Employment and the Commodity Composition of Trade

The general praise of exports and disparagement of imports was consistent
with a host of objectives, and did not merely reflect anxiety about the balance of trade. By the end of the seventeenth century, the commodity composition of a country's trade had come to dominate the balance of trade
doctrine as the method of determining the good and bad channels of trade.
Pollexfen (1697b, 15) proposed that "from a due consideration of what
sorts of commodities are exported, and imported, a true judgment can only
be made, whether the trade to any country be good or bad." Virtually all
mercantilists would agree with the following proposition: exports of manufactured goods were beneficial and exports of raw materials (for use by
foreign manufacturers abroad) were harmful; imports of raw materials
were advantageous and imports of manufactured goods were damaging.
According to Cary (1695, 129–30), "'Tis a certain rule that so far as any
nation furnishes us with things already manufactured, or only to be spent
among ourselves, so much less is our advantage by the trade . . . especially
if those manufactures interfere with our own." Other trades are "very advantageous, as they vend great quantities of our product and manufactures,
and furnish us with materials to be wrought up here."

The underlying rationale was described by Petyt (1680, 24) as follows:

> If any nation hath naturally any materials of manufacture, it is far more advan-
> tageous to export them in manufacture, rather than the raw materials, because
> the manufacture is so much more valuable, and will make a return of five, ten,
> or twenty times more treasure to the nation than the raw materials. Besides, it
> is most dangerous to export the materials of manufacture, since it may transfer
> the manufacture itself into some neighboring nation. . . . But if foreigners will
> vend their raw materials of manufacture, it is necessary, or highly convenient,
> for a nation to import them, and put them into manufacture at home.

In essence, mercantilists argued that economic activities generating high
value-added or involving extensive processing and manufacturing should
be produced in the home market. Because processing activities generated
more value and employment than other sectors, the economy should be
oriented toward importing raw materials and exporting finished goods.

This objective, rather than the balance of trade doctrine (though they are
not incompatible as Petyt's statement makes clear), should be more closely
associated with mercantilist views on trade because the implication for

commercial policy was clear: low import duties on inputs and raw materials, high import duties on processed goods. Fortrey (1663, 28–29) described his position this way: "All foreign commodities that are useful, to improve our own manufactures and trade abroad, and cannot be raised here, should be brought into us under easy customs," whereas foreign goods, especially luxury and consumption items, "should pay extraordinary customs, but should not be forbidden to be brought in." This line of reasoning also supported export taxes on raw materials to ensure a cheap and plentiful domestic supply for further processing, and to prevent foreign manufacturers from acquiring those supplies.

Repeated stress was put on the importance of domestic manufacturing and the dangers posed by importing such goods from abroad. A few quotations will illustrate this point. Child (1693, [xii]) argued that "the expense of foreign commodities, especially foreign manufactures, is the worst expense a nation can be inclinable to, and ought to be prevented as much as possible." "A trade that takes of little from us in commodities, and furnishes us with little or no goods for our foreign vent in other places [i.e., reexports], but with abundance of either unnecessary and superfluous things to feed our vain humours and fancies, or with such, though useful, as hinder the consumption of our own manufactures, can never be profitable but destructive," concluded Thomas Papillon (1680, 2). "That trade is advantageous to the kingdom of England which exports our product and manufactures [and] which imports to us such commodities as may be manufactured here, or be used in making our manufactures," stated Cary (1695, 48–49), and "it would be great wisdom of our government to regulate all foreign trades by such methods as may best make them useful in the promoting our manufactures."

This view continues to be expressed in the eighteenth century as well. Joshua Gee (1729, 111) stated that "it will be a maxim to be observed by all prudent governments who are capable of manufactures within themselves, to lay such duties on the foreign as they may favor their own and discourage the importation of any of the like sort from abroad." David Clayton (1719, 18) argued that "whatever trade, or branches of trade, bring in any manufactured goods that interfere with what is being made among our selves, is in its direct tendency and consequences injurious to the nation." "That trade is eminently bad, which supplies us with the same goods as we manufacture ourselves, especially if we can make enough for our consumption," the *British Merchant* (King 1714, 1: 4–5) pronounced. "The importation upon easy terms of such manufactures as are already introduced into a country must be of bad consequence, and check their progress . . . if those commodities were suffered to be brought in without paying very high duties." Postlethwayt (1757, 2: 371) concluded that "the importation of foreign commodities, whereby the consumption of national commodities is hurt, or the progress of a nation's manufactures and the culture of its lands prejudiced, must necessarily bring on the ruin of that nation."

To mercantilists, the advantage of manufacturing was not simply the gain from exchanging more valuable processed goods for less valuable unprocessed goods, but that industry was capable of generating greater employment. And the wages of those employed in export-oriented industries were believed to be "foreign paid incomes."[27] "The profit of trade consists in employing our hands, or selling the goods made by those hands abroad to our advantage," as Clayton (1719, 22) put it. King (1714, 1: 22) noted that "the trade of that country which contributes most to the employment and subsistence of our people, and to the improvement of our lands, is the most valuable." Richard Cantillon, an acute economic thinker of the period, was relatively undistinguished in his views on trade policy. As "by examining the results of each branch of commerce singly that foreign trade can be usefully regulated," Cantillon ([1755] 1931, 233–35) argued that "it will always be found . . . that the exportation of all manufactured articles is advantageous to the state, because in this case the foreigner always pays and supports workmen useful to the state. . . . It would not be profitable to put the state into the annual custom of sending abroad large quantities of its raw produce in return for foreign manufactures." Paxton (1704, 10) stated that "the great business of trade is the employing of our people, and the great advantage of it is the enriching them." Petty (1690, 37) even argued that a tariff could remedy unemployment: "If the people of any country, who have not already a full employment, should be enjoyned or taxed to work upon such commodities as are imported from abroad; I say, that such a tax, also doth improve the commonwealth."[28]

Thus, the underlying purpose of the mercantilists' focus on the commodity composition of trade was to promote economic development by encouraging the expansion of manufacturing and thereby creating greater employment.[29] Commercial policy was an important mechanism for manipulating economic incentives in such a way as to spur this development. John Asgill (1719, 10) wrote of using government policies for the "protection and encouragement" of domestic industry, thus introducing the term "protection" to the discourse over trade policy. That protection could secure greater employment and output in manufacturing became the standard argument

[27] E.A.J. Johnson (1932) elaborates on this point.

[28] Chapter 13 considers John Maynard Keynes's argument for protection in the face of severe unemployment.

[29] As Richard Wilkes (1987, 155) points out: "A review of the literature reveals scarcely a tract or work of the time that does not contain in its title or contents the ideal of the possibility of an 'increase,' 'improvement,' or 'advancement' of trade in general or of certain sectors of the economic system in particular. Or as a corollary, the work will attempt an explanation of the reason or reasons for the decay, decline, or stagnation of trade."

that free trade theories had to overcome after the mid-seventeenth century.[30] The particular obstacle for free trade ideas was that protectionist tariff policies were likely to be effective in achieving this objective, or at least give some appearance of success in terms of enhancing the production of import-competing industries. Under the balance of trade doctrine, mercantilists were quite uncertain whether an unfavorable balance could be reversed by import duties, or at least conceded that tariffs were not always the most efficient instrument for achieving a favorable balance of trade. But tariffs that reduced import penetration were almost assured of increasing domestic production and employment in the favored sectors.[31]

Promotion of economic development through the use of trade interventions (such as import tariffs and export subsidies) reached an exaggerate form in the work of James Steuart, whose *An Inquiry into the Principles of Political Oeconomy* was published in 1767, just nine years before Adam Smith's *Wealth of Nations*. In a sense, Steuart's *Principles* was an example of a mercantilist trade doctrine taken to extremes. Steuart started with the presumption that a wise and benevolent statesmen served as a caretaker and guardian of the economy. The statesman, through judicious administration and with various economic policies, could manipulate the economy at will, promoting certain activities here and discouraging others there.

Steuart's ([1767] 1966, 1: 291) criteria for assessing trade was not fundamentally different from those who had written before him:

> If the value of the matter imported be greater than the value of what is exported, the country gains. If a greater value of labour be imported than exported, the country loses. Why? Because in the first case, strangers must have paid, *in matter*, the surplus of the labour exported; and in the second case, because the country must have paid to strangers, *in matter*, the surplus of labour imported. It is therefore a general maxim, to discourage the importation of work, and to encourage the exportation of it.

If imports of a certain commodity began to increase, the statesman must respond by laying duties on those imports. "If these do not prove sufficient," Steuart said, "[the duties] will be increased; and if the augmentation produces frauds, difficult to be prevented, the articles will be prohibited altogether" (292). Any violent or sharp changes in policy would be unwise, Stuart counseled, but pernicious branches of trade must be regulated in a manner that led to a more desirable commodity composition of trade.

---

[30] At one level, there is little novelty to the idea. Sir Thomas Smith in the sixteenth century (and even earlier writers) had already described the employment rationale for import duties and even earlier writers can be found on this point.

[31] As Viner (1937, 52) notes, "Of all the mercantilist reasoning, [the employment argument] withstood criticism most successfully, and persisted into the nineteenth and twentieth centuries as an important element in the protectionist doctrine."

Because "the most profitable branches of exportation are those of work, the less profitable those of pure natural produce," it is an "object of the states-man's care" when a rich nation begins exporting natural produce "to pro-hibit the importation of all work, and even the natural produce of any other country conducive to luxury" (295).

In the field of agriculture, the statesman "must cut off all foreign com-petition . . . for that quantity of subsistence which is necessary for home consumption; and, by premiums upon exportation, he must discharge the farmers of any superfluous load, which may remain upon their hands when prices fall too low." Indeed, Steuart advocated a much more extensive pro-gram of export subsidies than earlier mercantilists probably would have accepted. One passage is worth quoting at length:

> Let me suppose a nation which is accustomed to export the value of a million sterling of fish every year, to be undersold in this article by another which has found a fishery on its own coasts, so abundant as to enable it to undersell the first by 20 *per cent*. In this case, let the statesman buy up all the fish of his subjects, and undersell his competitors at every foreign market, at the loss to himself of perhaps 250,000l. What is the consequence? That the million he paid for the fish remains at home, and that 750,000l. comes in from abroad for the prices of them. How is the 250,000l to be made up? By a general imposi-tion upon all the inhabitants. This returns into the public coffers, and all stands as it was. If this expedient is not to be followed, what will be the consequence? That those employed in the fishery will starve; that the fish taken will either remain upon hand, or be sold by the proprietors at a great loss; they will be undone, and the nation for the future will lose the acquisition of 750,000l. a year. (256–57)

This statement implies that export subsides (financed through general taxa-tion) should be dispensed as an insurance program to insulate domestic producers from any adjustments that might result from other countries ac-quiring a cost advantage in trade.

Steuart even ruled out the desirability of worldwide free trade so long as "there are different [nation] states, [because then] there must be separate interests; and when no one statesman is found at the head of these interests, there can be no such thing as a common good; and when there is no com-mon good, every interest must be considered separately." A world govern-ment "governed by the same laws, and administered according to one plan well concerted, can be compatible with an universally open trade." But with different governments, "any nation who would open its ports to all manner of foreign importation, without being assured of a reciprocal per-mission from all its neighbors, would, I think, very soon be ruined. . . . Laying, therefore, trade quite open would have this effect; it would destroy, at first at least, all the luxurious arts; consequently, it would diminish consumption; consequently, diminish the quantity of circulating cash; consequently, it would promote hoarding; and consequently, would bring on poverty in all the *states* of Europe" (364–65).

Steuart's *Principles* can be viewed as an extreme culmination of mercantilist foreign trade doctrines, one that went to much greater lengths than other tracts in outlining the necessity for a highly interventionist trade policy.[32] But the type of analysis embodied in Steuart's work was not suited to persuade the minds of his contemporaries, let alone minds of the future. Even before the publication of Smith's *Wealth of Nations*, Steuart's treatise was not well received. "When the *Principles* appeared in 1767," Andrew Skinner (1981, 36) notes, "the *Critical* and *Monthly* reviews were unanimous in their rejection of the role ascribed to the statesman." The next chapter documents the growing skepticism, even at the turn of the eighteenth century, among economic writers about whether trade restrictions, however well designed, serve a worthwhile economic purpose. Steuart's embrace of an omnipotent and wise statesman judiciously intervening in trade for the national interest seemed quaintly antiquated even in 1767.

． ． ．

In concluding this synopsis of the mercantilist trade literature, one is struck by how little ideas about commercial policy changed between Sir Thomas Smith's *Discourse* of the mid-1500s and, say, Charles King's *The British Merchant* of the early 1700s or even Steuart's *Principles* in 1767. The short pamphlets on trade grew into tracts and then into full-blown folios where trade was discussed at great length, but the space devoted to genuine analysis of trade, as opposed to describing the minute factual details of England's trade with various regions of the world, was sparse. In fact, although one can detect a greater sophistication in the economic tracts as the seventeenth century progresses, there is a marked decline in the quality of reasoning in most tracts on trade in the early eighteenth century. There is a return to the simple balance-of-trade-type reasoning, with little analysis or criticism, and one senses a complacency creeping in among economic writers, which made stereotyping and criticism by Adam Smith and the classical school that much easier.

In Joseph Schumpeter's (1954, 348) view, "Though pieces of genuine analytic work can be found occasionally and attempts at analysis more frequently, the bulk of the [mercantilist] literature is still essentially preanalytic; and not only that, it is crude." Perhaps expecting greater sophistication from the outpouring of works on trade would be unreasonable, for as

---

[32] Adam Smith (1987, 167) wrote just before publication of the *Wealth of Nations* that "without mentioning [Steuart's book] once, I flatter myself, that every false principle in it, will meet with a clear and distinct confutation in mine." See also Gary Anderson and Robert Tollison (1984).

D. C. Coleman (1980, 787) observes, "Much of the content of mercantilist writings is a compound of popular maxims and vague expositions held together by a cement in which logic, and what classical economics and its modern derivatives regard as rationality were very variable ingredients." This chapter, in fact, may convey a misleading impression of the coherence of the literature as there is more logic to this synthesis than was in any one particular work.

The mercantilist eulogy of international trade clearly makes it a mistake to interpret them as being crude protectionists whose program was akin to autarky. The mercantilists were sharply critical of restrictions on merchants's activities and commercial policies that hindered export growth. They held no anti-trade bias, indeed the opposite was true, and their anti-import bias was tempered by the recognition that trade was essentially barter between countries and that goods could not be sold abroad without the purchase of foreign goods in return. In terms of commercial policy, what we have in the end from the mercantilist literature is the simple employment argument for protection combined with the promotion of economic development through manufacturing, similar to the import-substitution policies proposed for developing countries in the 1950s.

But the mercantilist consensus that governments should use tariff policy to protect manufacturing and discourage raw material exports belies the emergence of other writers who questioned this received wisdom. Both of the reasons mercantilist writers set down for regulating trade, to promote a favorable balance of trade and to secure greater manufacturing production, were derivative of a more general view of trade where a disharmony between private and public interests led to a misallocation of economic resources, a misallocation that could be remedied by proper government intervention. Free trade thought emerged not only to question the particular goals and the particular concerns of mercantilists, but also confronted this more general question of the role of the state in directing the country's economic affairs and its international commerce in particular.

Chapter Three

THE EMERGENCE OF FREE TRADE THOUGHT

THE IDEAS and themes described in the previous chapter dominated the discussion of commercial policy in the English economics literature from the late sixteenth century until well into the eighteenth century. By the end of the seventeenth century, however, skepticism of state regulation of trade was increasingly evident and the benefits of free trade came to be recognized, at least by a few writers.

· · ·

Over the course of the seventeenth century, some individuals may have believed in free trade, but this position is not represented in the economic literature of the period. Thomas Violet (1651, 24) attests to how such beliefs remained obscure: "And whereas some men are of an opinion, that they would have trade free, to import all commodities, and export all without restraint. . . . I would not write it, but I have it affirmed by men of great quality, that this is the opinion of some men in place and power." But then he quickly added: "Truly I humbly conceive, there cannot be a more destructive thing to this Commonwealth, than that those men's principles should be followed."

The pro-commercial stance of mercantilists often led them to make statements on trade that have a decidedly liberal flavor. They pressed for many reforms of government policy, particularly those needlessly inhibiting exports, and sought to liberate commerce from the remnants of feudal and medieval restrictions. They often commented on the importance of a free and stable domestic environment for merchants and of establishing the security of property rights under the rule of law. Mercantilists frequently noted how trade thrived in countries where political liberties were respected and spoke of how this freedom was conducive to commerce. They also tended to take liberal stances on questions of immigration and religious tolerance because these too promoted commerce.

Just because there was much discussion about how trade flourished when free did not mean that "free trade" was advanced as the best policy of the state. Edward Misselden (1623, 112), for example, wrote that "trade hath in it such a kind of natural liberty in the course and use thereof, as it will not endure to be forced by any." Read in its context, however, he is simply putting forth the notion that sellers cannot force buyers to buy and buyers cannot force sellers to sell, not that regulatory burdens that force trade in certain directions are unwise or unnecessary, or that these burdens violate an individual's natural liberty.

The term "free trade" apparently originated at the end of the sixteenth century in parliamentary debates over foreign trade monopolies. In England, royal grants giving select merchants the exclusive privilege to engage in trade with a particular region of the world dated back to the thirteenth century. Although well established in the vocabulary of those writing on economic issues by the dawn of the seventeenth century, the term free trade initially carried a different meaning than what we now attach to it. "A free trade" was a commercial activity in which entry was unrestricted, where the liberty of the merchant to participate in trade was unhindered by exclusionary guild regulations or government grants of monopoly rights and privileges. Calls for "a free trade"—or, more precisely, "freedom to trade"—arose in an antimonopoly movement that opposed such government restraints on either domestic or foreign commerce. This movement was geared exclusively toward freeing trade from medieval controls and establishing the right to carry on trade without official permission or approval, and decidedly *not* with the abolition of import tariffs and the like.

English notions of individual liberty and natural rights under common law to employ one's labor in any activity that one saw fit underpinned the case against monopolies. The scholastic hostility to monopolies of all sorts was also deeply entrenched in the economic thought of the day, as Raymond de Roover (1951) points out, and there was little rhetorically or analytically new about these calls for freedom to trade. Indeed, monopoly trading companies provoked such ill feeling that those defending them either denied that they were really monopolies or justified the exclusive grants on other grounds. Misselden (1622, 63), for example, agreed that such grants reduced the liberty of subjects to engage in any trade they wished, but argued that the resulting security against competitors would increase traffic above what it otherwise would have been, and therefore concluded that "the utility that hereby arose to the commonwealth, did far exceed the restraint of the public liberty." A common defense of foreign trade monopolies was that long-distance trade required expenditures on certain public goods, such as navigational guides or defense establishments to protect person and property abroad, and government entry restrictions were required to prevent free riders from undermining the financing of such goods. An exclusive company, for example, could raise the requisite capital to pay for these required expenditures or use their trading profits to ensure the safety of cargo, whereas interlopers who did not contribute to the fund might reduce profits and could ultimately subvert the basis for all such trade.

Samuel Fortrey (1673, 41) objected to freedom to trade on the advanced grounds that it would turn the terms of trade, the price of exports relative to the price of imports, or the ratio at which goods are exchanged on world markets, against England. With trading companies, "our own commodities are sold the dearer to strangers, and foreign commodities bought much the cheaper; when both would happen contrary in a free trade; where each will undersell the other, to vent most; and also purchase at any rates, to prevent the rest." Others fell back on claims that the companies brought skill and experience to the trade which newcomers lacked; order and stability was good for a company's trade and was therefore good for country. An "ill-governed and disorderly trade" is "the bane of good government, . . . For want of government in trade, opens a gap and lets in all sorts of unskillful and disorderly persons," wrote John Wheeler (1601, 26), a prominent defender of the corporations. "I think no man doubteth . . . that the state and commonwealth reapeth more profit, then if men were suffered to run a loose and irregular course without order, command, and oversight of any."

Despite these arguments, the case for freedom to trade gradually achieved greater success in the English political arena. Wealthy merchants excluded from trade could also influence government policy, and in arguing for freedom to trade pointed to the mismanagement of the monopoly companies, the greater shipping that would result from an open trade, and the violation of their personal liberty that resulted from commercial restrictions. Yet advocates of "a free trade" or "freedom to trade" usually did not support the distinct notion of "free trade," that is, the absence of import barriers or export subsidies. Eli Heckscher (1935, 1: 296) put it this way: "The 'freedom of trade' had precisely this idea among the mercantilists: one was free to do what one wished without prevention or compulsion by governmental regulation, but the activity of the individual was to be directed along the right lines through economic rewards and penalties, the weapons of a wise government." These economic rewards and penalties included, obviously, commercial policies such as tariffs, subsidies, and even prohibitions. Regardless of one's position on freedom to trade, the central premise of mercantilist trade policy remained that government regulation of trade through such instruments was essential both to promote the expansion and prevent the decay of trade in general and to ensure that such trade was profitable or gainful to the country as a whole. R. Kayll (1615, 51) offered "a freedom of traffic for all his Majesty's subjects to all places" to stimulate trade, but insisted that "my proposition [of a free trade] is not any way so tumultuous as that thereby I would exclude all order and form from government in trades." Violet (1653, 16ff) similarly predicted that "a free trade will treble the importation and exportation of goods into all the sea-ports of this nation," but still advocated duties on "unnecessary" imports and prohibitions on certain manufactures to establish their production in England.

Support for free trade, defined as the absence of protectionist trade policies that discriminated against foreign goods, emerged in several ways in reaction to mercantilist doctrine. Mercantilist regulations could be unnecessary because there was no divergence in the economic interests of merchants and the general interests of society. A number of writers argued along with Henry Parker (1648, 13) that the actions of merchants always benefited the nation and society at large. Lewes Roberts (1641, 2) praised "the judicious merchant, whose labour is to profit himself, yet in all his actions doth therewith benefit his King, Country, and fellow subjects." Josiah Child (1693, 148–49, 154) maintained that "if our trade and shipping increase, how small or low soever the profits are to private men, it is an infallible indication that the nation in general thrives . . . if trade be great, and much English shipping employed, it will be good for the nation in general, whatever it may be for the private merchant." These scattered statements, left undeveloped in any length or detail at all, fell far short of establishing even the preconditions for a case for free trade. Most such statements were probably *obiter dicta* because not only did these same authors frequently contradict themselves, they certainly did not feel constrained from also arguing that import restrictions would be beneficial. This scattered discussion about the harmony of public and private interests in the economic realm was later taken up at length by moral philosophers in the eighteenth century and harnessed by Adam Smith in his case for free trade.

Initially, the strongest objections to mercantilism were not so ambitious as to attack its intellectual underpinnings, but instead eroded its credibility by questioning the twin objectives of a favorable balance of trade and a particular commodity composition of trade. A common concern by the end of the seventeenth century was whether the balance of trade really indicated the profitability of trade. A growing number of writers noted that numerous problems plagued the gathering of accurate data on the balance and misinformation about either exports or imports could lead to false conclusions about the state of trade. Child (1693, 137), for example, granted the basic truth of the balance of trade doctrine, but remained skeptical owing to difficulties in practice: "It will appear too doubtful and uncertain as to our general trade, and in reference to particular trades fallible and erroneous." Even if something approaching certainty about the balance of trade could be established, critics began to question whether an "unfavorable" balance implied anything about the well-being of the country. Roger Coke (1670, [x]) observed the following contradiction: "The Dutch we see import all, yet thrive upon trade, and the Irish export eight times more than they import, yet grow poorer."

Serious doubts about the reliability of the balance of trade doctrine preceded by many decades the mid-eighteenth-century theory that the price-specie flow mechanism would ensure the automatic self-correction of trade imbalances. According to this theory, any country with an initial cost advantage in trade might achieve a trade surplus, but the resulting inflow of precious metals would inflate prices in that country, erode the cost advantage, and ultimately eliminate the surplus. Jacob Vanderlint anticipated David Hume's famous description of this mechanism and helped undermine the theoretical basis for the mercantilists' pursuit of a protracted balance of trade surplus. Vanderlint (1734, 46) argued that free trade with France and its low cost manufactured goods would be beneficial to England: "Therefore if we were to open up trade with them, they would bring us all sorts of goods so cheap, that our manufactures would be at an end, till the money they would by this means get of us raised the prices of their things so much, and our want of money should fall ours to such a degree, that we could go on with our manufactures as cheap as they; and then trade would stand between that nation and us, as it does both between us and other nations who mutually take goods of each other; and I think this would enlarge the maritime trade of both nations, together with all the trades relating thereto (i.e., would furnish still further means of employing abundance of people of both nations this way); and at last, this will terminate in the particular advantages each nation hath in the produce of their respective countries."

Hume receives most of the credit for this idea in his justly famous essay, "Of the Balance of Trade." Here Hume (1752, 80) noted that "there still prevails, even in nations well acquainted with commerce, a strong jealousy with regard to the balance of trade, and a fear, that all their gold and silver may be leaving them. This seems to me, almost in every case, a groundless apprehension." As long as "we preserve our people and our industry," England (or any other country) need not fear this loss of specie. Hume (1955, 188–89) succinctly stated the reason why in a letter to Montesquieu in 1749:

If half the money in England were suddenly destroyed, labour and goods would suddenly become so cheap that there would suddenly follow a great quantity of exports which would attract to us the money of all our neighbors. If half the money which is in England were suddenly to double, goods would suddenly become more expensive, imports would rise to the disadvantage of exports and our money would be spread among all our neighbors. It does not seem that money, any more than water, can be raised or lowered anywhere much beyond the level it has in places where communication is open, but that it must rise and fall in proportion to the goods and labour contained in each state.

In his published essay, Hume (1752, 84) elaborated on this idea and used the example of Spain, which could not contrive a way of keeping at home the massive inflow of precious metals from the New World: "Can one imagine, that it had ever been possible, by any laws, or even by any art or industry, to have kept all the money in Spain, which the galleons have brought from the Indies?"

Yet demolishing the conceptual basis of the balance of trade rationale for mercantilist policies did nothing to undercut the argument that import barriers were necessary to protect domestic industries from foreign competition. (As discussed in the previous chapter, mercantilists had little faith that import duties alone could bring about a balance of trade surplus anyway.) Therefore, important though those developments were to the monetary aspects of mercantilist doctrine, the price specie-flow mechanism did little to resolve controversies about free trade itself. There was still almost unequivocal support for the proposition that imported goods, especially manufactures but possibly excepting raw materials, should be subject to special duties. This idea was not threatened by the new monetary theories.

Another reaction to the mercantilist orthodoxy was to cast doubt on the ability of government to administer regulations in a way that would improve national welfare. They did not question the idea that government should take a leading role in trade, but argued that government should simply do a better job, sometimes nominating themselves, as merchants, as the class which should regulate trade. Roberts (1641, 64, 67) denied that statesmen knew trade well enough to regulate it in promotion of the national interest: "Our ordinary statesmen do neither seriously consider, nor truly weight the real benefits that arise to a kingdom and people by the hand of traffic . . . a mere statesmen conceives not what commodities are fittest to be eased, and which are to be raised for the common good, and profit of the trade of that country." He proposed that a council of merchants should determine commercial policy because of their superior knowledge about such matters. John Cary (1695, 139–40) added, "Yet our Parliaments generally handle [trade policy] very coarsely, and usually do more hurt than good when they meddle with it, for foreseeing the ill consequences of what they do . . . the reason whereof is because the conceptions they have of it are too gross for a thing so full of spirit as trade is." He recommended creating a committee on trade consisting of "honest and discrete men" whose only business would be to consider the nation's best commercial interests.

By contrast, Francis Brewster (1695, 38–39) had no problem with a governmental committee on trade, but objected to putting merchants on it because they would be "judges of their own complaints . . . no man in the actual part and course of trade can be equal and different in the determination of controverted matters in traffic." Others were still less optimistic about the government's ability to act wisely under any circumstances. Thomas Johnson (1646, i) scorned all public magistrates because of their "specious pretense of common good."

Yet those attacking government ineptness did not dispute the validity of the mercantilist framework, but merely objected to the current management of that framework. Even the occasional writer who recommended reducing the burden of import duties, such as John Bland (1659, 60), did not so much have free trade in mind as a practical desire to raise tax revenue by undercutting the incentive to smuggle goods. Such proposals were often to be selectively applied and were counterbalanced by calls for retaining or strengthening restrictions on trade in other goods or with other countries. In other words, almost all statements for freer trade during this period resulted from practical considerations in isolated cases, narrow in scope and applicability, with any general principles stated abruptly (if at all) without much reasoning or justification.

Still, the mercantilists were well aware of the gains from trade and there were several expressions of a different perspective on trade that later became part of the free trade case, even if the early statements fell short of arguing for free trade in the sense of eliminating all protective trade barriers. Consider the following statement by Samuel Fortrey (1673, 14), which comes fairly close to grasping the main insight of the classical theory of comparative advantage:

> Our care should therefore be to increase chiefly those things which are of least charge at home, and greatest value abroad; and cattle may be of far greater advantage to us, than corn can be, if we might make the best profit of them: for that the profit be can make of any corn by exportation, is much hindered by the plenty that neighbor country affords of that commodity, as good or better than we have any. Wherefore, we could employ our lands to anything of more worth, we could not want plenty of corn, though we had none of our own; for what we should increase in the room of it, of greater value by exportation, would not only bring us home as much corn as that land would have yielded, but plenty of money to boot.

A tract of remarkably liberal tone by Nicholas Barbon (1690) chided the inconsistency of pamphleteers who extolled the benefits of freer trade, but then supported other restrictions on trade that would serve their own financial interests. Barbon argued that men employed themselves to their own benefit, that this improved the wealth of the country, and that prodigality, though bad for men, was good for trade.

He agreed with contemporaries in that the impact of imports on total employment determined whether or not they are beneficial. But Barbon (1690, 71ff) understood the barter nature of trade—"for all foreign wares are brought in by the exchange of the native: so that the prohibiting of any foreign commodity, doth hinder the making and exportation of so much of the native." He also criticized protectionist measures: "If the suppressing or prohibiting of some sorts of goods, should prove an advantage to the trader, and increase the consumption of the same sort of native commodity: yet it may prove a loss to the nation," the loss arising from foregone customs revenue and lost employment overall.

Yet Barbon's views on trade and commercial policy turned out to be fairly conventional. He notes that all nations understand the advantage of exchanging wrought for unwrought goods, but argued that if all followed this policy, trade would dry up to the ruin of every trading nation. However, Barbon speaks here of prohibitions, and when he moved on to discuss tariffs he states something quite different: "If the bringing in of foreign goods, should hinder the making and consuming of the native, which will very seldom happen; this disadvantage is not to be remedied by a prohibition of those goods; but by laying on so great duties upon them, that they may always be dearer than those of our country make: the dearness will hinder the consumption of them" (78). Such a statement, of course, is incompatible with the free trade position.

In his *Discourses Upon Trade* (1691), Dudley North agreed with Barbon that too many writers extolled the general interest in an open, free, and growing trade but came down in favor of restrictions for particular projects. Like Barbon's, North's tract is clearly remarkable for its time, but is also overrated as an early statement of free trade views. North devoted his short pamphlet mainly to a critique of usury and restrictions on the export of specie, which he viewed as a commodity like any other. Commercial policy is discussed with the utmost brevity and free trade conclusions are stated abruptly, without any accompanying reasoning to justify the conclusions. North (1691, 2, [28]) views trade as "a commutation of superfluities" among nations and uses the analogy that a nation in world trade is like a city in a kingdom's trade or a family in a city's trade. He concludes that "laws to hamper trade, whether foreign, or domestic, relating to money, or other merchandises, are not ingredients to make a people rich . . . for no people ever yet grew rich by policies, but it is peace, industry, and freedom that brings trade and wealth." The irony is that most mercantilists would probably agree with this proposition in general, but still see a role for tariffs in ensuring trade was brought to an even greater advantage. In the end, North's treatment is much too cursory and too short on analysis to grant him much of a role in the history of free trade analysis.[1]

---

[1] The preface of the *Discourses*, apparently written by North's brother, according to William Letwin (1951), contains a more concise statement of the tract's free-trade point of view. "Now it may appear strange to hear it said, that the whole world as to trade, is but one nation or people, and therein nations are as persons. That the loss of a trade with one nation, is not that only, separately considered, but so much of the trade of the world rescinded and

The Barbon and North contributions, however, were quickly followed up by a number of important writings. The immediate impetus for the new debate on commercial policy, which paved the way for a clearer analysis of the benefits of free trade, came in the mid-1690s when the East India Company began shipping vast amounts of cotton calicoes from India to England. These imports adversely affected domestic production of cotton goods, sparked a clamor for restrictions on the East Indian imports, and triggered the first real debate in England, not over whether there should be "a free trade" in the sense of monopoly trading companies, but whether there should be "free trade" in allowing imports of these manufactured goods to continue unimpeded.[2]

Proponents of protection argued that imports were destroying domestic manufacturers and impoverishing the nation. Pollexfen (1697, 18) envisioned ruin should the imports go unchecked: "Those [goods] from India must otherwise be cheapest, and all people will go to the cheapest markets, which will affect the rents of land, and bring our working people to poverty, and force them either to fly to foreign ports, or to be maintained by the parishes." This was the essence of the anti-import position, a position that focused primarily on how cheap imports reduced domestic output and displaced domestic workers. Pollexfen made one concession in that "so long as the nation keeps to frugality and industry laws may not be absolutely necessary to limit the consumption of any foreign commodities, nor to increase or promote our own manufacturing" (47). Still, under pressing circumstances a tariff could raise the price of competing imports and allow domestic firms to sell more in the home market, thereby preventing a decline in employment in that manufacturing industry.

One anonymous author feared that the result of imports "would very [be] to extinguish [our] manufactures" and warned that "this sending out of our treasure to bring in this abundance of wrought goods, is like the drawing out the pure and spirituous blood of a man's veins, and filling them with hydropick humours."[3] The conventional view that continued import penetration would cause a loss of employment and impoverish the nation was later exquisitely summed up by David Clayton (1719, 9), who wrote, "You may as soon convince me that black is white, and that darkness is light, as to convince me that the making our hands idle is the way to make us thrive, and the carrying our cash abroad is the way to enrich us."

Novel arguments, however, arose in defense of the imports. Gardner

---

lost, for all is combined together. That there can be no trade unprofitable to the public; for if any prove so, men leave it off; and wherever the traders thrive, the public, of which they are a part, thrives also." This anticipates a number of points that free-trade advocates would make later on.

[2] This debate is reviewed by P. J. Thomas (1926).

[3] *The Great Necessity and Advantage of Preserving Our Own Manufactures* (1697, 9).

(1697, 3–4, 9) succinctly stated two key points of the emerging free trade doctrine. First, "If the proposed prohibition passes it will only enrich a few master silk weavers, and their factors, and at the same time take away the means of increasing the stock of the nation." Second, "The bringing in of foreign wares at half the price we can make them here at home, whilst at the same time we can find employment for our people, we by that means save so much money." Thus, Gardner makes the point that few stand to benefit directly from the import restriction, and that others who have to pay more for those goods will have less for other expenditures. Furthermore, workers displaced by imports could find employment in other industries, and the country would have saved resources because it would have acquired the imported goods at a cheaper price than would otherwise be the case.

In his celebrated *Essay on the East-India Trade* (1696), Charles Davenant addressed the charge that imported cotton goods interfered with domestic production of woolens and silks. Davenant (1696, 22) began by arguing that special trade policies for individual industries were unwise because one trade is interdependent with all others: "All trades have a mutual dependance one upon the other, and one begets another, and the loss of one frequently loses half the rest." In discussing the adverse impact on wool producers, Davenant opened with a sweeping statement:

> Trade is the general concern of this nation, but every distinct trade has a distinct interest. The wisdom of the legislative power consists, in keeping an even hand to promote all, and chiefly to encourage such trades, as increase the public stock, and add to the kingdom's wealth, considered as a collective body. Trade is in its nature free, finds its own channel, and best directs its own course: and all laws to give it rules and directions, and to limit and circumscribe it, may serve the particular ends private men, but are seldom advantageous to the public. Governments, in relation to it, are to take a providential care of the whole, but generally to let second causes work their own way; and considering all the links and chains, by which they hang together, . . . in the main, all traffics whatsoever are beneficial to a country. . . . Laws to compel the consumption of some commodities, and prohibit the use of others, may do well enough, where trade is forced, and only artificial. . . . But in countries inclin'd by genius, and adapted to it by situation, such laws are needless, unnatural, and can have no effect conducive to the public good. (25ff)

The best way to promote the wool industry, Davenant insisted, was not to contrive its production artificially by using laws and import duties that raise domestic prices, but to encourage inexpensive domestic production that would lead to lower prices. Cheap production would enable domestic producers to undersell competitors and would discourage entry by other foreign firms, "but this can never be if . . . we endeavour to give wool an unnatural price here at home." He concluded that "the East-India goods do sometimes interfere with the woollen manufacture must undoubtedly be granted; but the principal matter to be considered is, which way that nation in general is more cheaply supplied" (32ff).

Regarding silk, Davenant again made a sweeping statement:

Wisdom is most commonly in the wrong, when it pretends to direct nature. The various products of different soils and countries is an indication, that providence intended they should be helpful to each other, and mutually supply the necessities of one another. And as it is a great folly to compel a youth to that sort of study, to which he is not adopted by genius, and inclination: so it can never be wise, to endeavour the introducing into a country, either the growth of any commodity, or any manufacture, for which, nor the soil, nor the general bent of the people is proper. (34ff)

Trying to cultivate an industry where it would not naturally arise or was not well suited was ultimately harmful; "a trade forced in this manner, brings no natural profit, but is prejudicial to the public." Davenant argued that domestic production of silk was artificially contrived and unsuited to England—"whatever encouragement it meets with, it cannot thrive with us"—and thus detracted from more profitable employments. The dislocation caused by import competition was not consequential because labor could move between occupations; "In a time of peace, and full employment, these hands can shift from one work to another, without any great prejudice to themselves or the public." The fact that silk could be produced much cheaper abroad indicated that those in the domestic silk industry would be better employed elsewhere. Even if silk could be suited to England, Davenant was skeptical about (but did not elaborate on) such an infant industry policy: "But though with forcing nature, and by art and industry, we could bring it to greater perfection, yet upon other accounts it is perhaps not advisable, nor for the nation's interest, to promote it." Furthermore, restricting cotton imports from East India would merely enrich other competitors because England would be forced to buy similar goods elsewhere at a higher price.

This is as far as Davenant carries the case for free trade in terms of providing an underlying economic reasoning. His statement was as much a critique of protection as a positive case for free trade. Although he eloquently put forth the view that there is a natural course to commerce that government cannot improve upon but only detract from, Davenant (1696, 37–38) never went so far as to advocate *laissez-faire*: "An unforced and natural improvement may be made in our wealth and substance, and it is here the legislative power may, to good effect, interpose with its care and wisdom . . . it is the prudence of a state to see that this industry [of traders and manufacturers], and stock, be not diverted from things profitable to the whole, and turned upon objects unprofitable, and perhaps dangerous to the public." In other places, Davenant (1698, 128) reveals proclivities toward intervention: "If the trade of England, which is the common concern of all, was made the particular business of some one council of men experienced and knowing therein; and if that council were armed with sufficient powers from the law, our traffic might perhaps be managed more to the general interest and welfare of the kingdom" (133). Such management might include sumptuary laws "such as might prohibit the use of commodities from those countries where we lose in the balance, and where trade is hurtful to us."[4] Yet he (1698, 139) also mentions that "a nation that visibly loses in the balance of trade with any country, will find very little help by laying high duties at home" to block imports or in undertaking measures to encourage exports.[5]

It is one thing to make such free-trade statements and another to provide solid analytical reasoning that supports them. Davenant advances the free trade argument further than anyone thus far in this particular debate, and both he and Gardner had briefly mentioned (but did not elaborate upon) a key point: rather than viewing imports as a loss or a cost to the nation for sustaining exports, imports were viewed as being a cheap way of acquiring certain goods indirectly via exports. But what has yet to be encountered is a tract that employs this idea to develop sound analytical reasoning in favor of free trade. The first such performance, and what a tremendous achievement it was, is Henry Martyn's *Considerations upon the East India Trade*, first published in 1701.[6] Martyn's work is highly unusual for the period in which it appeared. His treatment is thorough, systematic, and—most unusually—acutely analytical, with his subject discussed with great clarity

---

[4] On the other hand, Davenant (1696, 49) wrote that "there is no country without a multitude of sumptuary laws, but hardly a place can be instanced, where they are observed, or produce any public good."

[5] Waddell (1958, 281) and others have insisted that Davenant was a mercantilist because of his concern over the general balance of trade. For our purposes, the real question is not whether a writer expresses concern over the balance of payments under certain circumstances, but whether they entertain recourse to import restrictions. For this reason, Davenant was by and large a free trader in his day, or at least an antiprotectionist—even if he operated in the context of somewhat conventional balance of trade reasoning and even though he was against freedom to trade in the sense of abolishing exclusive companies. What gives particular force to this interpretation is that Davenant promulgated a fiscal proposal that called for customs duties to be replaced by consumption taxes, a key feature of any free trade proposal in the days when tariffs raised a significant amount of government revenue. Davenant (1695, 30–31) first mentions such a scheme, which he (1698, 230) later elaborated on in arguing "to contrive some way of easing the customs, and to give an equal encouragement, by laying duties that may be tantamount upon the commodities when they come into the retailers hands; and so to charge the consumption, instead of the importation." However, in this tract he also contradicts this position, arguing for "moderate duties, such as may not discourage other countries from dealing with us, and encourage our own people to place their efforts in trade where their wealth best operates to the public good." This brief retraction, however, does not reflect the overall tenor of his other statements.

[6] Martyn's authorship of the book has long been suspected and is now firmly established by Christine Macleod (1983). It should be noted that Viner (1937, 104–5) and Schumpeter (1954, 373–74) devote only ten sentences between them to Martyn's impressive reasoning.

and tenacity. Martyn's crisp economic reasoning is well in advance of his contemporaries, and it would not be unreasonable to suggest that he surpasses even Adam Smith in his analytical contribution to the case for free trade. Like Smith, Martyn also had a keen eye for the beneficial economic effects of rivalry and competition.

In the preface, Martyn alerts the reader that "most of the things in these papers are directly contrary to the received opinions." In this tract Martyn supports free trade in both the contemporary and the current sense of the word: he opposed both monopoly restraints on the East India trade and restrictions on manufactured imports from India. Martyn wanted to open the East India trade to all merchants, objecting to restricting trade to just those licensed by the government because this diminished competition: "In an open trade, every merchant is upon his good behaviour, always afraid of being undersold at home, always seeking out for new markets in foreign countries; in the meantime, trade is carried on with less expense: This is the effect of necessity and emulation, things unknown to a single company" (21). Martyn clearly explained how such freedom will make the East India trade less profitable for existing merchants, because open trade will drive the rate of profit down to that of other comparable lines of commerce, but more advantageous for the nation as the volume of trade expands. To the objection that exclusive companies were needed to generate monopoly profits that would finance the protection of trade, Martyn proposed that government provision of such goods would permit an open trade: "The necessary forts and castles may be as well maintained at the public charge; and this may be better paid by the greater gain of an open trade" (28).

The most compelling and original feature of Martyn's work was applying the principle of the division of labor to international trade. The gains arising from the division of labor, of course, had been noted by Plato and Xenephon and in Martyn's time by William Petty in a few scant paragraphs, but not directly in the context of international exchange. Martyn likened England's importation of cheap Indian cotton goods to a labor-saving invention, or to a new technology for producing manufactured goods, wherein more cotton goods could be obtained through less labor than before by exporting other products. "Things may be imported from India by fewer hands than as good would be made in England, so that to permit the consumption of Indian manufactures is to permit the loss of few men's labour . . . a law to restrain us to use only English manufactures, is to oblige us to make them first, is to oblige us to provide for our consumption by the labor of many, what might as well be done by that of few, is to oblige us to consume the labour of many when that of few might be sufficient" (47–48). Martyn's analogy was this: "If the same work is done by one, which was done before by three; if the other two are forced to sit still, the Kingdom got nothing before by the labour of the two, and therefore loses nothing by their sitting still" (24).

In the context of international trade: "If nine cannot produce above three bushels of wheat in England, if by equal labour they might procure nine bushels from another country, to employ these in agriculture at home, is to employ nine to do no more work than might be done as well by three" (55). Protection was wasteful and tantamount to throwing away useful labor; "It is to oblige the things to be provided by the labour of many, which might as well be done by few; tis to oblige many to labor to no purpose, to no profit of the kingdom, nay, to throw away their labour, which otherwise might be profitable" (57). "To employ to make manufactures here, more hands than are necessary to procure the like things from the East Indies, is not only to employ so many to no profit, it is also to lose the labor of so many hands which might be employed [elsewhere] to the profit of the Kingdom" (54).

Like Davenant but wholly out of the temper of the period, Martyn was unconcerned about the displacement of labor from import competition: "Manufactures are procured from the East Indies by the labour of fewer hands than the like can be made in England; if by this means any number of people are disabled to follow their former business, the East India trade has only disabled so many to work to no profit of the kingdom; by the loss of such manufactures, of such ways of employing the people, the public loses nothing" (59). "The East India trade destroys no profitable English manufacture, it deprives the people of no employment which we should wish to be preserved" (34). Martyn pressed his case by insisting that an open trade "is the most likely way to make work for all the people." Labor could be gainfully employed in other sectors because competition from India would reduce the price of similar English manufactures and thereby improve their ability to export overseas. He forcefully denied that a lower price of English manufactures would reduce the wages of labor, and distinguished sharply between the wage paid to labor and the cost of labor in production, again likening the East India trade to a productivity increase which lowers effective labor costs but not the wage received by labor. Import competition also forces productivity to advance in other industries. "And thus the East India trade by procuring things with less, and consequently cheaper labour, is a very likely way of forcing men upon the invention of arts and engines, by which other things may be also done with less and cheaper labor, and therefore may abate the price of manufactures, though the wages of men should not be abated" (66).

Gains from increasing the productivity of labor were also set out in his particular interpretation and invocation of the doctrine of universal economy: God bestowed his blessings on people by creating the sea so

> that our wants at home might be supplied by our navigation into other countries, the least and easiest labor. By this we taste the spices of Arabia, yet never

feel the scorching sun which brings them forth; we shine in silks which our hands never wrought; we drink of vineyards which we never planted; the treasures of those mines are ours, in which we have never digged; we only plough the deep, and reap the harvest of every country in the world. (58–59)

Martyn's tract was reprinted in 1720 and therefore could not have been completely ignored by his contemporaries. But his arguments appear not to have generated any discussion or rebuttals in print. By concentrating the reader's attention on the fundamental economic notions of opportunity cost, efficiency, and productivity, Martyn thereby advanced the theory of international trade to a new level. Trade was more than just an exchange of superfluities, as implied by weaker versions of the doctrine of universal economy. Even when imports competed directly with domestic production trade was found to be beneficial in increasing competition and improving economic efficiency. Trade enhanced the productivity of domestic labor in terms of the goods it could ultimately procure and was a means by which more goods could be had from the same domestic resources.

The writings of Gardner, Davenant, and Martyn were the best to emerge in the turn of the century debate over commercial policy in England. As the eighteenth century moved on, more and more contributors were willing to express their sentiment in favor of free trade in goods, even if their level of analysis is not up to Martyn's standards and no one followed up on Martyn's compelling analysis in any significant way. A short tract by Isaac Gervaise has received acclaim for its analysis of the equilibrating mechanism in international payments, and his discussion of commercial policy is perceptive, if less outstanding. Gervaise (1720, 22) employed the notion of opportunity cost (the sacrifice of alternatives) to cast doubt on the ability of government intervention to increase aggregate wealth: "No nation can encourage or enlarge its proportion of any private and natural manufacture, without discouraging the rest; because whether an allowance be given, either to the manufacturer, or transport, that allowance serves, and is employed to attract the workmen from those other manufacture, which have some likeness to the encouraged manufacture."

Applying this to trade policy, Gervaise wrote:

When the natural proportion of one, or more manufactures, although necessary, is not large enough to answer the entire demand of the inhabitants, the best and safest way is freely to suffer their importation from there of the world; taxes on imports being no more than a degree of prohibition, and prohibition only forcing those manufactures to extend themselves beyond their natural proportions, to the prejudice of those, which are, according to the dispositions of the country, natural beyond the entire demand of the inhabitants; which lessens or hinders their exportation, in proportion to the prejudice they receive by the increase of those manufactures, which are but in part natural, and whereof the importation is prohibited. This considered we may conclude, that trade is never in a better condition, than when it's natural and free; the forcing it either by laws, or taxes, being always dangerous: because though the intended benefit or advantage be perceived, it is difficult to perceive its countrecoup; which ever is at least in full proportion to the benefit: Nature not yielding at once, sharpens those countrecoup, and commonly causes a greater evil, than the intended benefit can balance. (22–23)

The implication is that trade promotion in one sector amounts to trade constriction for other sectors, and this cost may be unrecognized but is not unimportant. Once again, like Davenant, an appeal to a seemingly biological concept of balance across economic activities is made in developing the argument that government merely upsets this balance and disturbs these natural interrelationships.

Jacob Vanderlint's (1734, 26) qualified acceptance of the balance of trade criterion for determining beneficial trades did not prevent him from arguing that, "in general, there should never be any restraints of any kind on trade, nor any greater taxes than are unavoidable; for if any trade be restrained in any degree, by taxes or otherwise, many people, who subsisted by the business which now hath restraints laid upon it, will be rendered incapable of pursuing it, and of consequence they must be employed some other way, or drove out of the kingdom, or maintained at the public charge; which last is always a great and unreasonable burden." Vanderlint turned the usual employment argument on its head by stressing the employment loss from trade restrictions rather than the loss from import competition. "All nations of the world, therefore, should be regarded as one body of tradesmen, exercising their various occupations for the mutual benefit and advantage of each other. . . . Now since mankind never complained of having too much trade, but many do really want business sufficient to get a livelihood, prohibitions do in the very nature of things, cut off so much employment from the people, as there would be more, if there were no such prohibitions (42–3). . . . No inconvenience can arise by an unrestrained trade, but very great advantage" (78). This suggested an "invincible argument for a free and unrestrained trade, since if any nation makes goods for us, we must be making others for them or some other nation, and so mutually for each other, provided our goods are made cheap enough to maintain such commerce . . . it is impossible any body should be the poorer, for using any foreign goods at cheaper rates than we can raise them ourselves" (99).[7]

---

[7] Vanderlint still admitted, "Yet I must own, I am entirely for preventing the importation of all foreign commodities, as much as possible; but not by acts of parliament, which never can do any good to trade; but by raising such goods ourselves, so cheap as to make it impossible for other nations to find their account in bringing them to us" (54).

Vanderlint also envisioned a retaliatory dynamic in which trade restraints in one country beget trade restraints in another, with employment suffering in all countries as a result. "When any branch of commerce lessens the cash of a nation, I expect it will be thought fit by high duties or prohibitions to restrain or suppress it, but this I take the liberty to deny, because it will hence become fit for other nations to lay such restraints or prohibitions, as they never to let us have a gainful trade, if they can help it, it being just so far a losing trade to them as it's gainful to us; and as maritime commerce must be, and certainly is now, very much lessened by these mutual restraints, so many people must have lost their employment in every such nation." By avoiding high duties, "this might demonstrate to others the folly of restraining trade in any degree whatsoever" (79–80). Thus, Vanderlint's important contribution complements Martyn's; the latter focused on how trade strengthened the productiveness of domestic labor, whereas the former pointed out the employment costs of trade restraints.

That such ideas were now intellectually credible is evident in Matthew Decker's (1744, 56) call for Britain to become a free port, "by which I mean, that all sorts of merchandise be imported and exported at all times without paying any customs or fees." Though he made no analytical contribution to the case for free trade, Decker ranks as a prominent reformer who reacted against the high import duties of the day.[8] To gain support for his proposals, Decker (1743, 27–28) argued for something similar to what was later known as the compensation principle: the beneficiaries of free trade could compensate those harmed by free trade, ensuring that everyone was better off.

> Since I would willingly calculate my scheme for the good of the whole community and at the same time not to the prejudice of any individual member, if it could be avoided; I would be very willing that the parliament should consider all those who, by this scheme, would lose their present employment. Let their salary be continued to them upon the same foot they have it now, or during their lives, and this perhaps would induce them to look with a favorable eye on our design.

Several other mid-eighteenth-century writers echoed Decker's call for lower tariffs, although this came more as a reaction to the high level of taxation than from a reasoned analysis. This support for more liberal com-

---

[8] Yet elsewhere Decker (1743, 29) contradicts himself, suggesting that "I see very clearly that there must be some regulation upon some certain species of goods which may be imported from abroad, and would interfere with our own manufactures." Joseph Massie (1757, 63) castigated Decker with tremendous spirit and venom for this one exception, arguing not only that it undercut everything else he had said, but that it reduced his work to a "downright bare-faced piece of sophistry."

mercial policies also revealed itself in a debate over the merits of establishing free trade between England, Scotland, and Ireland, and in proposals to make the British isles "free ports," the traffic through which would be exempt from duties to spur trade. These reformist views are most often made in reference to specific cases rather than as general propositions, and were often qualified or contradicted by the author elsewhere. Most of these statements of a free trade position are made without supporting analysis and are too brief and skimpy to merit much consideration.[9]

To ask, therefore, whether one early author was or was not a consistent free trader is to overlook the more meaningful question: which authors, regardless of the consistency of their stand on free trade, contributed to the economic analysis and reasoning that buttressed the case for free trade thereafter. By this standard, Martyn stands out as exceptional among the pre-Smith writers. Other economic writers, such as North and Davenant and Decker, may have asserted that free trade is the best policy to be pursued or described how it could be implemented, but all too frequently their analysis ended there. Martyn's analysis was a tremendous advance, even if never followed or cited until the classical economist J. R. McCulloch rescued him from possible oblivion in the early nineteenth century. This does not imply by any means, however, that such ideas were widely accepted: as Arthur Young (1774, 262) argued, "A general free trade, as there has been no example of it in history, so is it contrary to reason."

. . .

While many of the essential elements of the economic analysis behind free trade predate Adam Smith, none of these writers were able to overthrow established notions of trade and commercial policy and create a new presumption that free trade was the most beneficial policy to be pursued. In creating a compelling case for free trade, Smith, perhaps somewhat surprisingly, did not draw much on these dissenting notions that existed within the

---

[9] As Jacob Viner (1937, 92) once suggested, "there has been great exaggeration of the extent to which free-trade views already prevailed in the English literature before Adam Smith." Many of these authors advocated free trade not as a matter of principle or solely on the basis of economic reasoning, but to achieve some political objective. Henry Martyn, who in many ways expounded the logic of free trade with more profound reasoning than Adam Smith, was also a contributor to the *British Merchant*, a compendium of typical mercantilist doctrine published during the debates over the clauses of the Treaty of Utrecht in 1713–14 that would have liberalized trade with France. Did Martyn contradict himself or merely change his mind between 1701 and 1713? Macleod (1983) suggests that neither is the case: Martyn was politically active and took standard Whig positions in both the East India trade debate at the turn of the century (favoring free imports from India via the East India company) and the French trade debate in 1713–14 (against freer trade with France). That his advocacy was politically driven, of course, takes nothing away from his analytical accomplishments.

mercantilist orthodoxy. Instead, he approached free trade from an entirely different angle, that of the moral philosophy that emerged in the eighteenth-century enlightenment. This approach, married to a more analytical inquiry similar to that of Martyn, ultimately proved successful in establishing a presumption in favor of free trade.

Chapter Four

PHYSIOCRACY AND MORAL PHILOSOPHY

"THE ANTECEDENTS of [Adam] Smith's *laissez-faire* and free trade views," Jacob Viner (1937, 91) once suggested, "are probably rightly to be sought mainly in the philosophic literature, and perhaps also in the writings of the physiocrats, rather than in the earlier English economics literature." This chapter briefly considers French physiocracy and English and Scottish moral philosophy only as they were possible sources for Smith's views on free trade, so as not to stray too far from ideas about commercial policy. Both groups addressed, in different ways, the mercantilist (but really age-old) contention that the state had to direct merchants toward activities that promoted the public good. The physiocrats advocated free trade in the context of a general *laissez-faire* approach that proclaimed the harmony of private actions with the public welfare. The moral philosophers held to a more nuanced position that competition within the framework of natural liberty ensured a broad but imperfect harmony of these interests, with the state creating an institutional framework (a system of justice) that would facilitate this convergence without actually directing the activities of individuals. Although these antecedents provided a philosophical approach to society and the market that Smith found indispensable, the physiocrats and the moral philosophers did not provide much guidance to Smith either in terms of providing an appealing justification for free trade or in improving the quality of economic analysis that could be used to support free trade.

PHYSIOCRACY

In the late seventeenth century, critics of mercantilism multiplied in France just as they had in England. Businessmen and merchants demanded that trade be set free from government interferences. "The greatest secret is to leave trade entirely free; men are sufficiently attracted to it by their own interests. . . . Never have [manufacturers] been so depressed, and trade also, since we have taken it into our heads to increase them by way of authority," stated one report of merchants's views in 1685. "Trade can flourish and subsist only when merchants are free to procure the merchandise they need in the places where they are [sold] at the lowest price, and every time we wish to compel them to buy in one place at the exclusion of all others, merchandise will become more expensive and trade will consequently fall into ruin," read another statement from 1686.[1]

In France, perhaps even more than in England, this period saw the emergence of ideas about economic liberty, later summarized in the maxim *laissez-faire et laissez-passer* (implying freedom to produce and freedom to trade). The economic context to this tradition owes much to Pierre de Boisguilbert, whose writings around 1690–1710 reflected a perspective that Adam Smith later developed.[2] According to Boisguilbert, individuals motivated by their own self-interest unintentionally perform a public service by directing their efforts toward activities that have high private rewards, rewards which can arise only when others value those efforts and hence are willing to pay a high price for them. As he put it, "All are occupied night and day with their own particular interests, but, at the same time, although it is what they care about least, they are contributing to the general good, while, nevertheless, attending to their own individual utility." Boisguilbert provided an excellent analysis of how the price system links, coordinates, and ensures competition between buyers and sellers in the market. Markets free of government restrictions will operate naturally to the benefit of both participants: "It is this reciprocal utility which makes for the harmony of the world and the maintenance of the state; each individual cares only for procuring his personal interest to the maximum extent, and with the greatest possible ease; and when he goes four leagues from home to buy a good, it is because it is not for sale three leagues away, or because it is better value and worth the extra distance."[3] Other than preserving justice, Boisguilbert argued, little government intervention is required to maintain this prosperous system.

These philosophically based notions about natural freedom and economic activity were adopted by one of the first "schools" of economics, the physiocrats, led by François Quesnay in the 1750s. The physiocrats joined in fervent calls for free commerce, although their contribution to the actual economic analysis of free trade was minimal. Indeed, the physiocratic school advocated free trade more as a matter of convenience than conviction. This convenience was based on the strongly held view that the natural produce of the earth, mainly agriculture, was the source of all wealth in society and that free trade would lead to a natural distribution of this produce, thereby tending (in their view) to raise grain prices and benefit agriculture in France. Quesnay's *Tableau Économique* ([1758–59] 1972, 4ff), for example, opened by contrasting the "productive" activities of the agri-

---

[1] Quoted in Lionel Rothkrug (1965, 231–32).

[2] For a fuller discussion of Boisguilbert, see Hazel Roberts (1935) and Terence Hutchison (1988, 107–15).

[3] Quoted in Hutchison (1988, 111).

cultural and raw materials sector with the "sterile" occupations of manufacturing and services. Produce from the land was taken to be the most important of all economic assets and the ultimate source of economic wealth, with all other activities derivative and ultimately dependent upon it. The physiocrats aimed to enact policies that would increase investment in agriculture and draw resources away from other "improper occupations." The agricultural expansion would increase exports and in turn enable greater imports of "sterile" goods for consumption.

In asserting the economic primacy of products from the earth and land, like earlier pro-agrarian, antimercantilist French writers of the seventeenth century, the physiocrats turned the mercantilist view of the ideal commodity composition of trade on its head. For the physiocrats, exporting raw materials and agricultural goods and importing manufactured goods was much more desirable than the reverse. As Quesnay ([1758–59] 1972, 4) put it: "In the mutual trade of the raw produce which is purchased from abroad and the manufactured commodities which are sold abroad, the disadvantage usually lies on the side of the latter commodities, because much more profit is yielded by the sale of raw produce." Indeed, Quesnay ([1757] 1963, 75) believed that countries specializing in manufactures were at risk: "A nation which has little trade in raw produce, and which is reduced to trade in industrial goods in order to subsist, is in a precarious and uncertain position" because new competitors could easily emerge to displace one's export position. Contrary to mercantilist suppositions, any government policy that reduces the price of raw produce in an effort to promote manufactures would led to an extreme chain of events (reminiscent of some of the mercantilist reasoning) whereby "the kingdom's strength is destroyed, its wealth is wiped out, the people are overburdened with taxes, and the sovereign's revenue diminishes."

Quesnay's disciple, the Marquis de Mirabeau (1766, 171–73), also disparaged manufacturing: "Manufactures for home consumption are no better than an object of expence, and by no means a source of income; nor can the exportation of them afford any net profit." Indeed, he urges readers not to confound "the general net produce or income belonging to the nation, with the profits of merchants" because "these profits are to be considered as barren expences, with respect to the nation." Yet he encouraged free trade in manufactures, arguing that a country should export manufactured goods only if it also has the raw materials with which to produce them at home and should expect to gain only to the extent that those manufactures (directly or indirectly) improve the market for produce from the earth.

Because mercantilist policy tended to favor the development of manufacturing relative to agriculture, physiocratic calls for the elimination of all government interference, particularly internal barriers to the grain trade (local policies of provision) and price ceilings on grain, were consistent with their philosophical position and would act to promote agricultural interests. Loath to make an exception to the principle of *laissez-faire*, the physiocrats recognized that consistency dictated that the removal of government restrictions be extended to international trade as well and they concluded that free trade was the best policy. As Quesnay ([1757] 1963, 79) contended, "A state should sacrifice certain of the less important branches of trade in favor of other branches which are more profitable to her and which would increase and assure the revenue of the kingdom's landed property. . . . Nevertheless, all trade ought to be free, because it is in the interests of merchants to devote themselves to those branches of external trade which are the safest and most profitable."[4] This advocacy of free trade was disingenuously convenient because free trade in France suited the physiocrats's objective of promoting greater output of agricultural goods. It is not at all clear that the physiocrats would have been as enthusiastic supporters of free trade had their country been in a different position; one can easily envision them having a more protectionist bent in grain-importing countries.

But aside from the occasional broad, sweeping statements favoring complete liberty in trade, the physiocrats did not devote much attention to international trade or commercial policy, except in the context of removing impediments on the export of grain. They were often unenthusiastic about the role that international trade played in an economy, asserting that internal trade was of greater importance. As Arthur Bloomfield (1938, 731) has noted, "In reaction to the mercantilist stress on foreign trade, the physiocrats were led to belittle its importance and to view it with disdain." Far from "presenting a comprehensive case for free trade on the basis of international specialization," the physiocrats "considered [trade] as a last resort which should be avoided as far as possible." Thus, while the *laissez-faire* views of the physiocrats were adopted to some extent by Smith, their views on free trade did not provide the general conceptual reasoning that Smith would find compelling.[5]

---

[4] "External trade should always be quite free, cleared of all encumbrances and exempted from all impositions, because it is only by means of the communication between nations which it maintains that we can make sure of always having the best possible price for the territory's products in internal trade, and the highest possible revenue for the sovereign and the state" Quesnay ([1766] 1963, 163).

[5] For more details on the intellectual relationships between the physiocrats and Smith and the physiocrats and the classical economists, see Ian Ross (1984) and Ronald Meek (1951), respectively. A.R.J. Turgot, another well-known free trade advocate in France but not a physiocrat, made few substantial contributions to the economic analysis behind free trade. His principal work in economics, *Reflections on the Formation and Distribution of Wealth* (1766), neglects international trade almost completely. But Turgot wrote policy-oriented letters calling for free trade in grain and a noted letter to L'Abbé Terray on the "Marque des Fers" opposing import duties for iron manufacturers. In this letter, as he had elsewhere, Turgot

MORAL PHILOSOPHY

The second, and more important, inspiration for Smith's work stemmed from the philosophical literature sparked in part by Thomas Hobbes's *Leviathan* in 1651. Hobbes argued that self-interest ruled the passions of men and was essentially destructive and chaotic. Men, consulting their reason, however, would delegate authority to a powerful state that could rein in these harmful tendencies for the common good. Hobbes's work sparked a wide debate with philosophers and others striving to refute or support his theory about the destructive nature of self-interest.

One opponent, the English theologian Richard Cumberland ([1672] 1727), argued instead that self-interest was tempered by benevolence and a constructive materialism that enabled the voluntary actions of social individuals to promote the public welfare.[6] Other opponents in the early eighteenth century included Lord Bolingbroke, Joseph Butler, and the Earl of Shaftsbury, who envisioned a self-governing order in which the designer of the universe arranged for there to be harmony between the various elements of social interaction. In this debate about the nature of self-interest, these thinkers began to resolve the conundrum of how the economic self-interest of individuals could conform to the best interests of the greater society. In so doing, they provided a key to uncovering the origins of Smith's thought, as well as creating a rich intellectual debate discussed in more detail by Albert Hirschman (1977) and Milton Meyers (1983).

Early eighteenth-century philosophers addressed the motivational psychology of man and asked whether certain passions should be suppressed or given free reign, but did not always relate these questions to economic behavior. This link became more explicit in Bernard Mandeville's controversial *Fable of the Bees*, first published in 1714 with the suggestive subtitle "Private Vices, Publick Benefits." Mandeville argued that the pursuit of luxury and self-love made for an industrious society and a flourishing economy. Though he described the economic benefits of vice and self-interest in what was then a provocative way, Mandeville was not quite an early *laissez-faire* theorist and he made no direct contribution to the free trade doctrine. Mandeville ([1714] 1924, 1: 111–12) eloquently described the exchange nature of trade: "Buying is bartering and no nation can buy goods of others that has not of her own to purchase them with . . . if we

---

([1773] 1977, 182–88) called for complete liberty in commerce because "this forced increase in price for all buyers necessarily diminishes the sum total of enjoyment, the amount of disposable revenues, the wealth of the proprietors and of the sovereign, and the amount of wages to be distributed to the people." Peter Groenewegen (1969) discusses Turgot's relationship with Adam Smith.

   [6] See Linda Kirk (1987) for a discussion of Cumberland's thought.

continue to refuse taking their commodities in payment for our manufactures, they can trade no longer with us, but must content themselves with buying what they want of such nations as are willing to take what we refuse." But his thoughts on commercial policy were entirely conventional:

> Every government ought to be thoroughly acquainted with, and steadfastly to pursue the interests of the country. Good politicians by dexterous management, laying heavy impositions on some goods, or totally prohibiting them, and lowering the duties on others, may always turn and divert the course of trade which way they please, . . . so they will always carefully prevent the traffic with such nations as refuse the goods of others, and will taking nothing but money for their own. (115–16)

Another philosopher who bridged the gap between moral philosophy and economic behavior, and had a direct association with Adam Smith as his teacher, was Francis Hutcheson. Hutcheson drew upon the natural law tradition of Grotius and Pufendorf and provided Smith as a student with a rich intellectual background from which to help build his economic system.[7] Hutcheson disputed the central place of "self-love" in Mandeville's discussion of human motivation, arguing that natural feelings for others provided a moral sense that tempered self-interest. He linked the eighteenth-century notion of "virtue" to commercial activity in this way and embedded it in a natural law framework. According to Hutcheson (1755, 1: 293–94), "As nature has implanted in each man a desire of his own happiness, and many tender affections toward other in some nearer relations of life . . . tis plain each one has a natural right to exert his powers, according to his own judgment and inclination, for these purposes, in all such industry, labour, or amusements, as are not hurtful to others in their persons or goods, while no more public interest necessarily requires this labours, or requires that his actions should be under the direction of others." "This right," he wrote, "was called *natural liberty*" and should not be deprived as "it would generally create more misery to deprive men of it, because of their imprudence, than what is to be feared from their imprudent use of it."

Hutcheson made a very basic but powerful case for economic freedom, but he completely failed to employ this logic in favor of free trade. In part because a country achieving an export surplus "must increase in its wealth and power," Hutcheson (1755, 2: 318–19) argued that "foreign manufactures and products ready for consumption, should be made dear to the consumer by high duties, if we cannot altogether prohibit the consumption." Exports should be free of hindrances, except when the country had market power to exploit in foreign markets: "Where one country alone has certain materials, they may safely impose duties upon them when exported; but

[7] These connections are explored most recently by Richard Teichgraeber (1986).

such moderate ones as shall not prevent the consumption of them abroad."
Smith was clearly influenced by Hutcheson's ideas about natural liberty
in the economic realm, but was not attracted to his conventional treatment
of commercial policy.

Lord Kames (Henry Home) (1774, 1: 496), a jurist and philosopher of
the Scottish Enlightenment, also approved of government regulation of
trade, warning that "nor ought we ever to rely entirely on our natural advantages [in trade]; for it is not easy to foresee what may occur to overbal-
ance them." After noting that "all nations should benefit by commerce as
by sunshine," Kames proposed a system of export bounties and import
restraints in part because there "is no cause more cogent for regulating
importation, than an unfavorable balance [of trade]" (81, 498). He also
welcomed protection for domestic industries: "To favour a new manufacture of our own, it is proper to lay a duty on the same manufacture imported." But Kames warned that "measures of government ought to be
sparingly exercised, for fear of retaliation" and that government promotion
efforts "ought to be taken with great circumspection, lest it recoil against
ourselves" (498–99).

Josiah Tucker, a prolific economic and religious writer, also played an
important role in describing the harmony of private and public interests in
the economic arena. In one manuscript Tucker (1755, 4ff) described the
philosophical precepts of his economic doctrine, "setting forth the natural
disposition, or instinctive inclination of mankind towards commerce."
Tucker took "self-love" as the "greater mover of human nature" and argued
that it was essentially selfish: "Self-Love is narrow and confined in its
views, and admits of no *sharers* or *competitors*." Tucker conceded that "the
social instinct of *benevolence* is some check upon this selfish *monopolizing*
principle; but it is so very feeble, that it would be quite ineffectual to prevent the mischiefs arising from inordinate self-love, were there no stronger
curb to rein it in: For the love of self is implanted in mankind much more
strongly than the love of benevolence."

But there should be no effort to weaken the power of self-love because
it provides the motivation for improvement and exertion. Therefore, "the
main point to be aimed at, is neither to extinguish nor enfeeble self-love,
but to give it such a direction, that it may promote the public interest by
pursuing its own: and then the very spirit of monopoly will operate for the
good of the whole." Thus the public wisdom of the state and community
can "divert . . . the pursuits of self-love from vicious and improper objects,
to those that are commendable and virtuous; grant no privileges to indolence and ignorance; give no assistance to the ingrossing schemes of monopolists; but raise a general emulation among all ranks and professions in
things relating to the public good." Then the "country will be blessed by
plenty, and abound in commerce." Tucker does not advocate *laissez-faire*;

the proper role of government is neither to repress nor to ignore self-interest, but to harness and channel it into socially desirable directions.[8] This belief, combined with Hutcheson's view that natural liberty should permit all actions that are not harmful to others, very much represents Smith's conceptual approach.

On commercial policy, Tucker was a vitriolic opponent of monopoly trading companies and therefore made a strong case for "a free trade." But when it came to import duties, Tucker adhered to conventional mercantilist thinking, as the following passage illustrates:

> Let him suppose the state to be a living personage, standing on the key of some great seaport and examining goods as loading or unloading. In the former case, if the goods to be exported are completely manufactured, having undergone the full industry and labor of his own people, he ought to lay no embargo whatever upon them, but to show exporters all the favor he can and to protect them in that good work. Whereas, if the goods are only manufactured in part, or, what is worse still, if they are absolutely raw materials, he should lay such taxes upon them to check and discourage their going out of the kingdom in that condition as may be proportionate to their unmanufactured or raw-material state. That is, if they are absolutely raw materials, they ought to have the highest tax laid upon them, and, in some cases, even such as may amount to a prohibition. But if they are partly manufactured and partly otherwise, the tax should be lessened in proportion as they recede from the state of raw materials and approach to complete manufactures. In regard to goods imported, his conduct ought to be just the very reverse of the former; that his, he ought to lay the highest and most discouraging taxes upon foreign complete manufactures, in order to prevent their being worn or used in his kingdom, a less discouraging upon others that are incomplete, and still less upon those that are but little removed from raw-material state. As to raw materials themselves, they ought to be admitted into every port of the kingdom duty-free, unless there are some very peculiar circumstances to create an exception to this general rule. Now, the grounds or foundation of all this reasoning is national industry and labor, because these are the only riches of a kingdom. [Tucker (1758, 58–59)][9]

---

[8] "The great view of the divinely inspired legislator, Moses, seems to have been, to turn the principle of self-love into such a channel that it should always operate for the public good. And, indeed, this ought to be the sole aim of every government, if either good morals or national prosperity are expected." See Tucker (1753, 37n).

[9] Tucker (1755, 96) also had stated: "But of all taxes, this is the worst and most pernicious in its consequences; for a tax upon the *exportation of our own manufactures*, is a tax upon our own industry and labour; and a tax upon the *importation of raw materials*, is no other than a method of tying men's hands behind them, lest they should do themselves and the country service.—The only tax of this nature that is justifiable is that which our *East India* Company lays upon tea, and such other articles and foreign manufactures as do not promote general industry *at home*."

Tucker (1749, 63–64) opposed as too hazardous Matthew Decker's proposal for free trade: "Were we to abolish all duties on *French* goods, and they to do the same on *English* ... the consequence would be ... that *England* would be overrun with *French* silks, laces, wines, brandies, cloths, stuffs, ribbands, fans, toys, &c. And the *French* would take very little or nothing in return."

Thus far, we have briefly considered how the economic implications of the late eighteenth-century debate over self-interest affected conventional views on commercial policy, and the answer is very little. Hutcheson, Tucker, and others described a system of natural liberty in which the public interest would be served by private interests. But they could not see private self-interest operating entirely to the benefit of the public interest in international trade and consequently they never advocated free trade. Yet a coherent intellectual framework is in evidence: the natural liberty view dictating that freedom be given wide reign in the economic realm is supported by the view that commerce, although driven by self-interested participants, can ultimately perform a public service. Adam Smith used this framework to advance the case for free trade and fill the incongruous void that his predecessors had failed to close.

A slightly different intellectual tradition also appeared in mid-eighteenth-century France and Britain that led to pervasive liberal views on trade. The European enlightenment as an intellectual movement was accompanied by a greater cosmopolitan outlook, although it remained more a political doctrine than an economic one.[10] David Hume, the eminent philosopher and Smith's close friend, eloquently set forth this perspective in a series of essays on economic themes. In "Of Commerce," Hume (1752, 15–16) praised foreign trade (as the mercantilists before him had) for "augmenting the power of the state, as well as the riches and happiness of the subject ... a kingdom, that has a large import and export, must abound with more industry, and that employed upon delicacies and luxuries, than a kingdom which rests contented with its native commodities. It is, therefore, more powerful, as well as richer and happier."[11]

Hume's cosmopolitan outlook came to the fore in the essay "Of the Balance of Trade," a sharp retort against trade restrictions bred by national antagonisms. All this would seem to lead to a free trade conclusion, but Hume (1752, 98) spoke of tariffs as a convenient revenue-raising device and also hedged in this way: "All taxes, however, upon foreign commodi-

---

[10] The cosmopolitanism of the enlightenment is examined by Thomas Schlereth (1977).

[11] "[P]erhaps ... the chief advantage which arises from a commerce with strangers," Hume added, is that it "rouses men from their indolence." They "become acquainted with the *pleasures* of luxury and the *profits* of commerce; and their *delicacy* and *industry*, being once awakened, carry them on to farther improvements, in every branch of domestic as well as foreign trade."

ties, are not to be regarded as prejudicial or useless, but those only which are founded on the jealousy above-mentioned. A tax on German linen encourages home manufactures, and thereby multiplies our people and industry. A tax on brandy encreases the sale of rum, and supports our southern colonies." However cosmopolitan in outlook, the Hume who speaks favorably of tariffs to encourage home manufactures is not the Hume that influenced Adam Smith's views on trade policy.

About five years later, however, Hume to some extent withdrew or compensated for these views in an essay "Of the Jealousy of Trade," published around 1758. Here he (1955, 78–82) opposed the "narrow and malignant opinion" that looked upon the economic success of neighbors with jealousy. What if foreign products arose to compete with those produced at home? "I answer, that, when any commodity is denominated the staple of a kingdom, it is supposed that this kingdom has some peculiar and natural advantages for raising the commodity; and if, notwithstanding these advantages, they lose such a manufacture, they ought to blame their own idleness, or bad government, not the industry of their neighbours." If the industry does shrink, opportunities are always available in other sectors: "If the spirit of industry be preserved, it may easily be diverted from one branch to another; and the manufacturers of wool, for instance, be employed in linen, silk, iron, or any other commodities, for which there appears to be a demand." No nation should fear being locked out of the international market: "Nature, by giving a diversity of geniuses, climates, and soils, to different nations, has secured their mutual intercourses and commerce, as long as they all remain industrious and civilized."

This passage is more in tune with Adam Smith's later writings, and in fact may have been written as a result of a controversy with Tucker (described in chapter 10 below). But despite his well-articulated writings in favor of a liberal view of trade, Hume's case for free trade reflects more a moral and philosophical temperament than an acute or novel economic analysis.[12]

·   ·   ·

This exceedingly brief synopsis of the physiocratic and moral philosophic contributions bearing on commercial policy illustrates Jacob Viner's (1937, 92) conclusion that "certain elements of doctrine tending to lead to free-trade views were fairly widely prevalent before the publication of the *Wealth of Nations*." Free trade sentiment in the form of calls for greater liberty in commerce flourished among intellectuals in France and Britain.

---

[12] Hume's development of the automatic price-specie-flow mechanism, as noted in the previous chapter, did much to undermine certain mercantilist predilections about the balance of trade, but as argued previously, these views are conceptually distinct from those relating to free trade.

But this opinion did not have a particularly strong economic basis and was sometimes founded upon a vague cosmopolitanism that had little economic content and therefore could be easily dismissed. Most remarkably, even those who argued that suitably tempered private interests promoted the public welfare failed to reach the conclusion that free trade was warranted. Adam Smith's stupendous accomplishment was in providing a more soundly based economic logic to accompany the philosophically derived compatibility of private interests and public benefits. With this combination in hand, he could speak in a more compelling way on the issue of free trade.

Chapter Five

ADAM SMITH'S CASE FOR FREE TRADE

ANY COMPARISON of the economics literature in the decades before and after the publication of Adam Smith's *Wealth of Nations* in 1776 reveals a sharp break in the treatment of commercial policy. Although "all the important elements in Smith's free-trade doctrine had been presented prior to the *Wealth of Nations*," Jacob Viner (1937, 108) rightly notes that "these were often, however, to be found only in isolated passages not wholly consistent with the views expounded in the surrounding text." While drawing upon the work of others, Smith created such a compelling and complete case for free trade that commercial policy could no longer be seriously discussed without contending with his views, and herein lies one of Smith's foremost contributions to economics. That "the *Wealth of Nations* does not contain a single *analytic* idea, principle, or method that was entirely new in 1776," as Joseph Schumpeter (1954, 184) put it, is less important than what Andrew Skinner (1990, 157) has described as "the presence of *system*; the fact that Smith gave political economy a distinctive analytical *shape* which was a dramatic step forward." Smith achieved what others before him had failed to do: present a systematic, coherent framework for thinking about the economics of trade policy.[1]

.   .   .

Early evidence of Smith's support of free trade comes from compilations of his lectures at Glasgow University in the 1760s. Smith (1978, 391–92) stated that all countries engaged in trade benefited from such exchange and he repeated the cosmopolitan viewpoint prevailing among intellectuals: "All these national jealousy(s) which prompt them to spite and ill-will each other, and refuse to be supplied by them in any convenience of life, must lessen the exchange of commodities, hurt the division of labour, and diminish the opulence of both." Smith unequivocally supported free trade and concluded that "it appears that Britain should by all means be made a free port, that there should be no interruptions of any kind made to foreign trade, that if it were possible to defray the expences of government by any other method, all duties, customs, and excise should be abolished, and that

---

[1] For an overview of Smith's contribution to trade theory in general, including many topics not covered here, such as the vent-for-surplus description of trade, see Arthur Bloomfield (1975).

free commerce and liberty of exchange should be allowed with all nations and for all things" (268).[2]

But the cursory discussion of trade in these lectures was just a sketch of what was to come. The economic analysis of commercial policy was fundamentally changed with the publication of *An Inquiry into the Nature and Causes of the Wealth of Nations* on March 9, 1776. Smith's discussion of trade policy is concentrated in Book IV, "Of Systems of Political Oeconomy."[3] Smith first described "the great object" of mercantilist policies as "to diminish as much as possible the importation of foreign goods for home consumption, and to increase as much as possible the exportation of the produce of domestic industry. Its two great engines for enriching the country, therefore, were restraints upon importation, and encouragements to exportation" (IV.i.35, 45). Smith then set out to "examine chiefly what are likely to be the effects of [such policies] upon the annual produce of [a country's] industry," because "according as they tend either to increase or diminish the value of this annual produce, they must evidently tend either to increase or diminish the real wealth and revenue of the country." In other words, Smith set up a specific criterion to evaluate the effects of various commercial policies in a consistent way. In assessing such policies, Smith argued that one must examine the economy-wide impact of such a policy on the real value of a country's national income (or output), or what he called the real annual revenue of society (or produce).[4] Simply by stating and then consistently applying this standard, Smith had already established a seminal contribution to the theory of commercial policy: no longer was it sufficient to conclude that an import tariff was beneficial simply because employment and output increased in the sector receiving such protection.

Smith first considered protection of domestic industries from foreign

---

[2] Smith (1978, 534–35) also argued that export taxes were more pernicious than import tariffs because the "motives to industry are diminished" with the former, a contention he did not repeat in the *Wealth of Nations*.

[3] All references will be to the Glasgow Edition of the Works and Correspondence of Adam Smith, edited by R. H. Campbell and A. S. Skinner. Quotations will be referenced using the Glasgow convention of citing the book, chapter, and paragraph in the *Wealth of Nations*.

[4] Thus, Smith's case for free trade was based on its being in the national economic interest, not on some cosmopolitan ideal as he was later accused by Friedrich List (see chapter 8) and others. As Smith ([1759] 1976, 229) put it in the *Theory of Moral Sentiments*: "The love of our own country seems not to be derived from the love of mankind. . . . France may contain, perhaps, near three times the number of inhabitants which Great Britain contains. In the great society of mankind, therefore, the prosperity of France should appear to be an object of much greater importance than that of Great Britain. The British subject, however, who, upon that account, should prefer upon all occasions the prosperity of the former to that of the latter country, would not be thought a good citizen of Great Britain. We do not love our country merely as part of the great society of mankind: we love it for its own sake, and independently of any such consideration."

competition, or "restraints upon the importation from foreign countries of such goods as can be produced at home." He contends that high duties or prohibitions on imports diminished competition and gave domestic producers a monopoly of the home market, enabling them to charge higher prices and leading to sloth and mismanagement. Agreeing with mercantilists that a tariff would expand domestic output in the import-competing sector, Smith posed a more penetrating consideration rarely raised by earlier writers:

> That this monopoly of the home-market frequently gives great encouragement to that particular species of industry which enjoys it, and frequently turns toward that employment a greater share of both the labour and stock of the society than would otherwise have gone to it, cannot be doubted. But whether it tends either to increase that general industry of the society, or to give it the most advantageous direction, is not, perhaps, altogether so evident. (IV.ii.2)

To evaluate the impact of trade restrictions on real income, one needed a way of thinking about how real income was determined. To address this point, Smith clarified the philosophical underpinnings of his views of commerce and the economic interactions of individuals in the marketplace. Smith started with the proposition that individuals always direct their labor to their best possible advantage; that is, they "endeavour to employ it in the support of that industry of which the produce is likely to be of the greatest value, or to exchange for the greatest quantity either of money or of other goods" (IV.ii.8). "Every individual is continually exerting himself to find out the most advantageous employment for whatever capital he can command. It is his own advantage, indeed, and not that of the society, which he has in view. But the study of his own advantage naturally, or rather necessarily leads him to prefer that employment which is most advantageous to the society" (IV.ii.4). This led to Smith's classic statement:

> As every individual, therefore, endeavours as much as he can both to employ his capital in the support of domestic industry, and so to direct that industry that its produce may be of the greatest value; every individual necessarily labours to render the annual revenue of the society as great as he can. He generally, indeed, neither intends to promote the public interest, nor knows how much he is promoting it. By preferring the support of domestic to that of foreign industry, he intends only his own security; and by directing that industry in such a manner as its produce may be of the greatest value, he intends only his own gain, and he is in this, as in many other cases, led by an invisible hand to promote an end which was no part of his intention. Nor is it always the worse for the society that it was no part of it. By pursuing his own interest he frequently promotes that of the society more effectually than when he really

intends to promote it. I have never known much good done by those who affected to trade for the public good. (IV.ii.9)

That self-interested individuals perform a beneficial service to society had, of course, been noted early on by the Greeks and scholastics, who contended that profit-seeking merchants in carrying grain from low to high price regions transported it from abundant to scarce markets to the general benefit, and among his contemporaries, as indicated in the previous chapter. Smith made this point the cornerstone of his economic framework. With clarity and persuasiveness he maintained that the natural liberty of individuals interacting in the economic realm, each seeking their own betterment by providing goods and services to others, would lead to an efficient allocation of resources from the standpoint of society; the wants and desires of individuals would be met, if it was profitable to do so, and the annual revenue of society (real national income) would be raised to its highest level. Both for this reason, and because respect for the natural liberty of citizens dictated it, the competitive market (rather than the government) was the best mechanism for determining profitable lines of activities and allocating resources to those ends.

Although Smith did not envision much of a role for government in directing market processes or in dictating market outcomes, he was far from a full-fledged adherent to the *laissez-faire* doctrine. Smith believed that government did have an important role in supporting the market mechanism as a social institution.[5] He outlined many circumstances in which government policies, such as the provision of certain public goods and the establishment of a system of law and justice, could allow the "invisible hand" of the market to operate more effectively. Thus, unlike what some critics would later charge, Smith's case for free trade did not rest upon the case for *laissez-faire*. At the same time, the existence of circumstances in which there might be a productive role for government policy did not justify or necessitate any departures from free international trade.

In this general context, Smith argued forcefully that the key concept in assessing economic policy is the notion of opportunity costs, or the trade-offs between alternative activities under resource constraints. Stated simply, because the amount of capital and labor was fixed in an economy at any given point in time, increasing the output in one sector could only come at the cost of using resources already employed elsewhere in the economy. This had clear and immediate implications for policies that aimed to promote certain industries or sectors. "No regulation of commerce can increase the quantity of industry in any society beyond what its capital can maintain," Smith wrote (IV.ii.3). "It can only divert a part of it into a

---

[5] The two classic articles on this theme are by Jacob Viner (1927) and Nathan Rosenberg (1960).

direction into which it might not otherwise have gone; and it is by no means certain that this artificial direction is likely to be more advantageous to the society than that into which it would have gone of its own accord." This fundamental principle of Smith's work departed entirely from mercantilist doctrine which implicitly held that government interference could either produce a more desirable mix of output than the free market, or produce a greater volume of total output, or both.

Thus far Smith's reasoning was not based on any particularly new ideas about trade, but rather was derived from a different conception of the economic organization of society and the role of natural liberty in promoting national wealth. Finally, Smith linked these ideas to commercial policy:

> If a foreign country can supply us with a commodity cheaper than we ourselves can make it, better buy it of them with some part of the produce of our own industry, employed in a way in which we have some advantage. . . . It is certainly not employed to the greatest advantage, when it is thus directed towards an object which it can buy cheaper than it can make. The value of its annual produce is certainly more or less diminished, when it is thus turned away from producing commodities evidently of more value than the commodity which it is directed to produce. According to the supposition, that commodity could be purchased from foreign countries cheaper than it can be made at home. It could, therefore, have been purchased with a part only of the commodities, or, what is the same thing, with a part only of the price of the commodities, which the industry employed by an equal capital, would have produced at home, had it been left to follow its natural course. The industry of the country, therefore, is thus turned away from a more, to a less advantageous employment, and the exchangeable value of its annual produce, instead of being increased, according to the intention of the lawgiver, must necessarily be diminished by every such regulation. (IV.ii.12)

This is a powerful and bold conclusion. Employing the concept of opportunity cost in terms of national income, Smith asserted with unwavering confidence that free trade permits the best allocation of society's resources and that protective tariffs interfere with this allocation and consequently reduce national income. (Note, however, that Henry Martyn was more explicit about the efficiency of free trade than Smith is in this paragraph.) Furthermore, the statement is backed up by a systematic framework of economic reasoning which, however flawed or subject to qualification, proved (not surprisingly) to be much more compelling than the exceedingly loose statements that characterized much of the mercantilist literature. This particular conclusion about trade policy actually pushed Smith's logic farther than he previously implied. Earlier he wrote that "it is by no means certain" that government interference "is likely to be more advantageous to the society than that into which it would have gone of its own accord." But in

the context of trade policy he wrote that the annual produce "must necessarily be diminished by every such regulation." This certitude perhaps
came from the demonstrable fact that certain goods could be acquired more
cheaply from imports than through domestic production.

Establishing this static notion of economic efficiency was clearly compelling, but it was by no means the sole or even the principal gain from
trade, according to Smith. "Between whatever places foreign trade is carried on, they all of them derive two distinct benefits from it." The first is the
exchange of superfluities which "satisfy a part of their wants, and increase
their enjoyments." The second, and more powerful force, was that "by
opening a more extensive market for whatever part of the produce of their
labour may exceed the home consumption, it encourages them to improve
its productive powers, and to augment its annual produce to the utmost, and
thereby to increase the real revenue and wealth of the society" (IV.i.31).
The division of labor, which Smith emphasized in Book I on "the Causes
of Improvement in the Productive Powers of Labour," spurred productivity
improvements such that a given amount of capital and labor could produce
more output. This force was particularly potent in the context of international trade. Because "the division of labor is limited by the extent of the
market," free trade widened the extent of the market and permitted a more
refined division of labor. In addition, free trade facilitated the exchange of
knowledge about new methods of production and new business practices:
"Nothing seems more likely to establish this equality of force than that
mutual communication of knowledge and of all sorts of improvements
which an extensive commerce from all countries to all countries naturally,
or rather necessarily, carries along with it" (IV.viii.c.80). The worldwide
division of labor brought about by international trade stimulated additional
improvements in production that fueled the productivity of domestic labor
and capital and thereby advanced the well-being of individuals.

Smith's exposition of the static gains from free trade and dynamic effects of the division of labor and technology transfer were outstanding for
the period in which he was writing. However, critics could argue that tariffs
could alter the incentives to accumulate new capital and thus lead to higher
output, although they would have to specify precisely the mechanism
which would generate this result to make their argument compelling. Smith
dismissed the likelihood that growth could increase by pursuing a policy of
protection:

> The industry of society can augment only in proportion as its capital augments,
> and its capital can augment only in proportion to what can be gradually saved
> out of its revenue. But the immediate effect of every such regulation is to
> diminish its revenue, and what diminishes its revenue, is certainly not very
> likely to augment its capital faster than it would have augmented of its own

accord, had both capital and industry been left to find out their natural employments. (IV.ii.13)

Smith also attacked the balance of trade motive for government interference with trade:

There is no commercial country in Europe of which the approaching ruin has not frequently been foretold by the pretended doctors of this system, from an unfavourable balance of trade. After all the anxiety, however, which they have excited about this, after all the vain attempts of almost all trading nations to turn that balance in their own favour and against their neighbors, it doest not appear that any one nation in Europe has been in any respect impoverished by this cause. Every town and country, on the contrary, in proportion as they have opened their ports to all nations; instead of being ruined by this free trade, as the principles of the commercial system would lead us to expect, have been enriched by it. (IV.iii.c.14)

Smith conceded two cases in which, to his mind, import duties were justifiable. "The first," he wrote, "is when some particular sort of industry is necessary for the defence of the country" (IV.ii.23). The reason, quite simply, is that "defense . . . is of much more importance than opulence." This statement implicitly recognizes that national security could be purchased only through the material sacrifice of other desirable goods. By accepting this trade-off in principle, Smith believed that protecting defense-related industries justified tariff protection against import competition, although this constituted a noneconomic argument for tariffs rather than one arising from economic analysis.

The second exception concerned cases in which domestic goods were subject to taxes not levied on foreign goods. Imposing equivalent import duties would then equalize the tax treatment of domestic and foreign goods and, according to Smith,

would not give the monopoly of the home market to domestic industry, nor turn towards a particular employment a greater share of the stock and labour of the country, than what would naturally go to it. It would only hinder any part of what would naturally go to it from being turned away by the tax, into a less natural direction, and would leave the competition between foreign and domestic industry, after the tax, as nearly as possible upon the same footing as before it. (IV.ii.31)

Smith also mentioned two other practical considerations "in which it may sometimes be a matter of deliberation" about how import duties should be eliminated. The first concerned reciprocity, or "when some foreign nation restrains by high duties or prohibitions the importation of some of our manufactures into their country" (IV.ii.38). "Revenge in this case naturally dictates retaliation, and that we should impose the like duties and prohibitions upon the importation of some or all of their manufactures into our," Smith wrote, adding that "[n]ations, accordingly[,] seldom fail to retaliate in this manner." But Smith's own advice was characteristically practical:

> There may be a good policy in retaliations of this kind, when there is a probability that they will procure the repeal of the high duties or prohibitions complained of. The recovery of a great foreign market will generally more than compensate the transitory inconveniency of paying dearer during a short time for some sorts of goods. To judge whether such retaliations are likely to produce such an effect, does not, perhaps, belong so much to the science of a legislator, whose deliberations ought to be governed by general principles which are always the same, as to the skill of that insidious and crafty animal, vulgarly called the statesman or politician, whose councils are directed by the momentary fluctuations of affairs. When there is no probability that any such repeal can be procured, it seems a bad method of compensating the injury done to certain classes of our people, to do another injury ourselves, not only to those classes, but to almost all the other classes of them. (IV.ii.39)[6]

Smith essentially states that reciprocity (temporary retaliation to reduce foreign trade restrictions) is a noneconomic question. If trade policies are interdependent, in the sense that the policies of one country can affect the policies of another, then a tactical issue is introduced that complicates the basic free trade issue. Economic analysis in itself is of little guidance because it cannot indicate the circumstances under which a given retaliatory action will or will not reduce a foreign trade barrier. Smith clearly viewed retaliation as a question of tactics, not of strategy. The fundamental principle was still clear: free trade should be pursued independently of other countries' policies.

The second "matter of deliberation" concerned the speed of introducing free trade. If lower duties promise to bring about a severe dislocation of domestic labor and capital (which is "much less [a problem] than is commonly imagined"), then "freedom of trade should be restored only by small gradations, with a good deal of reserve and circumspection" (IV.ii.40).

Smith then briefly turned to consider export policies such as bounties or subsidies, scoffing at such artificial efforts to increase exports:

---

[6] "When our neighbours prohibit some manufacture of ours, we generally prohibit, not only the same, for that alone would seldom affect them considerably, but some other manufacture of theirs. This may no doubt give encouragement to some particular class of workmen among ourselves, and by excluding some of their rivals, may enable them to raise their price in the home-market. Those workmen, however, who suffered by our neighbours' prohibitions will not be benefited by ours."

We cannot force foreigners to buy their goods, as we have done our own countrymen. The next best expedient it has been thought, therefore, is to pay them for buying. It is in this manner that the mercantile system proposed to enrich the whole country, and to put money into all our pockets . . . if the bounty did not repay to the merchant what he would otherwise lose upon the price of his goods, his own interest would soon oblige him to employ his stock in another way. . . . The effect of bounties, like that of all the other expedients of the mercantile system, can only be to force the trade of a country into a channel much less advantageous than that in which it would naturally run of its own accord. (IV.v.a.1,3)[7]

Smith closed out his discussion of trade policy in Book IV of the *Wealth of Nations* with a broad statement that put his case into perspective. "The laudable motive of all these [mercantilist] regulations," he declared, "is to extend our own manufactures, not by their own improvement, but by the depression of those of all our neighbours, and by putting an end, as much as possible, to the troublesome competition of such odious and disagreeable rivals." The problem with mercantilism was not the laudable motive of encouraging economic progress, but the way in which that end was achieved. That motive became distorted by special business interests to the detriment of the national welfare. Smith held that

consumption is the sole end and purpose of all production; and the interests of the producer ought to be attended to, only so far as it may be necessary for promoting that of the consumer. . . . But in the mercantile system, the interest of the consumer is almost constantly sacrificed to that of the producer; and it seems to consider production, and not consumption, as the ultimate end and object of all industry and commerce. In the restraints upon the importation of all foreign commodities which can come into competition with those of our own growth, or manufacture, the interest of the home-consumer is evidently sacrificed to that of the producer. It is altogether for the benefit of the latter, that the former is obliged to pay that enhancement of price which this monopoly almost always occasions. (IV.viii.48–50)

In a later passage, Smith summed up his case for natural liberty in commerce:

[7] "Bounties upon the exportation of any home-made commodity are liable, first, to that general objection which may be made to all the different expedients of the mercantile system; the objection of forcing some part of the industry of the country into a channel less advantageous than that in which it would run of its own accord; and, secondly, to the particular objection of forcing it, not only into a channel that is less advantageous, but into one that is actually disadvantageous; the trade which cannot be carried on but by means of a bounty being necessarily a losing trade" (IV.v.a.24).

It is thus that every system which endeavours, either, by extraordinary encouragements, to draw towards a particular species of industry a greater share of the capital of the society than what would naturally go to it; or, by extraordinary restraints, to force from a particular species of industry some share of the capital which would otherwise be employed in it; is in reality a great subversion of the great purpose which it means to promote. It retards, instead of accelerating, the progress of the society towards real wealth and greatness; and diminishes, instead of increasing, the real value of the annual produce of its land and labour. All systems either of preference or of restraint, therefore, being thus completely taken away, the obvious and simple system of natural liberty establishes itself of its own accord. Every man, as long as he does not violate the laws of justice, is left perfectly free to pursue his own interest his own way, and to bring both his industry and capital into competition with those of any other man, or order of men. The sovereign is completely discharged from a duty, in the attempting to perform which he must always be exposed to innumerable delusions, and for the proper performance of which no human wisdom or knowledge could ever be sufficient; the duty of superintending the industry of private people, and of directing it towards the employments most suitable to the interest of society. (IV.ix.50–51)

To understand just how sharp a break Smith's approach was with mercantilist thinking, one also needs to consider what is *not* in his writings. Smith does not exaggerate the role of trade in the domestic economy.[8] He ridiculed barriers to the importation of the luxury goods that mercantilists abhorred.[9] Most strikingly, stark judgments about the desirability of a particular commodity composition of trade are absent. The commodity composition of a country's external trade reflected its stage of economic development and the natural conditions (such as factor endowments) in which it operated.[10] Smith took a more balanced position than either the mercantilists, who magnified the importance of manufacturing, or the physiocrats, who embellished the importance of agriculture. In his discussion of the domestic economic relationship between town and country, which ex-

---

[8] In several places in the *Wealth of Nations*, Smith ranks domestic trade as being more useful than international trade. But as George Stigler (1976) points out, this is one of Smith's "proper failures."

[9] "It is the highest impertinence and presumption, therefore, in kings and ministers, to pretend to watch over the oeconomy of private people, and to restrain their expense either by sumptuary laws, or by prohibiting the importation of foreign luxuries. They are themselves always, and without any exception, the greatest spendthrifts in the society. Let them look well after their own expense, and they may safely trust private people with theirs. If their own extravagance does not ruin the state, that of their subjects never will" (II.iii.36).

[10] In the words of Hla Myint (1977, 240), who considers Smith's views on economic development, free trade in developing countries was, for Smith, "a method of bringing out more fully the longer-run productive potentialities of countries provided by an increasing division of labour, capital accumulation and changing supplies of factors of production."

changed manufactured goods and raw produce with each other, Smith denied that "the gain of the town is the loss of the country."

> The gains of both are mutual and reciprocal, and the division of labour is in this, as in all other cases, advantageous to all the different persons employed in the various occupations into which it is subdivided. . . . The inhabitants of the town and those of the country are mutually the servants of one another. The town is a continual fair or market, to which the inhabitants of the country resort, in order to exchange their rude for manufactured produce. It is this commerce which supplies the inhabitants of the two both with the materials of their work, and the means of their subsistence. The quantity of the finished work which they sell to the inhabitants of the country, necessarily regulates the quantity of the materials and provisions which they buy. Neither their employment nor subsistence, therefore, can augment, but in proportion to the augmentation of the demand from the country for finished work; and this demand can augment only in proportion to the extension of improvement and cultivation. (III.i.1, 4)

Like the town and country, different countries specialize in the export of different goods based on natural advantages that came from their factor endowments and stage of economic development. Countries exporting raw produce did so to their advantage but were not necessarily destined to continue forever in that state as long as stable governance was conducive to freedom and commerce and accumulation, thereby enabling individuals to invest in physical and human capital. This was best achieved not through the artificial contrivance of commercial policy, which merely shuffled resources from one sector to another and which Smith thought distorted incentives and was unlikely to succeed in increasing national wealth. Instead, private individuals seeking to better their condition would naturally engage in the types of activities and improvements that would enrich the economy if only government had the wisdom not to stifle the process.[11]

---

[11] According to Smith, "The uniform, constant, and uninterrupted effort of every man to better his condition, the principle from which publick and national, as well as private opulence is originally derived, is frequently powerful enough to maintain the natural progress of things toward improvement, in spite both of the extravagance of government, and of the greatest errors of administration." England's success was in allowing this process to operate unchecked: "When we compare, therefore, the state of a nation at two different periods, and find, that the annual produce of its land and labour is evidently greater at the latter than at the former, that its lands are better cultivated, its manufactures more numerous and more flourishing, and its trade more extensive, we may be assured that its capital must have increased during the interval between those two periods. . . . In the midst of all the exactions of government, this capital has been silently and gradually accumulated by the private frugality and good conduct of individuals, by their universal, continual, and uninterrupted effort to better their own condition. It is this effort, protected by law and allowed by liberty to exert itself in the manner that is most advantageous, which has maintained the progress of England towards opulence and improvement in almost all former times. . . ." (II.iii.31–32, 36)

Smith's policy of free trade, therefore, applied to all countries regardless of their state of economic development.

. . .

Other writers had stated free trade conclusions before Adam Smith, but none (with the possible exception of Henry Martyn) had provided a firm conceptual framework in which to sustain such a conclusion. In so doing, Smith inflicted substantial damage on mercantilist doctrines and irrevocably changed the economic analysis of commercial policy.

Chapter Six

FREE TRADE IN CLASSICAL ECONOMICS

THE FIRST QUARTER of the nineteenth century saw a tremendous outpouring of works on economics, particularly on trade, from a legion of intellectuals who became known as the classical economists. These economists developed Smith's ideas in theoretical detail and consolidated the case for free trade through the theory of comparative advantage. This period established beyond a doubt among theoretically inclined analysts of economic policy the presumption that free trade enabled a country to acquire a much greater quantity of goods than would otherwise be available.

. . .

The reception of the *Wealth of Nations* upon publication was respectable but not overwhelming, although immediate public approval is surely not a useful indicator of a book's importance. Roughly a quarter century elapsed after publication of the *Wealth of Nations* before clear evidence begins to establish it as the authoritative work among leading economic thinkers.[1]

But several works written in the 1780s indicate that Adam Smith's analysis had begun to recast the basic ideas about trade and commercial policy. An anonymously written tract entitled *Considerations on the Effects of Protecting Duties* (1783, 18ff) argued that "wherever a protecting duty has been enacted, an increase in the *particular manufacture* has followed; yet I deny that thereby the wealth of the *whole community* has been increased." Protection forces consumers to purchase the same goods at higher prices or inferior goods at the same price, the author stated, and operates "as if [the consumer] were transported to a climate less friendly, and a soil less fertile than that in which he had lived. . . . It operates as a tax upon every consumer in the country, the amount of which is put into the pockets of a few manufacturers." The implication for commercial policy was unambiguous: "The policy of every legislature should be, to enable its people to obtain the

---

[1] As Richard Teichgraeber (1987, 365) points out: "We still know astonishingly little about the process by which Smith's book was canonized. In 1793, Dugald Stewart talked of a hope that 'in due time' Smith's example would be followed by other students of political economy. Only ten years later, Francis Horner, a former pupil of Stewart's and a founder of the *Edinburgh Review*, spoke of a 'superstitious worship' that had come to be attached to Smith's name." The *Wealth of Nations* was out of temper with the times when it first appeared, but it did benefit from the growing sentiment in favor of a more liberal trade policy. See Kirk Willis (1979) and Salim Rashid (1982).

greatest possible quantity of every kind of consumable commodity, by the smallest possible exertion of labour"; in other words, by adopting free trade.

In 1788 a short, exceedingly well-argued book (revealingly entitled *New and Old Principles of Trade Compared*) put together a cogent attack on the "monopoly theory of trade," and contained one of the clearest statements yet to appear on the advantages from trade based on a division of labor across countries. Benjamin Vaughan (1788, 2, 25–26) forcefully described how a country could acquire more goods with trade: "The system of FREE TRADE . . . preferring abundance to ostentation, would force nothing but a disposition to industry; concluding, that if one nation raises flax with most success, and another wool, the sum of these commodities must be augmented in the world, when each nation devotes itself to its separate talents; and that, upon exchanging the two commodities, each nation will have a greater share of the two conjunctively, than if each had attempted to raise them both at home." Protection, by contrast, resulted in a net social loss: "Where a restraint is imposed to favor the class of producers, its direct operation is to injure the class of consumers, whereas these two classes ought to flourish conjunctively; and what makes this case still more unfortunate and unequal is, that the class of consumers in each instance is usually the most numerous, and that the loss sustained by the consumers generally *far exceeds* the gain secured to the producers." By reiterating the advantages of the territorial division of labor, the author strongly reinforced the idea that free trade is the most desirable policy.

The political turmoil across Europe in the 1790s was not conducive to calm reflection on matters of trade policy, at least in terms of much published work that built on or challenged Smith's ideas. William Spence stirred up a controversy in 1807 with his tract *Britain Independent of Commerce*, which argued, using physiocratic-type reasoning, that the cutting off of Britain's external trade during wartime would not adversely affect the economy because agriculture and internal trade formed the basis for all wealth. This prompted replies from James Mill (1808, 36–37) and Robert Torrens (1808, 53), both of whom described the productivity and efficiency benefits of trade much in the manner that Henry Martyn had in 1701. Mill (1808, 38–39), for example, reiterated Smith's discussion of the international division of labor:

> The commerce of one country with another, is in fact merely an extension of that division of labour by which so many benefits are conferred upon the human race. As the same country is rendered the richer by the trade of one province with another; as its labour becomes thus infinitely more divided, and more productive than it could otherwise have been; and as the mutual supply to each other of all the accommodations which one province has and another

wants, multiplies the accommodations of the whole, and the country becomes thus in a wonderful degree more opulent and happy; the same beautiful train of consequences is observable in the world at large, that great empire, of which the different kingdoms and tribes of men may be regarded as the provinces. In this magnificent empire too one province is favourable to the production of one species of accommodation and another province to another, by their mutual intercourse they are enabled to sort and distribute their labour as most peculiarly suits the genius of each particular spot. The labour of the human race thus becomes much more productive, and every species of accommodation is afforded in much greater abundance.

The notion that imported goods could be acquired more cheaply abroad because the absolute cost of production was lower than at home has come to be known as the "eighteenth-century rule," owing to its occasional use during that century. After Adam Smith, however, the eighteenth-century rule became an integral part of the case for free trade, whereas prior to Smith (with the exception of those such as Henry Martyn) it was sometimes employed to show how cheaper imports could not be excluded from the home market except by raising their price through import duties. As Mill's statement above indicates, the division of labor among nations could be a mechanism whereby goods would be produced where their cost of production was lowest.

But Mill and Torrens were on the verge of an even more important insight. The question as they posed it was the choice between acquiring a given quantity of a good, say corn, by using labor and capital to produce the corn at home, or by using that labor and capital to make other products, such as manufactures, that could be exchanged via trade for corn. Both Mill and Torrens pointed out that it was more efficient to allow free trade to determine how a given amount of resources should be used to generate the largest amount of corn for consumption. This manner of thinking about trade, as an indirect way of producing certain goods for consumption, was stated by Mill (1814, 4–5), which is cited for its clarity of expression:

> If we import, we must pay for what we import, with the produce of a portion of our labour exported. But why not employ that labour in raising the same portion at home? The answer is, because it will procure more corn by going in the shape of commodities to purchase corn abroad, than if it had been employed in raising it at home. . . . A law, therefore, to prevent the importation of corn, can have only one effect,—to make a greater portion of the labour of the community necessary for the production of its food.

This indirect way of thinking about trade led to the most important analytical contribution of classical economics relating to the free trade doctrine, the theory of comparative costs, or comparative advantage.[2] This theory stated that certain goods could be advantageously imported from abroad *even if* the home country had an absolute cost advantage in producing the good. Robert Torrens (1815, 263–64) first recognized the essence of the comparative advantage argument when he wrote:

> Let us suppose, that there are, in England, unreclaimed districts, from which corn might be raised at as small an expense of labour and capital, as from the fertile plains of Poland. This being the case, and all other things the same, the person who should cultivate our unreclaimed districts, could afford to sell his produce at as cheap a rate as the cultivator of Poland; and it seems natural to conclude, that if industry were left to take its most profitable direction, capital would be employed in raising corn at home, rather than bringing it in from Poland at an equal prime cost, and at much greater expense of carriage. But this conclusion, however obvious and natural it may, at first sight, appear, might, on closer examination, be found entirely erroneous. If England should have acquired such a degree of skill in manufactures, that, with any given portion of her capital, she could prepare a quantity of cloth, for which the Polish cultivator would give a greater quantity of corn, than she [England] could, with the same portion of capital, raise from her own soil, then, tracts of her territory, though they should be equal, nay, even though they should be superior, to the lands in Poland, will be neglected; and a part of her supply of corn will be imported from that country.

As has been pointed out by Lionel Robbins and others, this formulation lacks only the comparison of the cost ratios in both countries (that is, in Poland as well) whereby the theory is stated in its entirety. David Ricardo ([1817] 1951, 1: 128) provided this finishing touch in his *On the Principles of Political Economy and Taxation* in 1817 and James Mill (1824) in an article on colonies written in 1817 but first published in early 1818.

Why was the theory of comparative costs such an advance over the eighteenth-century rule? The latter illustrated the gains from specialization and trade when countries differed in their ability to produce different goods. But what if one country was superior to another in producing all goods? In other words, why should a country import corn when it could produce that corn with less expense of capital and labor at home than the foreign country could? (Or, conversely, how could a country gain from trade if that country was inferior in the production of all goods?) The theory of comparative costs demonstrated that there would still be mutual gains from specialization and trade even under those circumstances. Countries would specialize in the production of the good in which their opportunity cost (in terms of the implicit sacrifice of other, forgone goods, not in terms of absolute cost) was lowest. Combined with some simple numerical examples, the classical

---

[2] For an overview of classical thought on trade, see Denis P. O'Brien (1975, 170–205).

economists showed how both countries could potentially consume more of both goods as a result of free trade.

David Ricardo, perhaps the most illustrious member of the classical school, has traditionally received virtually all the credit for expounding the theory of comparative costs. The *Principles* contains the famous chapter 7 example of Portugal and England exchanging wine and cloth, wherein Portugal has an absolute cost advantage in the production of both commodities but comparative cost advantage in wine. Yet Ricardo's mere three-paragraph discussion was poorly expressed, awkwardly placed in the chapter, and failed to bring out the essence of the theory. John Chipman (1965, 480) has even stated that Ricardo's "statement of the law is quite wanting, so much so as to cast some doubt as to whether he truly understood it." William Thweatt (1976) has suggested that James Mill was actually responsible for Ricardo's three-paragraph example, either because he read Torrens's passage and recognized its significance or because he developed the theory in elaborating on the eighteenth-century rule for his article on colonies.[3] Indeed, in his *Elements of Political Economy*, Mill (1821, 87, 89) set out the comparative costs example with tremendous clarity and even conveyed the intuition for the theory in two simple sentences:

> When a country can either import a commodity or produce it at home, it compares the cost of producing at home with the cost of procuring from abroad; if the latter cost is less than the first, it imports. The cost at which a country can import from abroad depends, not upon the cost at which the foreign country produces the commodity, but upon what the commodity costs which it sends in exchange, compared with the cost which it must be at to produce the commodity in question, if it did not import it.

Mill staunchly advocated free trade and firmly stated that "the benefit which is derived from exchanging one commodity for another, arises, in all cases, from the commodity *received*, not from the commodity given." Because a country "gains nothing in parting with its commodities," what is given away in the form of exports is the *cost* of acquiring imports. This conception of international trade, a hallmark of classical thought, is in direct opposition to that of mercantilist doctrine even though that doctrine too recognized that trade was a form of barter.

In arguing for free trade in policy debates, however, most economists

---

[3] Thweatt's case is plausible because Mill worked closely with Ricardo on the *Principles* and commented extensively on drafts. Inconclusive evidence against his interpretation comes in a letter from Mill to Ricardo in which he states: ". . . that it may be good for a country to import commodities from a country where the production of those same commodities costs more, than it would cost at home: that a change in manufacturing skill in one country, produces a new distribution of the precious metals, are new propositions of the highest importance, and which you fully prove." See David Ricardo (1952, 7: 99). Furthermore, in his article on colonies Mill also credits Ricardo with the theory.

relied not on the abstract theory of comparative advantage, but on the more
simple and intuitive efficiency argument associated with absolute advantage (for example, that Poland was the lowest cost source of grain). The
theory of comparative advantage, however striking, did not become a leading part of the classical canon until John Stuart Mill (James Mill's brilliant
son) gave it prominence in his *Principles of Political Economy*, a book that
educated several generations of students. The first edition of Mill's *Principles* appeared in 1848 and contained a concise yet penetrating account of
the benefits of trade and the costs of protection. Mill lucidly illustrated the
static argument of how total world output and each country's consumption
could increase with international specialization and trade. He ([1848]
1909, 581) also considered the "indirect effects [of trade], which must be
mentioned as benefits of a high order," and counted chief among these "the
tendency of every extension of the market to improve the processes of production." The extension of the market through trade led to greater refinements in production and advances in technology and productivity. These
advances spilled over across countries, according to the younger Mill, for
"whatever causes a greater quantity of anything to be produced in the same
place, tends to the general increase of the productive powers of the world."
But Mill went further to assert, in direct opposition to the ancient Greeks
and Romans, that

> the economical benefits of commerce are surpassed in importance by those of
> its effects which are intellectual and moral. It is hardly possible to overrate the
> value, for the improvement of human beings, of things which bring them into
> contact with persons dissimilar to themselves, and with modes of thought and
> action unlike those with which they are familiar . . . it is indispensable to be
> perpetually comparing [one's] own notions and customs with the experience
> and example of persons in different circumstances . . . there is no nation which
> does not need to borrow from others. (581–82)

John Stuart Mill argued strongly against protection to domestic producers because such policies "render the labour and capital of the country less
efficient in production than they would otherwise be; and compel a waste.
. . . All is sheer loss, to the country as well as to the consumer." He leveled
the employment argument for protection: "The alternative is not between
employing our own country-people and foreigners, but between employing
one class and another of our own country-people," because "the imported
commodity is always paid for, directly or indirectly, with the produce of
our own industry."

Despite their unanimity in extolling the virtues of free trade, the classical
economists were acutely aware that certain groups were harmed by the
policy and they did not entirely overlook those interests. Virtually all of
them agreed with Adam Smith that protection should be phased out to

allow factors of production to adapt and shift to other employments in anticipation of complete free trade. John Stuart Mill even advocated compensating those adversely affected by tariffs, if need be. Writing on agricultural protection (the Corn Laws, which in the first half of the nineteenth century were a lightening rod for controversy, just as Indian calicoes had been in 1690s), Mill (1825, 399ff) argued that "if there were nothing in the whole process but a transfer; if whatever is lost by the consumer and by the capitalist were gains by the landlord; there might be robbery, but there would not be waste, there might be a worse distribution of the national wealth, but there would be no positive diminution of this aggregate wealth." But protectionist duties "occasion in all cases an absolute loss, greatly exceeding the gain which can be derived from them by the receivers of rent; and for every pound which finds its way into the pockets of the landlords, . . . the community is robbed of several." If landlords demand this public transfer, Mill stated that a direct tax is less costly than an indirect one and that financial compensation be paid to the landlords. "It would be better, however, to have a repeal of the Corn Laws, even clogged by a compensation, than not to have it at all; and if this were our only alternative, no one could complain of a change, by which, though an enormous amount of evil would be prevented, no one would lose."

Yet trade was considered tantamount to an economy-wide productivity improvement, and it was thought that concern for those initially harmed by free trade should never delay or prevent that policy from being enacted. "If we should think it madness to prohibit, or to tax, the use of an improved steam-engine, because it must be injurious to those employed in raising coal, what pretence is there for prohibiting or taxing foreign ribands or velvets because their importation would be injurious to the English silk-weaver?" asked Nassau Senior (1828, 59–60). "[T]o prohibit every change which is accompanied by individual injury would be to prohibit every improvement whatever."

All the leading economists of the first half of the nineteenth century— James Mill, David Ricardo, Robert Torrens, John Stuart Mill, John Ramsay McCulloch, Nassau Senior, to mention but the most eminent—wrote, with varying degrees of sophistication, in favor of free trade and stood in virtual unanimity against protectionist import duties. The classical economists reserved particular hostility for the Corn Laws, which in restricting grain imports into Britain were the primary target of their popular writings that castigated protection. But while Ricardo illustrated the benefits of trade using absolute and (only once) comparative cost reasoning in his book and pamphlets and even in the halls of parliament (where he was briefly a member), his case for free trade in agricultural goods also had a distinctive theoretical twist. The Corn Laws assisted landowners by increasing the price of grain and inducing cultivation on less productive land, thereby driving up the rent of land. By increasing the price of grain, the major consumption good of laborers, Ricardo posited that the Corn Laws also produced an increase in economy-wide wages, which were assumed to be fixed in real terms in the short run. This increase in nominal wages adversely affected manufacturers and drove down the profit rate. Ricardo's case for free trade thus hinged on an inverse relationship between wages and profits. As Ricardo ([1815] 1951, 4: 25) put it:

> There are two ways in which a country may be benefited by trade—one by the increase of the general rate of profits, which, according to my opinion, can never take place but in consequence of cheap food, which is beneficial only to those who derive a revenue from the employment of their capital, either as farmers, manufacturers, merchants, or capitalists, lending their money at interest—the other by the abundance of commodities, and by a fall in their exchangeable value, in which the whole community participates. In the first case, the revenue of the country is augmented—in the second the same revenue becomes efficient in procuring a greater amount of the necessaries and luxuries of life.

To Ricardo, an additional and perhaps more significant benefit of trade beyond the static efficiency gain was that lower food prices increased profits and stimulated accumulation and economic growth. Ricardo ([1822] 1951, 4: 237–38) reiterated this argument and pointed out another problem with the Corn Laws:

> Besides the impolicy of devoting a greater portion of our labour to the production of food than would otherwise be necessary, thereby diminishing the sum of our enjoyments and the power of saving, by lowering profits, we offer an irresistible temptation to capitalists to quit this country, that they may take their capitals to places where wages are low and profits high. If landlords could be sure of the prices of corn remaining steadily high, which happily they cannot be, they would have an interest opposed to every other class in the community . . . to give a moderate advantage to one class, a most oppressive burthen must be laid on all the other classes.

While standing by Ricardo's opposition to the Corn Laws and his appreciation for its effects on income distribution, few economists endorsed this theory explicitly or elaborated upon it. John Ramsay McCulloch, for example, argued principally that free trade in grain would diminish price fluctuations, not that it would increase profits and spur capital accumulation.[4]

The most notable exception to this opposition to the Corn Laws among economists came from the Rev. Thomas Malthus. Already controversial because of his population theories, Malthus entered the debate over the

---

[4] See O'Brien (1970, 191–203, 217–28, 378–95).

Corn Laws with two pamphlets in 1815, the first merely laying out the advantages and disadvantages of the Corn Laws, the second setting down his case for import restrictions to secure an independent supply of grain in normal years. "It must be allowed that *a free trade in corn* would, in all ordinary cases, not only secure a cheaper, but a more steady, supply of grain," he (1815, 10) initially conceded. But if there were a general crop failure, other grain exporting countries (such as France) would act in their own interests and impose export restrictions. This would prevent Britain from purchasing any significant amount of grain abroad, exacerbate harmful price fluctuations, and jeopardize the food supply of the country since it unwisely depended upon the good behavior of other governments. Thus, if exporting countries were not committed to free exports during times of scarcity, then (to Malthus) grain-importing countries merited a special exception from the general rule of free trade.[5] "To open our ports, under these circumstances, is not to obtain a free trade in corn," Malthus stated. "Such a species of commerce in grain shakes the foundations, and alters entirely the *data* on which the general principles of free trade are established" (15).

Perhaps even more important, by adopting free trade unilaterally without obtaining free trade in corn elsewhere, Britain would inflict a tremendous loss on its agricultural capital and land, bringing about wrenching domestic adjustments ("the transfer of wealth and population [away from agriculture] will be slow, painful, and unfavorable to happiness") and having far-reaching macroeconomic consequences. Free imports would sharply reduce the rent on land that accrues to landlords, of whom, "it may truly be said, that though they do not so actively contribute to the production of wealth, as either of the classes just noticed [labor and capitalists], there is no class in society whose interests are more nearly and intimately connected with the prosperity of the state" (34). The reason is that the incomes and prosperity of the landlords supported the livelihoods of many others. As the income of landlords declined, "there is reason to fear that it may be accompanied with an actual diminution of home demand," in which case "the whole of the internal trade must severely suffer, and the wealth and enjoyments of the country be decidedly diminished" (33). The repercussions would be felt by manufacturers in particular since the consumption of landlords "affords the most steady home demand for the manufactures of the country, the most effective fund for its financial support, and the largest disposable force for its army and navy" (35). Having rejected Say's Law (that supply automatically creates its own demand and the economy would

---

[5] In fact, Adam Smith had also raised questions of this sort regarding the grain trade because few countries had free trade in corn. Should a large neighboring country have a crop failure, the small neighbor might restrict its exports to prevent domestic shortages. "The very bad policy of one country may thus render it in some measure dangerous and imprudent to establish what would otherwise be the best policy in another" *WN*, IV.v.b.39.

remain at full employment), Malthus envisioned a collapse of aggregate demand that would plunge the economy into a steep depression.[6]

Needless to say, Malthus's tract caused a tremendous controversy among economists. One critical review of his pamphlet believed his argument "insufficient" and maintained that there were "no grounds for apprehension" in the mutual dependence of countries in agricultural trade, calling the idea of dependence on France "chimerical" because Poland and America lay open for agricultural expansion.[7] In 1819, Ricardo (1952, 8: 142) spoke of Malthus's "dangerous heresy on the corn laws." Malthus's reputation suffered considerably, and "after his support of the Corn Bill," his biographer Patricia James (1979, 269) writes, "it was even easier than it had been before to make Mr. Malthus seem like an ogre who wanted large families of little children to be starved into extinction." Malthus's suffering was apparently compounded by the lack of any great conviction that his position was the correct one. Upon Malthus's death, his friend William Empson (1837, 496–97) noted that, in writing against free trade in corn, Malthus "was not on this occasion as sure as usual of the soundness of the judgment which he had pronounced . . . his general principles in favour of freedom of trade were so absolute that, at times, doubts came over him whether any exception ought to be admitted."

Despite his dissenting views on agricultural protection, Malthus generally advocated free trade and never again so openly championed protection for agriculture as he had in 1815. In the fifth (1817) and sixth (1826) editions of his *Essay on the Principle of Population*, Malthus introduced sections discussing import restrictions on corn in which he moderated his views. Here Malthus (1826, 2: 185–86) tried to maintain balance, noting only that "though we may reasonably therefore object to restrictions upon the importation of foreign corn, on the grounds of their tending to prevent the most profitable employment of the national capital and industry, to check population, and to discourage the export of our manufactures; yet we cannot deny their tendency to encourage the growth of corn at home, and to procure and maintain an independent supply." Malthus discussed the special position of agriculture in economy, the "evils" associated with manufacturing, and the problems associated with grain price fluctuations, but seemed to concede that protection was inefficient although possibly desirable on other grounds: "The question is not a question of the efficiency or inefficiency of the measure proposed, but of its policy or impolicy," and "it may not appear impolitic artificially to maintain a more equal balance between the agricultural and commercial classes by restricting the importation of foreign corn, and making agriculture keep pace with manufactures"

---

[6] Another macroeconomic case for protection, developed by John Maynard Keynes, is discussed in chapter 13.

[7] "Corn Laws" (1815, 498–99).

(191). In his *Principles of Political Economy*, Malthus (1820, 225) reiterated his clear bias toward landlords and agriculture by asserting that, unlike the case with other producers in society, "the interests of the state may not sometimes be the same as that of the landlords."

But his ultimate policy conclusion was uncertain in the *Essay*:

> I certainly think that, in reference to the interests of a particular state, a restriction upon the importation of foreign corn may sometimes be advantageous; but I feel still more certain that in reference to the interests of Europe in general the most perfect freedom of trade in corn, as well as in every other commodity, would be the most advantageous. . . . A perfect freedom of trade . . . should always be considered at the great general rule. And when any deviations from it are proposed, those who propose them are bound clearly to make out the exception. [Malthus (1826), 2: 209–10]

So unenthusiastically did Malthus argue for restrictions on grain imports that there is evidence in his correspondence that he later withdrew his support of the Corn Laws, albeit never explicitly in his published work.[8] At any rate, Malthus's arguments did not hold much sway over the classical economists, although his concern about dependence on foreign supply survived in many later arguments for protection.

· · ·

Adam Smith's compelling case for free trade swept up almost all economists in Britain in the first quarter of the nineteenth century, the age of what Karl Marx dubbed "classical economics." The doctrine of free trade became firmly established as orthodoxy among economists in Britain during this period and sustained this position thereafter, despite a gradual weakening toward the end of the century. As Cliffe Leslie (1888, 140) observed, "In the United Kingdom only a single professor of the science—the late Issac Butt, who for a time held the chair of Political Economy in the University of Dublin—has shown any leaning toward protection." (Butt's aim in advocating protection was to redistribute income to the poor.[9]) But this

---

[8] The evidence is marshalled in Samuel Hollander (1992), but has been disputed. See the exchange between J. M. Pullen (1995) and Hollander (1995).

[9] Butt (1846) based his case for protection on the fact that Ireland exported food yet suffered from poverty and unemployment. By imposing duties on imported manufactures consumed primarily by the rich, Ireland's external trade would contract, domestic food prices would fall, and the poor would be set to work: "Protective duties have, so far as they controlled the expenditure of the rich, been the means of giving our labouring classes a larger share in the revenue of the country than they could have had without them, and that in all relaxations of protective duties . . . we may seriously compromise the rights of the poor" (41). The tariff would not reduce food production because manufacturing could increase output by utilizing unemployed labor. "The effect of using Irish instead of imported manufactures would be, to leave all the present ability of paying for labour undisturbed—to leave, therefore,

minor exception aside, virtually all leading economic theorists of the century agreed with Adam Smith's principal conclusions regarding commercial policy and free trade, though they were far from slavish disciples of Adam Smith—Ricardo dissented from Smith's treatment of bounties and the colonial trade, for example. On top of this wide consensus, the classical economists treated the issue of free trade very seriously. As Senior (1828, 88) put it gravely, "The question of free trade is, next to the Reformation, next to the question of free religion, the most momentous that has ever been submitted to human decision."

But the economic analysis underlying the case for free trade did not go unquestioned even in Britain during this period, as we shall see. And outside Britain this consensus in favor of free trade was by no means as well established, with notable economic writers—Friedrich List in Germany, Augustine Cournot in France, Henry Carey in the United States—raising objections to the free trade doctrine. The intellectual scene in the mid-nineteenth century, however, was fundamentally different than it had been in the mid-eighteenth century. In the latter period, those rejecting free trade could not carry a debate merely by reiterating the mercantilist conventional wisdom. They had to make a new, positive case for protection in specific cases against the general presumption that free trade was beneficial. Some of these cases were even considered successful. As John Stuart Mill ([1848] 1909, 920) put it, "Defeated as a general theory, Protectionist doctrine finds support in some particular cases." To these particular cases, and the questions they raised about the validity and generality of the case for free trade, we now turn.

---

the amount of our produce the same, but to turn that produce from exportation to feeding our own people" (43). Butt pointed out that his arguments were "unquestionably much less unfavorable to a system of protection of home industry than is generally expected to be met with in the writings of one professing to be a student of political economy," although "they are not, however, intended as a general defense of protective duties" (14–15).

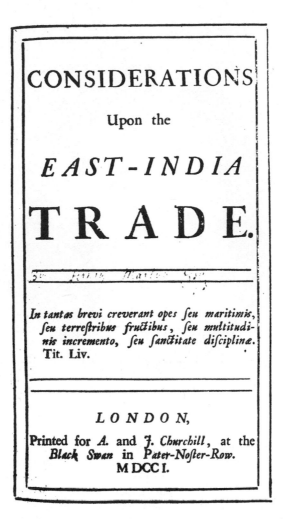

1. Title page of Henry Martyn's *Considerations upon the East India Trade*. (Permission from the Goldsmiths' Library, University of London.)

Originally published in 1701 (and republished in 1720), this brilliant tract by Henry Martyn argued strongly in favor of allowing free imports of Indian textiles into Britain. Martyn stated that trade was an indirect means of acquiring goods through exports rather than through domestic production. With ingenious reasoning, Martyn concluded that free trade would allow a country to acquire more goods with the same labor, and was therefore akin to an improvement in the country's productivity.

2. Adam Smith. (From the collection of the author.)

Published in 1776, Smith's *Wealth of Nations* stands as a landmark in the intellectual case for free trade. Smith sharply criticized policies that protected domestic producers from import competition on the grounds that this would reduce national income by diverting resources from other, more profitable uses. The *Wealth of Nations* proved so influential that it almost singlehandedly changed the presumption of economic thinkers in favor of free trade and against protection.

3. *Left*, James Mill. (From the collection of the author.)

Mill's keen intellect enabled him to provide logical rigor to early classical doctrines on international trade. It has been suggested that he developed the theory of comparative advantage before Ricardo, but at the very least Mill more than others recognized its significance as a major intellectual achievement that gave free trade a solid analytical basis.

4. *Right*, David Ricardo. (From the collection of the author.)

A London investor who turned economist upon reading the *Wealth of Nations* on vacation, Ricardo popularized the theory of comparative advantage in chapter 7 of his *Principles of Political Economy* (1817).

5. *Left*, Robert Torrens. (From the collection of the author.)

A military officer turned economist, Torrens deserves credit for publishing the first statement (in 1815) that conveys the essence of the theory of comparative advantage. Torrens triggered a hotly contested controversy in the early 1840s when he, despite his free trade views, developed the strongest economic case against free trade—the terms of trade argument, in which a country might employ a tariff to increase the purchasing power of a country's exports in terms of the imports they could procure. Torrens also sketched out what later became known as the "Australian" argument for protection.

6. *Right*, John Stuart Mill. (From the collection of the author.)

The brilliant son of James Mill, the younger Mill added to free trade arguments by proposing the "compensation principle," in which the beneficiaries of free trade could "compensate" the losers and potentially make everyone better off as a result. But much to the consternation of his contemporaries, Mill lent his support to the long-standing but controversial "infant industry" argument for protection, in which tariffs might prove beneficial in facilitating the development of new industries. Mill was also first to develop the terms of trade argument for protection, but his carefully reasoned work appeared in print only after Torrens had drawn attention to this case.

7. *Left*, Joseph Shield Nicholson. (Permission from the University of Edinburgh Library.)

A professor at the University of Edinburgh, Nicholson pointed out two potentially important weaknesses in the case for free trade at the end of the nineteenth century. Nicholson recognized that there might be a valid argument for protection if an industry operated under conditions of increasing returns to scale or if there were inefficient wage differentials between industries. Nicholson's insights were neglected until Frank Graham and Mihaïl Manoïlescu later achieved prominence by analyzing these two cases in greater detail.

8. *Right*, Henry Sidgwick. (From the collection of the author.)

A Cambridge economist and philosopher, Sidgwick exemplified the late nineteenth-century English reaction against what was perceived as the earlier "free trade dogmatism" of the classical economists. Sidgwick's influential textbook, for example, accepted without much critical scrutiny various weakly formulated arguments for protection.

9. *Left*, Friedrich List. (From the collection of the author.)

A German political activist and author of *The National System of Political Economy* (1841), List dismissed classical economic analysis as too cosmopolitan and argued that middle-income countries should foster industrialization through high import tariffs. List reached his conclusions on the basis of a "politico-historical" perspective, and consequently his arguments for protection were weak from the standpoint of economic theory. However, List became a cult figure for protectionists and achieved wide recognition and support for his ideas in the United States and elsewhere.

10. *Right*, Mihaïl Manoïlescu. (Permission from Anca E. Giurescu.)

A government minister and academic in Romania, Manoïlescu forcefully argued (in a book first published in 1929) that protection would correct the failure of market economies to employ enough labor in the high-wage, high-productivity manufacturing sector. Later economists suspected that wage differentials between sectors were not market failures and could be accounted for by trade unions, worker skills, or urban cost-of-living differences. But for genuine market failures, critics demonstrated that employment or production subsidies dominated the use of import protection to achieve the best allocation of labor across sectors.

11. *Left*, Frank Graham. (Permission from Archives of the University. Department of Rare Books and Special Collections. Princeton University Libraries.)

This Princeton University economist published a seminal article in 1923 questioning the desirability of free trade when some industries operate under increasing returns to scale. According to Graham, specialization in increasing returns industries would increase a country's productivity and thereby its national income, while countries specializing in decreasing returns industries would suffer losses from free trade. Critics showed that Graham's case failed if the increasing returns were internal to the firm, but a controversial case for protection has been proposed for certain types of external economies.

12. *Right*, James Brigden. (Permission from the National Library of Australia.)

An Australian economist and official, Brigden rehabilitated the argument (one previously considered by Torrens and Sidgwick) that protection might be beneficial in preventing a country from specializing in diminishing returns industries, such as natural resource extraction. Protection would thereby avoid an undesirable reduction in wages and an equally undesirable increase in emigration. Unless accompanied by a terms of trade improvement, however, such a policy would not augment national income. And later work showed that, even if the country had the ability to affect its terms of trade, protection might actually reduce wages.

13. *Left*, John Maynard Keynes. (From the collection of the author.)

Perhaps the most illustrious economist of the twentieth century, Keynes generated a storm of controversy in the early 1930s when he proposed the use of tariffs to alleviate unemployment if other remedies (such as a currency devaluation) were ruled out as infeasible. Keynes also pointed out the difficulties for free trade if labor was immobile between sectors and nominal wages were inflexible.

14. *Right*, James Brander and Barbara Spencer. (Permission from Robert Semeniuk/First Light.)

In the 1980s, these two economists from the University of British Columbia examined the strategic use of government trade policies (such as export promotion) to capture economic rents in international markets with few competitors. Under additional scrutiny, their novel case for activist trade policies was found to hinge crucially on numerous assumptions about market structure and conduct. As a result, unless the government had exacting information on an industry's cost and demand structure and the nature of competition, the optimal government intervention could not be easily determined. The uncertainty that surrounds the determination of strategic trade policies led many economists to doubt the wisdom of any type of intervention.

PART TWO

Controversies about the
Free Trade Doctrine

Chapter Seven

TORRENS AND THE
TERMS OF TRADE ARGUMENT

DESPITE SHARING with David Ricardo the credit for developing the concept of comparative advantage, Robert Torrens remains a relatively neglected member of the classical school of economists. A cogent and forceful advocate for free trade, Torrens also developed the most generally valid argument for tariffs. He described conditions under which a tariff could benefit a country by making the ratio at which it exchanged its products with the rest of the world—the terms of trade, or the purchasing power of a country's exports in terms of the imports it can procure—more advantageous. His strident and controversial criticism of unilateral free trade and advocacy of reciprocity in the 1840s triggered a sharp debate among economists. To argue against free trade was heresy in the minds of most economists of the day, and in crossing those bounds Torrens became a pariah for almost a century.[1] But the terms of trade argument for protection is the hardest to refute on theoretical grounds and remains the most durable and important exception to free trade ever conceived.

. . .

Torrens's early forays into economics were decidedly in favor of free trade. In his 1808 tract *The Economists Refuted*, he introduced the term "territorial division of labour" in rejecting the physiocratic notion that agriculture alone, and not international trade, contributes to wealth. In 1815, as discussed in chapter 6, he attacked protection to agriculture, stating that England's superiority in manufacturing was so great that it could import corn with advantage even if its own land was more productive than land in other countries. By this statement Torrens clearly anticipated the concept of comparative advantage as expounded by Ricardo in his *Principles of Political Economy*. Torrens also spoke out strongly in favor of free trade and dismissed any arguments for reciprocity. To the frequent contention

---

[1] The original *Palgrave Dictionary of Economics* dismissed Torrens's work as "devoid of permanent merit." Decades later the *New Palgrave* said that Torrens, "if not in the top rank of the classical economists, or in the class for example of Ricardo, Senior, or John Stuart Mill, certainly was of the second rank and was the equal of, or even above, James Mill and McCulloch in terms of originality, theoretical reasoning, and range of economic topics that he considered." See R.H.I. Palgrave (1913, 3: 550) and B. A. Corry (1987, 4: 659). For a masterful overview of Torrens's work, see Lionel Robbins (1958), especially chapter 7.

that it is "highly inexpedient in any one country to abandon the restrictive system [of import protection] while her neighbours continued to enforce it," Torrens (1821, 268ff) responded that "nothing can be more erroneous or absurd." A "mistaken policy on the part of France could furnish no conceivable reason why England should imitate the absurd example," he wrote, adding that foreign protection did not force a free trade country to pay any financial cost or tribute, something he would explicitly contend in later work.

While Torrens and the classical economists were united in believing that the free exchange of goods between countries was mutually beneficial, they lacked insight into what determined the ratio at which goods would be exchanged between countries. Early expositions of comparative costs examples presumed a ratio of exchange exactly between the autarky cost ratios, allowing both countries to share equally the gains from exchange.[2] As Torrens (1821, 260) put it, "The advantages of foreign trade are reciprocal, and equally divided between nations carrying it on." But the desirability of sacrificing a smaller rather than a larger bundle of goods through exports in exchange for a given quantity of imports (implying a high price of exports relative to imports) was also clearly recognized, even if there was little inkling about precisely how the terms of trade were established. Around 1820, Ricardo (1951, 2: 146) wrote that "it is undoubtedly true that if a country is to pay a certain money price for foreign necessaries and conveniences, it is for its interest to sell the commodities at a higher, rather than at a lower price; it is desirable that for a given quantity of its own commodity, it should obtain a large rather than a small quantity of foreign commodities in return, but in what way a nation can so regulate its affairs as to accomplish this by any means which it is in its power to adopt, I am totally at a loss to conceive."[3]

Despite the only rudimentary understanding of the determinants of the terms of trade, Torrens gradually came to discover that a country could shift the terms of trade in its favor by imposing a tariff. He used this theory to argue that tariffs should not be reduced unilaterally, as this would adversely affect the terms of trade, but in conjunction with other countries acting similarly under a policy of reciprocity. The groundwork for Torrens's theory was developed in a series of letters to the *Bolton Chronicle* in

---

[2] On early errors in determining how countries divided the gains from trade, see William Thweatt (1987).

[3] Ricardo (1951, 4: 71) staunchly supported free trade on a unilateral basis: "If foreign nations are not sufficiently enlightened to adopt this liberal system, and should continue their prohibitions and excessive duties on the importation of our commodities and manufactures, let England set them a good example by benefiting herself; and instead of meeting their prohibitions by similar exclusions, let her get rid, as soon as she can, of every vestige of so absurd and hurtful a policy."

1832 as part of his effort to get elected to Parliament.[4] Drawing on earlier ideas of Ricardo and Nassau Senior regarding the international distribution of precious metals, Torrens argued that tariffs could affect the movement of precious metals across countries. In particular, a country imposing a tariff would initially obtain a trade surplus, draw to itself a greater propor- tion of the world's precious metals, and thereby raise domestic prices, wages, and profits, and increase the purchasing power of its labor in terms of gold.

Holding his doctrines as immediately applicable to British circum- stances, Torrens (1833, 6) maintained that the prosperity of the country depended on a trade policy based not on free trade, but on reciprocity. The guiding principle of commercial policy should be "to lower the duties of customs upon the importation of goods produced in countries which con- sent to receive British goods upon terms equally favourable, and to pro- hibit, or to lay heavy duties upon, the importation of all goods, not con- sisting of first necessaries, produced in countries which prohibit, or lay heavy duties upon, British goods." Torrens accused the British government of departing from these principles, thereby reducing the price of British goods in foreign markets and undermining the country's superiority in manufacturing.

Torrens's initial, incomplete formulation neglected to stress the gain from improved terms of trade (or the international purchasing power of a country's exports) only to emphasize the deflationary consequences of uni- lateral free trade on domestic prices. Yet his heresy was evident and Tor- rens's ideas met broad resistance. Perronet Thompson (1833*a*) failed to understand how Torrens could argue that the nation as a whole could be worse off as the result of the free and profitable private trade of merchants. He further maintained that the export of specie was equivalent to the export of any other profitable commodity. Torrens (1833, 58) dismissed Thomp- son as having "no conception of the real question at issue."[5] J. L. Mallet's diary entry gives an indication of the suspicion and hostility with which Torrens's views were received in a Political Economy Club meeting in 1835: "The first question discussed was a question of Torrens, which was unanimously voted to turn upon an impossible case. He claimed the right to discuss any abstract proposition with a view to the establishing of princi- ple, but it was over-ruled in the present case which did not go to *establish* but to *disturb* a principle, that of Free Trade upon grounds altogether hypo- thetical" (Political Economy Club [1921, 270]).

[4] These letters were collected and republished in Torrens (1833).

[5] The meek reply is in Thompson (1933*b*). This exchange took a nasty turn. Torrens (1833, 57) called Thompson's work "correct, where not original, and where original, not correct," to which Thompson (1833*b*, 423) excoriated Torrens's "dishonest and in fact legally punishable action" of attacking his work in that way!

Torrens developed his views considerably more in a series of pamphlets addressed to leading political figures during the tariff debates of the early 1840s and later collected in a book entitled *The Budget: On Commercial and Colonial Policy*, published in 1844. Torrens became the leading exponent of the view that a unilateral tariff reduction would be detrimental to Britain's national welfare. His analysis hinged on two Ricardian concepts. First, international demand, and not costs of production alone, plays a role in determining the terms of trade.[6] Second, commercial policies affect the international distribution of precious metals through the price-specie-flow mechanism.

From these precepts, Torrens (1844, 28) argued that "when any particular country imposes import duties upon the productions of other countries, while those other countries continue to receive her products duty free, then such particular country draws to herself a larger proportion of the precious metals, maintains a higher range of general prices than her neighbours, and obtains, in exchange for the produce of a given quantity of her labour, the produce of a greater quantity of foreign labour." This last statement, regarding the quantity of goods a country's labor could procure on the world market, emphasized the efficiency of trade restrictions in possibly procuring a large quantity of goods. The neighboring countries could recover these precious metals, he wrote, by retaliatory tariffs that would restore the previous exchange ratio.

Torrens then introduced a numerical example of tariffs and trade between Cuba (representing the rest of the world) and Britain to illustrate the proposition. If Cuba imposes tariffs from a situation of perfectly free trade, Britain will initially find itself importing the same value of goods from Cuba but exporting less. The concomitant trade imbalance will be financed by a flow of specie from Britain to Cuba, thereby reducing British prices and raising Cuban prices. The volume of trade would also adjust to ensure balanced trade, with the volume of British exports becoming larger and the volume of Cuban exports smaller. In the end, a greater amount of British exports would be exchanged for a smaller amount of imports from Cuba, an inferior ratio of exchange from Britain's perspective. While Torrens's numerical example was produced under particular assumptions, such as constant nominal outlays on Cuban products by Britain (implying unit elastic demand), his proposition was later shown to be more general in nature. Torrens (1844, 36–37) concluded that his example proved that the "ultimate incidence of the import duty imposed upon Brit-

---

[6] As Ricardo ([1817] 1951, 1: 133) put it, "The same rule which regulates the relative value of commodities in one country, does not regulate the relative value of the commodities exchanged between two or more countries." Montiford Longfield (1835, 99–101) introduced demand more explicitly as a determinant of the terms of international exchange, but his contribution was incomplete and failed to attract much notice.

ish goods would be upon British producers. The wealth of England would be decreased by the amount of the duty—the wealth of Cuba would be increased by its amount." Yet Torrens believed that this terms of trade effect "would be the least portion of the evil inflicted upon England by the change which has been described," and instead the deflationary consequences were paramount—with "national bankruptcy and revolution . . . the probable result."

Torrens's policy recommendations sparked a controversy among economists that even spilled over into parliamentary debates. He (1844, 47–48) insisted that the following practical rules of commercial policy are "direct and necessary corollaries" from the principles he had described:

> First,—to adopt, with respect to all foreign powers, the principle of reciprocity.—Second,—To lower the import duties upon the goods produced in countries receiving British goods upon terms equally favourable.—Third,—To impose high or prohibitive duties upon goods, the produce of countries imposing high or prohibitive duties upon British goods.—Fourth,—To admit, duty free, all raw materials employed in the processes of reproduction.

These rules could hardly constitute the commercial policy recommendations of a cosmopolitan free trader. In fact, Torrens was acutely aware of the distinction between national and world welfare, for two paragraphs later he wrote that "unrestricted interchange of commodities between different countries, would increase the wealth of the world." Implicit in this statement is the recognition that the terms of trade improvement for Britain would imply a corresponding terms of trade deterioration for other countries, inflicting losses on others that exceeded Britain's gains as the volume of trade shrank. But as Britain's national welfare was at stake, he scolded the government for having "deprived the country of the advantages which our manufacturing superiority would otherwise have secured" and having "lowered the prices of British goods in foreign markets" (62). In addition, reciprocity would "hold out to [foreign countries] a powerful inducement to act upon the principles of reciprocal freedom" and perhaps lead to worldwide free trade (65). In sum, Torrens believed that "reciprocity should be the universal rule" and that "the sound principle of commercial policy is, to oppose foreign tariffs by retaliatory duties, and to lower our import duties in favour of those countries which may consent to trade with us on terms of reciprocity" (50).

Many economists, outraged at what they thought were Torrens's irresponsible views, dismissed as irrelevant his whole analysis. As one anonymous reviewer put it, Torrens's analysis was "without even a shadow of foundation."[7] Nassau Senior's (1843) lengthy critique made him the most

---

[7] "Colonel Torrens on Free Trade" (1843, 2).

prominent (and the most eminent) opponent of Torrens. Unfortunately for his cause, Senior's essay in support of unilateral free trade was a weak and desultory response.[8] Despite this, the essay scored some telling points. Senior first accused Torrens of rejuvenating the erroneous doctrines of mercantilism. He (1843, 12, 14) then said that Torrens, while highlighting the adverse terms-of-trade impact of reducing tariffs, ignored the costs entailed by trade restraints:

> Torrens assumes, first, that a country can exclude foreign commodities without diminishing the efficiency of its own labour. . . . It is a great mistake to suppose that a country which rejects the territorial division of labour, suffers merely by the greater dearness of the commodities which it is forced to produce instead of importing them. It incurs a further, and in many instances greater, injury—in the general diminution of the efficiency of its own industry, occasioned by the misdirection of capital and the diminished division of labour.

Senior accepted but dismissed Torrens's example of a tariff's impact on the terms of trade: "We believe this to be true; but we believe it to be one of those barren truths from which no practical inferences can be drawn. . . . In short, when he [Torrens] seriously urges us to act as if his hypothesis represented the actual state of things, we utterly dissent from, and repudiate his doctrine" (36–37). He also chided Torrens for assuming that Britain was the innocent victim of foreign tariffs when its own trade barriers were substantial as well.

Accurately noting that Senior was evasive in dealing with the main body of his argument, Torrens (1844, 350–51) jumped on the admission that Torrens's doctrine was true: "Your utter dissent and repudiation are utterly inconsistent with the facts and principles which you have yourself established . . . the doctrine which you admit to be true." Senior's review was also subject to a devastating attack by an anonymous author who laid out Torrens's ideas better than Torrens himself did.[9] The author lambasted Senior for accusing Torrens of rehabilitating mercantilism: movements of precious metals were introduced only to restore trade to barter, the author sharply reminded the reader, and tariffs brought national gain not from acquiring metals *per se* but from changing the effective productivity of British labor in acquiring goods through international trade. The author easily demonstrated how supply and demand, and not costs of production as Senior continued to maintain, regulated international values and how

---

[8] This opinion was held even by those who shared Senior's disdain for Torrens's views. "Senior's article contains very many just remarks, but he did not take the trouble thoroughly to understand T[orrens] before he sat down to answer him, therefore he is incomplete and unsatisfactory," opined S. J. Lloyd (Lord Overstone), a leading monetary theorist of the time. See the letter to G. W. Norman (December 13, 1843) in Denis O'Brien (1971, 345).

[9] "Reciprocal Free Trade" (1843).

Torrens's example could, in principle, be extended to many countries and many commodities.

Herman Merivale (1842, 2: 305–11), one of the most incisive critics to emerge, restated Torrens's example of Cuba in purely barter terms not only to focus on the essence of the tariff and terms of trade argument but to show that the result was robust even when ignoring monetary adjustments. Merivale then introduced a second country, Brazil, that could supply sugar to Britain at a slightly greater cost than Cuba. If Cuba placed duties on imports from Britain, thereby raising the relative price of its sugar, England could simply switch its source of supply to "the next cheapest country producing the same commodities as Cuba." In all, Britain would be hurt only in proportion to the gap between Cuba's original price and Brazil's price of sugar, the trade of Cuba would be ruined, and Brazil would be the real beneficiary of Cuba's tariff. By allowing competition among Britain's import suppliers, Merivale demonstrated that Torrens exaggerated the impact of foreign tariffs if not all other nations increased their tariffs.

Torrens (1844, 358) reluctantly conceded this point, admitting that if Merivale's "assumption bore any resemblance to actual circumstances, the Cuba tariff could have a very slender effect in altering the terms of international exchange to the disadvantage of England." Torrens was left to assert that his example of all foreign countries increasing their tariffs was more appropriate.

George Warde Norman, in a lengthy publication written around 1845 and privately published in 1860, granted only that Torrens's case was half true. The burden of imposing retaliatory or reciprocity tariffs would also fall in part on foreigners, but some of the burden would fall on Britain's producers and consumers. Even though the burden would probably be borne equally by both countries, Norman (1860, 36) argued, the lower volume of trade and diminution of the natural advantages of trade would ensure that any gain would be "almost nugatory." He also made the point that, in practice, retaliation would never take place on the grounds established by Torrens, who had excluded from the policy of reciprocity any tariffs on raw materials, which, Norman pointed out, comprised the overwhelming proportion of British imports.

Torrens's analysis survived the onslaught of other theorists. James Anthony Lawson (1843, 133–47) held that the distribution of precious metals between countries was governed only by labor productivity in the export sector and tried to come up with an arithmetic example of a Cuban tariff that improved Britain's terms of trade. Torrens (1844, lii–lvii) charged that the first was a direct contradiction of Ricardian doctrine and showed, along with an anonymous reviewer of Lawson's work, that the arithmetic example had a fatal inconsistency.[10] Implicitly assuming that the terms of

[10] "Professor Lawson's Lectures on Political Economy" (1844).

trade are fixed and given from the perspective of a country, J. R. McCulloch (1849, 166) thought such tariffs would be "futile" as the burden on import duties would always be on the country imposing such tariffs. But McCulloch fully granted Torrens's case for a country with a monopoly power in the export good, in which case a country could affect the international price of its exports.

This debate continued until John Stuart Mill weighed in with qualified support for Torrens. Mill had anonymously reviewed one of Torrens's pamphlets in 1843 and shared his concern that foreign tariffs would accelerate the decline of Britain's position as workshop of the world. While not directly discussing the terms-of-trade effects of tariffs, Mill (1843, 85–86) called foreign tariffs "the real source of alarm" for stifling British exports and potentially reducing the high wages commanded by British labor relative to competitors. He urged Britain's politicians to spread free trade to other countries.

But Mill's brilliant work on the determination of the terms of trade clinched Torrens's argument and essentially settled the debate among economists. In 1844 in his *Essays on Some Unsettled Questions of Political Economy*, Mill published "Of the Laws of Interchange between Nations; and the Distribution of the Gains of Commerce among the Countries of the Commercial World." This essay, originally written in 1829–30 according to Mill, described how world supply and demand determine the terms of trade between countries. In his preface to the collection of essays, Mill (1844, v–vi) wrote that they had been published "under the impression that the controversies excited by Colonel Torrens's *Budget* have again called the attention of political economists to the discussion of the abstract science. . . . It will be seen that opinions identical in principle to those promulgated by Colonel Torrens (there would probably be considerable difference as to the extent of their practical application) have been held by the writer for more than fifteen years."

"Of the Laws of Interchange between Nations" is the famous essay that set out the theory of reciprocal demand as the determinant of the equilibrium terms of trade. And it was here that Mill (1844, 21) questioned "whether any country, by its own legislative policy, can engross to itself a larger share of the benefits of foreign commerce than would fall to it in the natural or spontaneous course of trade." He answered affirmatively and explained more clearly than Torrens the advantages of trade taxes if foreign demand for a country's exports is not perfectly elastic. In such a case, the imposition of a tariff would reduce both import and export volume, with the reduction in export supply driving up the price of those exports on world markets. With the higher price, a given amount of exports could acquire a greater amount of imports than previously was the case.

Mill cautioned that while import duties may be advantageous under such circumstances, "the determining circumstances are of a nature so imperfectly ascertainable, that it must be almost impossible to decide with any certainty, even after the tax has been imposed, whether we have been gainers by it or losers" (25). Furthermore, because the tax could eliminate a country's trade if foreigners could buy from other sources, he argued that "even on the most selfish principles, therefore, the benefits of such a tax is always extremely precarious."[11]

Mill also endorsed a qualified version of a reciprocity-based trade policy, distinguishing between a protecting duty, which encourages a particular branch of domestic industry by attracting labor and capital to its production, and a revenue duty, levied on those goods not produced at home. A "protecting duty can never be a cause of gain, but always and necessarily of loss, to the country imposing it," but Mill stated that, with revenue duties,

> considerations of reciprocity, which are quite unessential when the matter in debate is a protecting duty, are of material importance when the repeal of duties of this other description is discussed. A country cannot be expected to renounce the power of taxing foreigners, unless foreigners will in return practise towards itself the same forbearance. The only mode in which a country can save itself from being a loser by the duties imposed by other countries on its commodities, is to impose corresponding duties on theirs. (28–29)

Mill noted that a country could only improve its terms of trade at the expense of other trading countries, and their losses would exceed the gains of the tariff-imposing country. Therefore, "it is evidently the common interest of all nations that each of them should abstain from every measure by which the aggregate wealth of the commercial world would be diminished, although of this smaller sum total it might thereby be enabled to attract to itself a larger share." But "until, by the common consent of nations, all restrictions upon trade are done away, a nation cannot be required to abolish those from which she derives a real advantage, without stipulating for an equivalent" (31–32). Still, Mill believed that import duties would bring harm to all countries, doubting that tariffs could be properly set to the advantage of any. He observed with concern the severely protectionist policies in France, the Netherlands, and the United States, arguing that such policies, "though chiefly injurious to the countries imposing them, have also been highly injurious to England" (38).

Thus Mill accepted (indeed originated, though Torrens popularized) the theoretical point that a tariff can improve a country's terms of trade. Mill

---

[11] Mill set out his example in both barter and monetary terms. On the latter, Mill (1844, 40–41) noted what Torrens had stressed, that tariff reductions may have a deflationary effect, but added that this gave "rise, as a general fall of prices always does, to an appearance, though a temporary and fallacious one, of general distress."

stressed that such tariffs were a negative sum game for the world as a whole (a point recognized but downplayed by Torrens, who was concerned about national gains). As a result, Mill exercised great restraint in drawing specific policy recommendations from the proposition. His (1843, 85) caveat was that Torrens, "as is not unusual with him, seems to us to overstate the importance and urgency of a portion of his doctrines in their application to the immediate circumstances of the country." That Torrens was correct in theory was confirmed when the controversy prompted Mill to publish his previously written essay on the subject. But as to the policy recommendations that Torrens considered natural conclusions of his analysis, Mill hesitated endorsing them and other economists rejected them entirely.

Torrens and Mill had developed a theory that consisted of two parts: first, under certain circumstances a tariff reduction could lead to a deterioration in the terms of trade (or, conversely, a tariff increase could improve the terms of trade); second, a country undertaking such a tariff reduction could conceivably suffer a net economic loss as a result. Mill and Torrens demonstrated the first proposition conclusively. The second proposition remained speculative: would the lower tariff bring about an adverse terms-of-trade effect sufficient to outweigh the gain from the expansion of trade resulting from a greater international division of labor? Torrens and Mill assumed that an improvement in the terms of trade by itself would necessarily imply greater economic wealth. But this ignored the equally important contribution of the volume of trade to the gains from trade, and hence their cost-benefit analysis was inadequate. As F. Y. Edgeworth (1894, 40) later noted, "Mill obscures the subject by taking as the measure of the gain of trade the alteration in the rate of exchange between exports and imports rather than the truer measure of advantage which the principles of consumers' and producers' rent afford"—or, in modern terms, consumer and producer surplus as a measure of economic welfare.

It was not until the late nineteenth century that Edgeworth, an economist and statistician at Oxford, demonstrated the validity of the second proposition on more rigorous analytical grounds. Edgeworth employed a construction called the offer curve, developed by Alfred Marshall in the early 1870s to illustrate various combinations of export and import volume that a country was willing to exchange with others, to represent graphically Mill's reciprocal demand theory.[12] Edgeworth (1894, 433ff) ingeniously combined these offer curves with a graphical representation of a country's aggregate economic welfare (through utility indifference curves, depicting the country's preferences across various goods). Edgeworth was thereby able to sketch out a proof that, if the foreign (rest of the world) offer curve

[12] Marshall privately distributed a manuscript describing these curves in 1879 but did not initially apply this apparatus to commercial policy. He later reprinted them in part and discussed tariff policy in Appendix J of Marshall (1923).

was anything but perfectly elastic (in which case the terms of trade would be fixed by the world market), there was the potential for tariffs to improve the terms of trade and increase national welfare. The "optimal" tariff became the term used to describe a tariff that exploited the terms of trade precisely to maximize national economic welfare. Edgeworth also confirmed the Mill-Torrens view that this gain arose entirely by imposing an even greater loss on other countries. Edgeworth appears not to have recognized the significance of his findings until later, but he secured for the terms of trade argument the final clinching verdict. Any lingering doubts about the theoretical possibility of achieving higher economic welfare under these conditions through tariffs was eliminated.

Edgeworth's work later convinced Alfred Marshall, the great Cambridge University economist, to repudiate use of the analytical tools he himself had developed. "In recent years, I have gradually gone away from the fundamental hypothesis on which the curves are based," Marshall (1925, 449) wrote to a correspondent in 1904. "They lead to the result that a great part of an import duty will probably fall on the export nation: and I have become convinced that, though the reasons which the old free-traders gave for the opinion that import duties are paid almost entirely by the consumer are wrong, yet their result is pretty well true." Despite Marshall's concern, his offer curve construction became a standard tool in the theoretical analysis of tariffs. Edgeworth's analysis was later revived and elaborated by Nicholas Kaldor (1940) and others in the 1940s. This approach culminated in the early 1950s with the derivation by Harry Johnson (1950–51) of a precise mathematical formula for the "optimal" tariff based on the elasticity of the foreign offer curve.

Aside from these advanced analytical deliberations, another debate concerning Torrens's and Mill's theory focused on the closely related question of tariff incidence—or "who pays the tariff?"—when a country possesses market power in its export or import markets and does not take world prices as given. Some classical economists, such as J. R. McCulloch (1849, 166) as we have seen, implicitly assumed that a country could not influence the prices of its imports as determined by world market, and therefore concluded that domestic consumers bore the full burden of the tariff. Under this scenario, the idea that tariff revenue could be extracted from foreign suppliers "is wholly visionary, and that duties on imports are always paid by the importers and never by the exporters" Advocates of tariffs, of course, took the other extreme position and asserted that the burden of import tariffs could be shifted entirely onto foreigners through lower import prices.

Mill, appropriately, took a middle path. As a result of his theory of reciprocal demand, Mill (1844, 27) pointed out, "it may, therefore, be laid down as a principle, that a tax on imported commodities, when it really operates as a tax, and not as a prohibition either total or partial, almost always falls in part upon the foreigners who consume our goods; and that this is a mode in which a nation may appropriate to itself, at the expense of foreigners, a larger share than would otherwise belong to it of the increase in the general productiveness of the labour and capital of the world, which results from the interchange of commodities among nations."

But the state of knowledge about the question of tariff incidence remained uncertain through most of the nineteenth century. Henry Sidgwick (1883, 492–93) argued that "there is no theoretical means of determining" the impact of a tariff on domestic consumers or producers, but "unless foreign products are completely excluded by import duties, such duties will partly have the effect of levying a tribute on foreign producers, the amount and duration of which may in certain cases be considerable." This arises either because the foreign costs of production (and hence its price) will fall as its export volume falls, or because profits could be extracted from foreign monopolists or cartels. On the export side, Edgeworth (1894, 42–43) reiterated Mill's argument about how export restraints could be advantageous in raising export prices (if foreign demand for a country's goods was somewhat inelastic), noting that "it is often stated with the unnecessary limitation that the home country must have an absolute monopoly of the exporting article," whereas "that she should furnish a considerable portion of the total supply might suffice." It was later pointed out that if domestic producers do not act as perfect competitors in the export market but recognize the market power that they collectively possess, these producers will collude to restrict their exports and hence mimic the optimal export tax, obviating the need for government intervention.

Yet outlining the possibility of such an outcome was quite different from actually proposing tariffs for this purpose. Joseph Shield Nicholson (1891, 465) summed up the view of many economists at the end of the nineteenth century in writing that

> taxing the foreigner is very like "shearing the wolf." It is quite true that *theoretically* under certain conditions one nation might obtain from other nations, either by export or by import duties, a considerable part of its revenue, but it is equally true that these conditions are extremely unlikely to arise; and even if they did arise, it is still more unlikely that the wisdom of statesmen would be equal to the task of taking advantage of them. It is important to observe that theoretical exceptions may be admitted whilst the practical application is denied, for no greater harm has been done to the spread of "Free Trade principles" in the broad sense of the terms than by the attempt to reduce them to a fictitious simplicity. To assert that every import-duty must *necessarily* fall on the home consumer is as false as to assert that every export-duty must necessarily fall on the foreign consumer; it is equally untrue to say that *necessarily* the import-duties fall on the foreign producer and the export-duties on the

home producer. As a matter of fact the incidence of export and import duties, especially when the indirect effects are considered, is the most complicated and difficult problems in economics.[13]

The "complicated and difficult problem" of determining tariff incidence and whether the tariff burden could be shifted onto foreigners soon gave way to an analytical breakthrough. Using Marshall's supply and demand schedules to represent the market for an imported good in partial equilibrium, Charles F. Bickerdike (1906, 529ff) raised the question of whether "a country, by means of taxes, can get more favourable terms of exchange with foreigners in such a way as to leave a net advantage, after allowing for the disadvantages involved in turning production from its 'natural' course." He answered affirmatively: "In pure theory advantage is always possible in normal circumstances from either import or export taxation when the taxes are small enough." Provided only that the foreign export supply curve is upward sloping, some of the revenue generated by a tariff is extracted from the producer surplus of foreign suppliers. Furthermore, this is "a general possibility of advantage not confined to exceptional circumstances." Bickerdike demonstrated with the simple Marshallian geometry that, for small or "incipient" taxes, a net gain results: the higher domestic price paid by consumers is largely a transfer to the government treasury, but the small deadweight loss of consumer surplus is exceeded by the gain from lower foreign prices over the entire volume of imports (and collected as tariff revenue) at the expense of foreign producers.

Bickerdike later extended these findings to derive a mathematical formula for the optimal tax based on export and import supply and demand elasticities. Under this formula, he (1907, 101) noted that "rather strong assumptions have to be made as to the elasticity of foreign supply and demand if the rate of the tax affording maximum advantage is to come below 10 per cent." In evaluating this theory, Edgeworth (1908, 392) praised Bickerdike for his having "accomplished a wonderful feat" of saying "something new about protection" and reinforced the point that Bickerdike was correct as a matter of theory. But Edgeworth was deeply skeptical about the practical application of the finding. Conceding that Bickerdike's result appeared to be quite general and only required information about supply and demand elasticities, Edgeworth (1908, 554) remarked that the theory seemed

> to justify the imposition of small customs duties, say from 2½ to 5 per cent, on a great number of articles. The objection that industry is thereby directed into less advantageous channels is not admissible; for by the theory the disad-

---

[13] Nicholson (1901, 306) later wrote that "certain exceptional conditions under which it is theoretically possible by the judicious manipulation of duties to extract a certain amount of revenue from the foreigner" although "practically they are of little importance."

vantage in the way of production is overbalanced by the gain accruing to the Treasury. Abstracting the practical difficulties to which we are coming, on the platform of pure theory the Free Trader must abandon his hectoring tone with respect to the defence of a Protectionist tax on the ground that it is a little one.

But Edgeworth went on to mention "weighty objections" that gave the theory "limited application." Aside from the frictions that many small taxes would entail in practice, the foremost obstacle was the threat of retaliation. Bickerdike's novel and ingenious sketch may imply a strong ability of hitting the foreigner with taxes because it "may be practiced by a country which has no special [monopoly] advantages" in trade, "but it equally increases the power of the foreigner to hit back." For these reasons, Edgeworth (1908, 555–56) continued,

> the direct use of the theory is likely to be small. But it is to be feared that its abuse will be considerable. It affords to unscrupulous advocates of vulgar Protection a peculiarly specious pretext for introducing the thin edge of the fiscal wedge. Mr. Bickerdike may be compared to a scientist who, by a new analysis, has discovered that strychnine may be administered in small doses with prospect of advantage in one or two more cases than was previously known; the result of this discovery may be to render the drug more easily procurable by those whose intention, or at least whose practice, is not medicinal. . . . Let us admire the skill of the analyst, but label the subject of his investigation POISON.

Just as the foreign reciprocal demand approach had been resurrected in the 1940s, the partial equilibrium "elasticities" approach to the optimal tariff was also resurrected then by, among others, Richard Kahn (1947–48), who supported Bickerdike's contention that the optimal tariff could be substantial based on what was believed about the magnitude of the elasticities.

Thus, although the terms of trade argument continued to undergo further refinements, few developments have seriously undermined its standing as a theoretically valid proposition. The most commonly proposed qualification is that foreign retaliation might undo the positive terms of trade effect of one country's optimal tariff. Since a country could only improve its terms of trade at the expense of other countries, an attempt to do so might incite the other countries into responding in kind to preserve their own position. And if all countries use tariffs in seeking to improve their terms of trade, the result would simply be a contraction in the volume of trade without anyone succeeding in their effort. One conceptual qualification to this argument was provided by Harry Johnson's (1953–54) finding that it was at least possible that, even after retaliation, one of the countries could still be better off than it would have been under free trade. Yet Johnson showed a possibility, not a likelihood, and the threat of foreign retaliation has been an oft-invoked practical argument against the terms-of-trade motive for trade intervention.[14]

The conclusion to be drawn from the terms of trade controversy is not that free trade is undesirable, but that, under certain circumstances, *unilateral* free trade is undesirable. Therefore, to avoid a situation in which countries seek to gain at the expense of others by imposing optimal tariffs, thereby diminishing the worldwide gains from trade, countries may wish to have a commitment mechanism, an agreement, in which all agree to forgo the use of tariffs for this purpose. In this context, contractual multilateral free trade avoids some of the problems associated with countries seeking to manipulate their terms of trade. And, of course, the cosmopolitan case for free trade remains unaffected. As John Stuart Mill (1844, 44) put it, "If international morality, therefore, were rightly understood and acted upon, such taxes, as being contrary to the universal weal, would not exist."

. . .

After a brief but intense debate, Torrens's speculations that tariffs could conceivably be beneficial in improving the terms of trade gradually become orthodoxy under Mill, who demonstrated the soundness of these speculations in terms of its underlying economic analysis. Although inadvisable from a global perspective for shifting the gains from trade to one country at the greater loss of others, few developments have detracted from its validity as a theoretical proposition. Indeed, of all the economic arguments against free trade, the terms of trade argument appears to be the most robust and least subject to qualification or exception, and it remains the most widely acknowledged and generally accepted restriction to free trade admitted by economic theory.

[14] Carlos Rodriguez (1974) showed that both countries would definitely be worse off if retaliation took place by means of import quotas instead of import tariffs.

Chapter Eight

MILL AND THE
INFANT INDUSTRY ARGUMENT

JOHN STUART MILL, the preeminent figure in mid-nineteenth-century economics, wrote the *Principles of Political Economy* (1848), which became the standard economics treatise for several generations of students. Yet one paragraph of Mill's influential text inspired a lasting controversy and earned him the scorn of many of his contemporaries. In a brief passage, Mill gave his qualified endorsement to temporary protection for "infant industries," defined as industries that were not initially capable of surviving in the face of import competition but with time and experience could grow to compete successfully in world markets. Mill caused great consternation among economists by sanctioning this argument for protection, although he eventually (but quietly) recanted his endorsement of tariffs as the means of supporting such industries. Despite its somewhat vague theoretical formulation, the infant industry argument survived many criticisms and continues to occupy an uneasy place in the theory of commercial policy.

· · ·

The infant industry argument, which is perhaps the oldest and longest-lived specific argument for protection, can be traced at least as far back as the Elizabethan period. Precise statement of the doctrine, involving temporary protection to establish a new industry, arises in the mercantilist period. Viner (1937, 71) finds a passage from 1645 arguing that monopoly privileges in a particular trade were no longer necessary because the domestic firm, having matured, was no longer in its infancy. More common were pleas for government support to assist fledgling manufacturers against foreign competition. Andrew Yarranton (1677, 62), for example, advocated

> that the linen and iron manufactures may be so encouraged here by a public law, as that we may draw these trades solely to us, which now foreign nations receive the benefit of, there ought in the first place to be a tax or customs at least of four shillings in the pound put on all linen yarn, threads, tapes, and twines for cordage that shall be imported into England . . . and this law to continue and be for seven years. And by virtue of this tax or imposition, there will be such advantage given to the linen manufacture in its infancy, that thereby it will take deep rooting and get a good foundation.

William Wood (1718, 224–25) repeated verbatim the statement by Theodore Jansssen (1713, 9) that "all wise nations are so fond of encouraging manufactures in their infancy, that they not only burden foreign manufactures of the like kind with high impositions, but often totally condemn and prohibit the consumption of them." Arthur Dobbs (1729, 2: 65ff) argued similarly: "Upon the whole, premiums are only to be given to encourage manufactures or other improvements in their infancy, to usher them into the world, and to give an encouragement to begin a commerce abroad; and if after their improvement they can't push their own way, by being wrought so cheap as to sell at par with others of the same kind, it is in vain to force it."

The infant industry case was a part, although by no means a pervasive part, of the mercantilist desire to promote domestic employment and industry. These few early statements adequately convey the main thrust of the infant industry doctrine, that before new industries could compete successfully against established foreign rivals, government assistance was required to help them overcome certain start-up obstacles and grow to maturity. The appealing and intuitive metaphor of an "infant" lured most eighteenth-century economic writers into accepting the case for infant industry protection without much serious questioning. Even Adam Smith's teacher, Francis Hutcheson (1753, 308), seemed to accept the doctrine when he wrote "all mechanick arts, either simpler, or more elegant, should be encouraged, lest our wealth be drained by our buying foreign manufactures."

The infant industry argument was so widely accepted that writers made their mark by pointing out qualifications to it. Josiah Tucker (1758, 50–51), for example, cautioned that protection should be temporary or else the infant industry may never mature:

> It is also easy to see, that such infant manufactures, or raw materials, as promise to become hereafter of general use and importance, ought to be reared and nursed during the weakness and difficulties of their infant state, by public encouragements and national premiums. But it doth by no means so clearly appear, that this nursing and supporting should be *continued forever*. On the contrary, it seems more natural to conclude, that after a reasonable course of years, attempts ought to be made to wean this commercial child by gentle degrees, and not to suffer it to contract a lazy habit of leaning continually on the leading strings . . . that trade is not worth the having, which never can be brought to support itself.

Others argued that the tariffs used to promote infant industries should not be set too high. In Malachy Postlethwayt's (1757, 2: 397) view:

> A manufacture, even in its infancy, seems not to have any reason to fear foreign competition, when the duties of entry are at 15 per cent; for the charges of

carriage, commission, and others, will come to 4 or 5 per cent more. If 18 or 20 per cent, besides the foreign manufacturer's profit, do not content the home manufacturer; one may readily conclude, either that such home manufacture wants to gain too much, or, that his undertaking is badly managed; or, in short, that there are such obstacles in the way at home, which must be removed before success can be expected.

On the other hand, James Steuart ([1767] 1966, 262–63) expounded the infant industry argument with great enthusiasm and little qualification: "The ruling principle, therefore, which ought to direct a statesman in promoting and improving the infant trade of his people, is to encourage the manufacturing of every branch of natural productions, by extending the home-consumption of them; by excluding all competition with strangers; by permitting the rise of profits, so far as to promote dexterity and emulation in invention and improvement; . . . and, until it can be exported to advantage, it may be exported with loss, at the expence of the public." Steuart had no concern that protection would produce slothfulness rather than promote improvement, for "as long as the gates of a kingdom are kept shut, and that no foreign communication is permitted, large profits do little harm, and tend to promote dexterity and refinement."

Although economic writers differed in the degree to which they qualified their support for infant industry policies, one is hard pressed to find anyone who actually disputed the basic argument prior to Adam Smith. It is a credit to his intellectual independence that Smith opposed government support for infant industries even though other Scottish philosophers (such as Lord Kames) endorsed it. Perhaps in response to unqualified statements like Steuart's, Smith reacted so strongly against the infant industry doctrine that, unlike his predecessors, he came close to denying that such protection could ever be beneficial:

> By means of such regulations, indeed, a particular manufacture may sometimes be acquired sooner than it could have been otherwise, and after a certain time may be made at home as cheap or cheaper than in the foreign country. But though the industry of the society may be thus carried with advantage into a particular channel sooner than it could have been otherwise, it will by no means follow that the sum total, either of its industry, or of its revenue, can ever be augmented by any such regulation. The industry of the society can augment only in proportion as its capital augments, and its capital can augment only in proportion to what can be gradually saved out of its revenue. But the immediate effect of every such regulation is to diminish its revenue, and what diminishes its revenue, is certainly not very likely to augment its capital faster than it would have augmented of its own accord, had both capital and industry been left to find out their natural employments. Though for want of such regulations the society should never acquire the proposed manufacture, it would

not, upon that account, necessarily be the poorer in any one period of its duration. In every period of its duration its whole capital and industry might still have been employed, though upon different objects, in the manner that was most advantageous at the time. In every period its revenue might have been the greatest which its capital could afford, and both capital and revenue might have been augmented with the greatest possible rapidity. [*WN*, IV.ii.13–14]

To Smith, the underlying cause of the foreign industry's superiority was irrelevant: "Whether the advantage which one country has over another, be natural or acquired, is in this respect of no consequence. As long as the one country has those advantages, and the other wants them, it will always be more advantageous for the latter, rather to buy of the former than to make" [*WN*, IV.ii.15]. Indeed, Smith was so deeply skeptical of the infant industry argument for protection that he conceded virtually nothing to it. Just because a country could acquire an industry by means of such protection did not imply that it should do so, or that the country would be better off for having done so. And even if a country could eventually produce that industry's good at a lower price than foreign producers, the policy still might be disadvantageous: protection would distort resource allocation, reduce national income, and thereby shrink the pool of investible savings available for capital accumulation. Smith also implicitly stressed the intertemporal balancing of the policy's costs and benefits, that the short-run costs must be offset by some distinct, long-run benefit, a point that was to be ignored for decades. However, by taking a fairly static view of infant industries, Smith was vulnerable to critics who would complain that he failed to deal with the essentially dynamic issues involved.

Other classical economists followed Smith's lead on the infant industry argument, either treating it unfavorably or ignoring it altogether. Jean-Charles-Léonard Simonde de Sismondi (1815, 70) focused on the opportunity costs of shifting by artificial means scarce resources into favored sectors at the expense of other sectors: "It ought to be recollected that each merchant knows his own business better than the government can do; that the whole nation's productive power is limited; that in a given time, it has but a given number of hands, and a given quantity of capital; that by forcing it to enter upon a kind of work which it did not previously execute, we almost always at the same time force it to abandon a kind of work which it did execute: whilst the most probable result of such a change is the abandonment of a more lucrative manufacture for another which is less so, and which personal interest had designedly overlooked."[1]

---

[1] See also Simonde de Sismondi ([1826] 1991, 327–42). This became an important theme in the classical critique. "In the infancy of any such employment, it is only by actual wealth, in the shape of additional capital, that any effectual assistance can be given to a new branch of industry," Jeremy Bentham (1843 [1821], 96) stated. "By removal of competition, increase

Others were skeptical of the infant industry argument on the grounds that protection would just create inefficient industries. J. R. McCulloch thought it unlikely that the domestic industry could ever succeed in reducing its price below the lowest import price, but according to D. P. O'Brien (1970, 221) was apparently inconsistent on this point. George Scrope (1833, 369) believed that import prohibitions could "raise some faint imitation of a foreign manufacture in a country unsuited for its production," but that "there is a waste of all the trouble and expense which the effort has cost. . . . In the sickly and confined atmosphere of the legislative forcing-frame [industry] loses its health and vigour, decays, and before long expires." Jean-Baptiste Say (1834, 131) accepted Smith's dictum in general, but then conceded that cases could exist wherein "a new channel of industry may ruin an unsupported speculator, though capable of yielding enormous profit, when the labourers shall have acquired practice, and the novelty has once been overcome."

The debate over infant industries from the mercantilists through the classicals (but prior to Mill's statement) hinged on three key issues: whether infant industry protection would (1) create new wealth and capital, or merely divert it from other more profitable activities; (2) stimulate domestic producers to acquire new technology and skills, or just stifled the incentive for such efforts; and (3) generate long-term net benefits, or simply foster costly industries that required ongoing government support. On the first issue, the conceptual framework of Smith and Bentham was structured in a way that emphasized resource constraints, whereas proponents (coming from a different perspective) disputed or ignored that point. On the second issue, the stimulating effect of infant industry protection envisioned by Steuart ("promotes dexterity and emulation in invention and improvement") was contrast with the depressing effect envisioned by Scrope ("loses its health and vigour, decays, . . ."). The third issue, the intertemporal cost-benefit analysis, was a crucial but neglected aspect of the economic case for infant industry protection.

Unfortunately, there was no agreement on how to determine which of these perspectives was most appropriate. Indeed, economic analysis alone was of little assistance in evaluating these issues: one could envision the successful maturation of the infant, and yet one could also entertain the possibility of protection breeding inefficiencies; *a priori*, neither outcome could be dismissed. Thus, the debate amounted to the exchange of claims and assertions about which effects were more likely. Indeed, for many de-

---

may indeed be given to the rate of profit, if profit be the result of the newly directed labour: but it is only by the employment of capital, which must necessarily be taken from other sources, that this result can be obtained; the prohibition of existing rival establishments will not create that capital."

cades, the problem afflicting the infant industry argument was the lack of a substantive economic structure behind it. Without such structure, economic theory could not provide a satisfactory resolution to the debate over whether government intervention was justified.

With some hedging, the classical economists broadly supported the view that infant industry policies were not advisable. They based this verdict on their observations about tariff policies in practice and on their view (following Adam Smith) that policies of "preference or restraint" could not improve upon the economic outcome that arose from a system of natural liberty. But if Smith and his followers believed that their criticisms were sufficient to undermine the infant industry argument, they were sorely mistaken. A decidedly different view of the issue was taken elsewhere in the world. Economic observers in America, Europe, and in other industrializing countries of the day saw no reason for importing manufactured goods from wealthy Britain when their own country seemed to have the skills and resources necessary to produce such goods at home. Far from suffering any inherent and immutable cost disadvantage, all their fledgling manufacturers apparently lacked was the accumulated experience and expertise required to produce such goods more efficiently. Three major figures—Alexander Hamilton, John Rae, and Friedrich List—gave renewed force to the infant industry argument even after Smith's scathing treatment.

As the first United States Secretary of the Treasury, Hamilton penned the famous "Report on Manufactures" in 1791. Hamilton objected to Smith's doctrine that, if left to itself, industry would automatically take the most profitable course of development.[2] Hamilton ([1791] 1966, 266–67) spoke of "the strong influence of habit and the spirit of imitation—the fear of want of success in untried enterprises—the intrinsic difficulties incident to first essays toward a competition with those who have previously attained to perfection in the business to be attempted—the bounties, premiums, and other artificial encouragements, with which foreign nations second the exertions of their own citizens in the branches, in which they are to be rivaled," all as obstacles to the establishment of new industries. Overcoming these obstacles "may therefore require the incitement and patronage of government." Although Hamilton recognized that import restrictions would increase domestic prices, "it is universally true, that the contrary is the ultimate effect with every successful manufacture. . . . Being free from the heavy charges, which attend the importation of foreign commodities, it can be afforded, and accordingly seldom or never fails to be sold cheaper, in process of time, than was the foreign article for which it is a substitute" (286).

[2] Hamilton drew quite extensively on the *Wealth of Nations*, even when he disagreed with it. See E. G. Bourne (1894).

Although Hamilton's discussion of infant industries was more detailed than any previous writer and his argument received widespread attention, there is little that is fundamentally new in his analysis. But his study of policy instruments is quite insightful for this period. Hamilton compared the effects of four policies to promote domestic manufactures: protective duties, prohibitions, export taxes on raw materials, and pecuniary bounties (subsidies). For three reasons, Hamilton's preferred method of intervention was a subsidy: first, bounties have a "more immediate tendency to stimulate and uphold new enterprises, increasing the chances of profit, and diminishing the risks of loss, in the first attempts"; second, "bounties have not like high protecting duties, a tendency to produce scarcity," that is, higher domestic prices; third, bounties also promote exports and thereby extend the size of the market for domestic producers (299). Alternatively, import duties raise revenue, but assist producers in the domestic market alone with no direct effect on exports. Recognizing the fiscal constraints to providing subsidies, Hamilton proposed the practical compromise of levying import duties with the resulting revenue being used to finance bounties on domestic production.

John Rae, a Scotsman who had migrated to Canada, provided a more acute analysis of infant industries. Disputing the notion of a harmony between the interests of an individual and the interests of society, Rae directly attacked Smith's claim that tariff protection would, by reducing national income, reduce capital accumulation.[3] But Rae framed his discussion of infant industries more in terms of the advisability of government assistance to the transfer of superior technologies from other countries. Rae (1834, 364) believed that the "general practical conclusion" about the desirability of government intervention to facilitate technology transfer must be granted. But, he added, the case "resolves itself into particulars, and the investigations of the political economist, would seem to be confined to the

[3] Although his response to Smith is not entirely clear, Rae (1834, 381–82) appears to imply that even if income were reduced slightly, the intensity of accumulation would increase and thereby bring about more capital. "It is said capital can only augment by accumulation, and, as the interference of the legislator takes something from individual revenue, it must also take from the power to accumulate, and, consequently, instead of augmenting, must tend to diminish the sum of the capitals of all the individuals in the society, that is the national capital or stock. . . . The answer to this objection is, that the proceedings of the legislator may increase the absolute capital and stock of the society, the provision, that is, for future wants, embodied in the stock of instruments possessed by it, though they may not increase, and may even a little diminish its relative capital, or the sum which would be brought out by measuring those instruments with one another. That is the amount of the absolute capital of the society, which is the proper measure of the wealth of the whole, and of each individual, and that whatever augments it not only directly, and of itself, advances national wealth, but ultimately, also, does so indirectly, through the stimulus given to the accumulation principle, and the addition thence arising to relative capital." For a more detailed discussion of Rae's critique of Smith, see Brewer (1991).

tracing out, from the principles of his science, rules determining when the passage of any art is practicable, and when the benefits derived from it will exceed, or fall short of the necessary expense in effecting the passage."

Rae suggested that technology transfer policies should be employed if domestic manufactures could be expected to produce the goods at the same or a lower price than foreign manufactures, but without explaining when such an expectation was reasonable. Three distinct advantages would result. First, the infant industry would save the costs of transporting the imported goods and thereby increase internal trade, generate additional technological improvements at home, and "so increase the absolute capital of the society." Second, the dislocation of domestic production caused by import supply disruptions, which causes a "great waste of resources," would be avoided. Finally, and most important, greater domestic production of the previously imported good would "stimulate invention and diminish the propensity to servile imitation." As he put it: "Every useful art is so connected with many, or with all others, that whatever renders its products more easily attainable, facilitates the operations of a whole circle of arts, and introduces change—the great agent in producing improvements—under the most favorable form" (365). Quoting Hamilton approvingly, Rae suggested that new arts, by "their very existence in any society, gives a powerful stimulus to the ingenuity of its members."

Therefore, Rae was broadly supportive of infant industry policies:

> The legislator effects his purpose by premiums for successful individual imitations of the foreign article; by general bounties on the home manufacture; or by duties on that imported from abroad. . . . it having been made sufficiently apparent that nothing prevents the branch of industry in question being established, but the difficulties attending new undertakings, the want of skilled labor, and a sufficiently accurate knowledge of the properties of the materials to be employed in the formation of the new instruments, it is then proper to proceed to direct and general encouragements by bounties or duties. In this way real capital, and healthy enterprise are directed to the art, the difficulties attending its introduction overcome in the shortest possible space, and the commodities yielded by it are produced at less outlay, and afforded at a less price than that, at which they were before imported. (368)

Rae sounded a note of caution in that the legislator "is never justifiable in attempt to transfer arts yielding utilities from foreign countries to his own, unless he has sufficient reason to conclude that they will ultimately lessen the cost of the commodities they produce. . . . When there are circumstances particularly unfavorable to the practice of the art, and no countervailing circumstances particularly favorable to it, the first introduction of it must always cost the society high, and the subsequent maintaining of it will in all probability be a burden on the common industry and stock."

Unfortunately, he added, "examples of injudicious conduct of the legislator from inattention to this particular have been not unfrequent" (367–68).

Although Rae is perhaps the most careful early analyst of infant industry protection, Friedrich List was by far the most popular proponent of protection in newly industrializing countries. A German political activist, writer, and sometime academic, List's book *The National System of Political Economy*, first published in German in 1841, attained the status within protectionist circles that the *Wealth of Nations* had achieved among free traders. List based his study largely on historical judgments rather than on economic analysis because he rejected classical theory, which he thought suggested that free trade was always beneficial. Instead, List argued that the appropriate commercial policy of a country depended on its particular stage of economic development.

List and the classical school agreed on many issues, such as, for example, the importance of freedom and stability in promoting investment and other forms of economic activity. But, in List's mind, two basic points separated his doctrines from those of the classicals. First, he attacked the "cosmopolitical economy" of Adam Smith and his followers which, in his view, wholly ignored the separate and distinct economic interests of a particular country in a world rife with conflict, fraught with insecurity, and seething with national identity. List accused Smith and his free-trade followers of examining only what is best for the world overall under conditions that he believed presumed an as yet unattained degree of international cooperation. List's harsh attacks on the "cosmopolitan school" of Smith frequently distorted the position of classical writers, who were not romantic cosmopolitans neglectful of the national interest, and even List admitted in his preface that his attacks were exaggerated for effect.

Second, List (1885, 133) stated that *"the power of producing wealth* is . . . infinitely more important than *wealth itself,"* and deemed this contrary to the approach of the classical school. The power of production, by which he apparently meant the ability to reproduce and augment certain factors of production such as capital and skilled labor, ensured not only "the possession and the increase of what has been gained, but also the replacement of what has been lost." He accused the classical school of taking a static view that valued only current wealth (exchangeable value) to the exclusion of factors that could be used to produce wealth. His ideas about productive powers were not obviously at variance with the views of the classical economists, however, because they also emphasized the importance of allowing capital and skills to accumulate. List believed that more attention should be devoted to production, however, because "production renders consumption possible" (233).

When it came to commercial policy, List endorsed many aspects of mercantilist doctrine. List (1885, 144) believed that the interests of merchants did not necessarily reflect the national interest in the development of a country's powers of production: "The foreign trade of a nation must not be estimated in the way in which individual merchants judge it, solely and only according to the theory of values (i.e., by regarding merely the gain at any particular moment of some material advantage); the nation is bound to keep steadily in view all these conditions on which its present and future existence, prosperity, and power depend." List repeatedly stressed the fundamental importance of manufacturing, the benefits of which were economic and noneconomic and included greater security and independence, greater division of labor with its impetus to developing skills and accumulating capital, and the like. Thus, the commodity composition of trade deserved watchful attention. "It may be stated as a principle," List (1854, 77) wrote, "that a nation is richer and more powerful, in proportion as it exports more manufactured products, imports more raw materials, and consumes more tropical commodities."

For these reasons, government support for infant industries was essential. "The fact that manufacturing industry transforms into productive capital, wealth, and national powers, explains mainly why protection exerts so powerful an influence upon the increase of national wealth." List (1885, 144–45) argued that future benefits from establishing domestic manufactures would more than compensate for what he fully acknowledged would be the short-run economic costs of protection:

> The nation must sacrifice and give up a measure of material property in order to gain culture, skill, and powers of united production; it must sacrifice some present advantages in order to insure to itself future ones. It is true that protective duties at first increase the price of manufactured goods; but it is just as true . . . that in the course of time, by the nation being enabled to build up a completely developed manufacturing power of its own, those goods are produced more cheaply at home than the price at which they can be imported from foreign parts. If, therefore, a sacrifice of *value* is caused by protective duties, it is made good by the gain of a *power of production*, which not only secures to the nation an infinitely greater amount of material goods, but also industrial independence in case of war. . . . A nation capable of developing a manufacturing power, if it makes use of the system of protection, thus acts quite in the same spirit as that landed proprietor did who by the sacrifice of some material wealth allowed some of his children to learn a productive trade.

List (1885, 226–27) strenuously disputed Smith's negative remarks about infant industries:

> He wrongly maintains that the revenues of the nation are dependent only on the sum of its material capital. His own work, on the contrary, contains a thousand proofs that these revenues are chiefly conditional on the sum of its

mental and bodily powers, and on the degree to which they are perfected, in social and political respects (especially by means of more perfect division of labour and confederation of the national productive powers), and that although measures of protection require sacrifices of material goods for a time, these sacrifices are made good a hundred-fold in powers, in the ability to acquire values of exchange, and are consequently merely reproductive outlay by the nation. . . . He has not considered the influence of manufactures on the internal and external commerce, on the civilisation and power of the nation, and on the maintenance of its independence, as well as on the capability arising from these of gaining material wealth.

However, not all countries were well suited for such policies. Indeed, List's case for protection was carefully circumscribed. Because manufactures only flourish in temperate climates, tropical countries must never attempt to acquire manufactures through artificial means.[4] And regardless of the stage of economic development, all countries should have free trade in agricultural goods and raw materials.[5] "The system of protection," List (1885, 188, 309) wrote, "can be justified solely and only for the purpose of the *industrial development* of the nation. . . . Measures of protection are justifiable only for the purpose of furthering and protecting the internal manufacturing power, and only in the case of nations which through an extensive and compact territory, large population, possession of natural resources, far advanced agriculture, a high degree of civilization and political development, are qualified to maintain an equal rank with the principal agricultural manufacturing commercial nations."

List drew upon his reading of history in proposing the best commercial policy for countries at different stages of economic development: "History teaches us how nations which have been endowed by Nature with all resources which are requisite for the attainment of the highest grade of wealth and power, may and must . . . modify their [commercial] systems according to the measure of their own progress: in the first stage, adopting free trade

---

[4] "A country of the torrid zone would make a very fatal mistake, should it try to become a manufacturing country. Having received no invitation to that vocation from nature, it will progress more rapidly in riches and civilization if it continues to exchange its agricultural productions for the manufactured products of the temperate zone. It is true that tropical countries sink thus into dependence upon those of the temperate zone, but that dependence will not be without compensation, if competition arises among the nations of temperate climates in their manufacturing industry in their trade with the former. . . . This competition will not only ensure a full supply of manufactures at low prices, but will prevent any one nation from taking advantage by its superiority over the weaker nations of the torrid zone" [List (1854, 75–76)].

[5] List (1885, 324, 187) wrote: "Free trade in agricultural products and raw materials is useful to all nations at all stages of their industrial development." He believed that production of "provisions and raw materials . . . needs no protection, and in which the restriction of commercial intercourse must be disadvantageous under all circumstances to both nations—to that which imposes, as well as to that which suffers from such restrictions."

with more advanced nations as a means of raising themselves from a state of barbarism, and of making advances in agriculture; in the second stage, promoting the growth of manufactures, fisheries, navigation, and foreign trade by means of commercial restrictions; and in the last stage, after reaching the highest degree of wealth and power, by gradually reverting to the principle of free trade and of unrestricted competition in the home as well as in foreign markets" (115).

Unlike Rae or Hamilton, List did not mention any preference for subsidies over tariffs as the way to promote industry. As for the height of protective tariffs, List observed that "it may in general be assumed that where any technical industry cannot be established by means of an original protection of forty to sixty per cent and cannot continue to maintain itself under a continued protection of twenty to thirty per cent the fundamental conditions of manufacturing power are lacking" (313). List was prepared to wait decades before allowing protection to expire, calling it "ridiculous to allow a nation merely a *few years* for the task of bringing to perfection one great branch of national industry" (319).

List never disparaged the ultimate goal of worldwide free trade; indeed, he embraced it.[6] He simply advocated temporary protective measures in countries passing through a certain stage of development to ensure that they could trade on an equal footing with more advanced countries in producing manufactured goods. As he (1885, 129, 131) put it, "The system of protection, inasmuch as it forms the only means of placing those nations which are far behind in civilisation on equal terms with the one predominating nation [England] (which, however, never received at the hands of Nature a perpetual right to a monopoly of manufacture, but which merely gained an advance over others in point of time), the system of protection regarded from this point of view appears to be the most efficient means of furthering the final union of nations, and hence also of promoting true freedom of trade. . . . In order to allow freedom of trade to operate naturally, the less advanced nations must first be raised by artificial means to that stage of cultivation to which the English nation has been artificially elevated."

Over the course of the nineteenth century, List came to have an immense popular impact. By the end of the century such eminent British economists as Alfred Marshall acknowledged and accepted many of List's basic ideas about infant industries in developing countries. But most economists did not accept the infant industry argument on List's terms and with reference to List's works. They were suspicious of his historical analysis, skeptical that it could provide a careful analysis of the problems faced by infant

---

[6] List (1885, 122) simply believed that there were important political prerequisites: "If . . . we assume a universal union or confederation of all nations as the guarantee for an everlasting peace, the principle of international free trade seems to be perfectly justified."

industries or useful guidance about the conditions under which protection was or was not advisable. Under ideal circumstances, the implications of economic theory did not depend upon historical circumstances, as was the case with comparative advantage. And List did nothing to advance the theory underlying the infant industry case because this was not his purpose.

Thus, the infant industry doctrine did not gain formal acceptance into classical trade theory until 1848, when John Stuart Mill published the first edition of his *Principles of Political Economy*. The endorsement by an economic theorist of first rank was not so easily dismissed as similar statements coming from a Hamilton or a List. Mill's ([1848] 1909, 922) original statement was as follows:

> The only case in which, on mere principles of political economy, protecting duties can be defensible, is when they are imposed temporarily (especially in a young and rising nation) in hopes of naturalizing a foreign industry, in itself perfectly suitable to the circumstances of the country. The superiority of one country over another in a branch of production often arises only from having begun it sooner. There may be no inherent advantage on one part, or disadvantage on the other, but only a present superiority of acquired skill and experience. A country which has this skill and experience yet to acquire, may in other respects be better adapted to the production than those which were earlier in the field: and besides, it is a just remark of Mr. Rae, that nothing has a greater tendency to promote improvements in any branch of production than its trial under a new set of conditions. But it cannot be expected that individuals should, at their own risk, or rather to their certain loss, introduce a new manufacture, and bear the burthen of carrying it on until the producers have been educated up to the level of those with whom the processes are traditional. A protecting duty, continued for a reasonable time, will sometimes be the least inconvenient mode in which the nation can tax itself for the support of such an experiment. But the protection should be confined to cases in which there is good ground of assurance that the industry which it fosters will after a time be able to dispense with it; nor should the domestic producers ever be allowed to expect that it will be continued to them beyond the time necessary for a fair trial of what they are capable of accomplishing.

Mill's standing and reputation among economists gave intellectual credibility to the infant industry argument for the first time. Economists and others who viewed free trade as the best policy for all countries regardless of the circumstances were dismayed by the respectability Mill lent to protection. Richard Cobden, the great free-trade activist in mid-nineteenth-century Britain, reportedly lamented on his deathbed that "I believe that the harm which Mill has done to the world by the passage in his book on *Political Economy* in which he favors the principle of protection in young communities has outweighed all the good which may have been caused by his other writings."[7] And Alfred Marshall ([1890] 1925, 259) later remarked that "when John Stuart Mill ventured to tell the English people that some arguments for protection in new countries were scientifically valid, his friends spoke of it in anger—but more in sorrow than in anger—as his one sad departure from the sound principles of economic rectitude."

Indeed, complaints soon reached Mill on how his statement was being distorted by protectionists to justify high tariffs in the United States, Canada, and Australia in the 1860s. In his correspondence, Mill condemned any general policy of protection—"an organized system of pillage of the many by the few," he called it—but reiterated that, in principle, the infant industry claim to protection was valid.[8] "It may sometimes be a good calculation for the future interests of the country to make a temporary sacrifice by granting a moderate protecting duty for a certain limited number of years, say ten, or at the very most twenty, during the latter part of which the duty should be on a gradually diminishing scale, and at the end of which it should expire."[9] But the complaints persisted and by the late 1860s Mill grew to question his own approval of the doctrine. To one correspondent Mill sighed, "But I confess that I almost despair of this general understanding [of the limits of the infant industry case] being ever practically established. I find that in Australia, protection is not advocated in this form or for this purpose, but that the vulgarest and most exploded fallacies are revived in its support."[10]

Eventually, Mill recanted his view that import protection was an appropriate means of promoting infant industries, although he never abandoned his belief that such industries could exist and that this in principle constituted a genuine exception to free trade. "Though I still think that the introduction of a foreign industry is often worth a sacrifice, and that a temporary protecting duty, if it were sure to remain temporary, would probably be the best shape in which that sacrifice can be made, I am inclined to believe that it is safer to make it by an annual grant from the public treasury, which is not nearly so likely to be continued indefinitely, to prop up an industry which has not so thriven as to be able to dispense with it."[11]

Curiously, Mill never incorporated these views into later editions of the

[7] Quoted in George Armitage-Smith (1898, 53).

[8] *JSM*, XVII, 1798. References to Mill's work are from *The Collected Works of John Stuart Mill* (Toronto: University of Toronto Press, 1965–91), hereafter referred to as *JSM* followed by volume and page number.

[9] *JSM*, XVI, 1044.

[10] *JSM*, XVI, 1420.

[11] *JSM*, XVI, 1516. "I am now much shaken in the opinion, which has so often been quoted for purposes which it did not warrant; and I am disposed to think that when it is advisable, as it may sometimes be, to subsidise a new industry in its commencement, this had better be done by a direct annual grant, which is far less likely to be continued after the conditions which alone justified it have ceased to exist" (*JSM*, XVI, 1520).

Principles. In the sixth edition of 1865, Mill (1909, 923) added the following passage to his infamous paragraph:

> The expenses of production being always greatest at first, it may happen that the home production, though really the most advantageous, may not become so until after a certain duration of pecuniary loss, which it is not to be expected that private speculators should incur in order that their successors may be benefited by their ruin. I have therefore conceded that in a new country a temporary protecting duty may sometimes be economically defensible; on condition, however, that it be strictly limited in point of time, and provision be made that during the latter part of its existence it be on a gradually decreasing scale. Such temporary protection is of the same nature as a patent, and should be governed by similar conditions.

Then, in the seventh and final edition of 1871, Mill added the further qualification that replaced "a protecting duty . . . *will* sometimes be" with "*might* sometimes be," and to add "*it is essential that* the protection should be confined. . . ."

In the decades after 1848, Mill's qualified endorsement of infant industry protection failed to attract much support among economists. Mill's paragraph succeeded in putting them on the defensive, but economists remained skeptical. Even Mill's foremost disciple, John E. Cairnes (1874, 403), dismissed infant industry protection because "the inevitable result is that industry becomes unprogressive wherever it is highly protected." Cairnes characterized Mill's statement as the "*obiter dictum* of a great writer" and called attention to the "strict limitations" Mill had set down with his case. But he added that "with or without such limitations, however, I cannot but think that the position is untenable." Henry Fawcett (1878, 111) agreed that Mill's argument would be conclusive "if there were a reasonable probability that the conditions under which he supposes that such a protective duty could be imposed would ever be realized." But it has been "incontestably shown" that "it is absolutely impossible to impose a protective duty under the stipulations on which Mr. Mill so emphatically insists."

William Graham Sumner (1885, 117) believed that Mill's case was "conceivable" and therefore not "absurd," but maintained that "I strenuously dissent from Mill's doctrine even as he limits it." "Manufactures grow up as population increases and capital accumulates, and, in the natural order of industry, are best developed in countries of dense population and accumulated wealth," observed Henry George (1886, 165) in rejecting the infant industry argument. "Seeing this connection, it is easy to mistake for cause what is really effect, and to imagine that manufacturing brings population and wealth." Finally, J. S. Nicholson (1901, 364–65) commented that "temporary protection is impossible owing to the creation of

vested interests, that new countries especially require capital, which is re-
pelled and diminished by protection, and that the artificial forcing of new
industries is not advantageous in the long run." Echoing George, Nicholson argued that "the best way to promote the higher forms of industry is not
by the simple process of exclusion, but rather by improvements in the edu-
cation of the people."

Despite such skepticism, key questions about the infant industry case for
protection remained unasked and unanswered. The first question related to
identifying the specific market failures that give rise to the necessity for
government intervention. The second question related to whether, given
the existence of some market failure, the expected value of government
action was positive. Yet these fundamental issues were virtually swept
aside toward the end of the nineteenth century when economists were reacting against what they viewed as dogmatic *laissez-faire* arguments
against government intervention that had become associated with political
economy. A greater willingness to accept market failures and concede a
greater economic role to the government served to insulate the infant industry argument from greater scrutiny, giving the infant industry doctrine the appearance of greater strength in economic analysis than it actually had.

In his widely read textbook, for example, Henry Sidgwick (1887, 489ff)
of Cambridge University strongly endorsed Mill's passage and even made
the incredibly bold claim that "the argument for temporary protection . . .
is theoretically valid from what I have called a 'cosmopolitan' point of
view," that is, from the standpoint of the world's overall economic welfare.
In Sidgwick's words, "It is quite possible that the cost incurred may be
compensated to the community by the ultimate economic gain accruing
from the domestic production of the commodity previously imported;
while yet the initial outlay, that would be required to establish the industry
without protection, could not be expected to be ultimately remunerative to
any private capitalists who undertook it." Here Sidgwick raised the first
key issue: if the government recognizes that a currently unprofitable industry is potentially successful after a period of protection, what prevents private firms and entrepreneurs from borrowing in capital markets to cover
their initial losses? Private action would fail, he argued, "if the difficulties
of introducing the industry were of such a kind that, when once overcome
by the original introducers, they would no longer exist for others or would
exist in a much smaller degree." This implied some externality, but regret-
tably he did not elaborate.

Sidgwick instead offered the example of two regions equally suited for
producing manufactures, one of which exported manufactures and the
other agricultural goods. The region exporting agricultural products could
then save on the transportation costs of imported manufactures by estab-

lishing domestic production itself; in other words, temporary protective duties would bring about a gain that would "consist chiefly" in saving the cost of transport.[12] Sidgwick did not explain why comparative advantage failed in this particular instance or how world welfare would increase as a result. This savings-of-transportation-costs argument for infant industry protection was not new (having been discussed by Rae and dating back to the mercantilists), and Sidgwick was essentially resurrecting the same case made by the well-known American protectionist, Henry Carey (1858).

Yet this savings-of-transportation-costs argument completely fails as a case for protection. From the 6th edition of his *Principles* in 1865, Mill (1909, 925ff) scornfully called Carey's widely read argument for protection "totally invalid."[13] Mill strenuously rejected it and had, in fact, totally demolished it in the *Principles*. The Carey-Sidgwick doctrine completely ignored the insights of comparative advantage and failed to recognize that, in spite of the transportation costs, there is a savings to the country from procuring the good from abroad. As Mill (1909, 923) put it, "The burthen [of transportation costs] is borne for a more than equivalence advantage. If the commodity is bought in a foreign country with domestic produce in spite of the double cost of carriage, the fact proves that, heavy as that cost may be, the saving in cost of production outweighs it, and the collective labour of the country is on the whole better remunerated than if the article were produced at home."

There had also been skirting around the issue of whether infant industry protection was justifiable on the basis of cost-benefit analysis. Charles F. Bastable (1887, 136–37), a professor at Trinity College (Dublin), conceded that the infant industry argument is "the most plausible case which can be made for protection." But Bastable pointed out that government intervention could not be called a success simply because it enabled an industry to overcome a historical handicap and survive. Rather, a more decisive question was posed: "Will the certain and immediate loss, resulting from protection, be outweighed by the future gains from the new industry?" This question not only applied a basic cost-benefit test to infant industry policies, but, in Bastable's opinion, the practical problems associated with such policies "strongly impress us with the belief that this special case is in reality no exception to the rule of freedom in international trade." Bastable agreed that arguments for protection of manufactures on noneconomic grounds were prevalent, but on the demonstrable criteria of economic gain, something even Mill himself had been vague about, was more stringent.

Until Bastable's statement, economists had noted the costs associated with infant industry protection, but failed to identify clearly the gains from

---

[12] As Jacques Melitz (1963) points out, transportation costs were an integral part of Sidgwick's trade theory.

[13] To one correspondent, Mill even wrote about Carey that his was "about the worst book on political economy I ever read" (*JSM*, XVII, 1589).

having an industry naturalized. If the rate of payments to factors of production was determined in other sectors of the economy and the infant industry
merely drew these factors away from other activities, factors would earn no
more than their opportunity cost and there would be no gain from having
created a new industry. Rather, the industry that developed due to protection must create some quasi-rents (or producer surplus) for it to prove
beneficial to the economy.

Once the costs and the benefits had been identified, then they could be
compared. Paul-Gustave Fauveau (1873), a French mathematician and
contributor to French economic journals, calculated the precise conditions
under which infant industry protection would bring a net gain. Suppose a
were the mean annual cost required to establish an infant industry and b
were the mean annual benefits generated by the industry after infant industry protection was removed. If x were the number of years of infant industry
protection, the present discounted value of the costs of the policy (assuming interest rate r):

$$a + \frac{a}{(1 + r)} + \frac{a}{(1 + r)^2} + \ldots + \frac{a}{(1 + r)^{x-1}},$$

which would sum to:

$$\frac{a}{r} \cdot (1 + r) \cdot \left[1 - \frac{1}{(1 + r)^x}\right].$$

The gains from the infant industry after year x would be an infinite sum of
b that would amount in present value terms to:

$$\frac{b}{r} \cdot (1 + r) \cdot \frac{1}{(1 + r)^x}.$$

Equating the discounted stream of future benefits from the infant industry
to the discounted sum of initial costs, such that there would be no net gain
from the infant industry policy, yields the following relationship:

$$x \cdot \log (1 + r) = \log \left(1 + \frac{a}{b}\right).$$

Assuming an interest rate of 5 percent, Fauveau calculated the mean annual
"break-even" gain that would be necessary to compensate exactly for the
loss from import duties. If protection lasts 5 years ($x = 5$), then the mean
annual gains (in perpetuity) from the infant industry must be 28 percent of
the mean annual loss to ensure no net gain or loss from the policy. If protection continues for 10 years, the mean annual gain must be 63 percent of the

mean annual loss; for 15 years, 108 percent of annual loss; for 20 years, 165 percent; for 30 years, 332 percent; for 50 years, 1,047 percent. This calculation demonstrates the cost-benefit hurdle that any infant industry policy has to surmount for the expected value of intervention to be positive. What economists including Mill had failed to do was to address the underlying economic structure of the infant industry argument in terms of specific market failures, specify the gains that accrue to a nation from naturalizing a certain industry, and then describe how these gains could compensate for the loss incurred while protecting the industry.

The infant industry argument received yet another lease on life, and again escaped careful scrutiny, when two leading economists of the next generation merely accepted the case in principle without dissecting it. Alfred Marshall (of Cambridge University) and Frank Taussig (of Harvard University) were both agnostic as to the underlying theory behind infant industries and pursued a case-study approach to assess such policies. In various writings, Marshall expressed his belief that the classical economists had been too dogmatically opposed to the infant industry argument and that protection in the newly industrializing countries of the United States and Australia was not an unmitigated evil.[14] Marshall ([1903] 1926, 392) went so far as to say that "protection to immature industries is a very great national good" and that, while costly in some instances, "it would have been foolish for nations with immature industries to adopt" free trade. Marshall would often describe his visit to America in 1875 during which he concluded that the overall costs and benefits of protection were roughly balanced.

Taussig also fully accepted the infant industry argument when the impediments to establishing an industry were artificial, not natural or permanent. In studying the cotton textile and iron industries in the early nineteenth-century United States, Taussig (1883, 66–68) found that although "the conditions existed under which it is most likely that protection to a young industry may be advantageously applied . . . little, if anything, was gained by the costly protection which the United States maintained in the first part of this century." As this constituted just one experiment, Taussig insisted that "the intrinsic soundness of the argument for protection to young industries is therefore not touched by the conclusions drawn from the history of its trial in the United States." Indeed, he maintained that whether protection is beneficial or not is "simply a question of probability for the given case."[15]

---

[14] Phyllis Deane (1990) provides an overview of Marshall's views on free trade.

[15] Certainly there was the danger that, as Taussig (1905, 47) put it, protection, "so far from leading to improvements and eventual cheapening, leads to the retention of antiquated and inefficient methods of production." But he also argued that ten years might be too brief a trial period for infant industry protection, with thirty years not necessarily being unreasonable.

Marshall and Taussig did nothing to advance or qualify the conceptual basis for the infant industry argument. While their own studies provided little support for infant industry policies in practice, their uncritical acceptance of the economic argument perpetuated the impression that the infant industry case constituted a valid and important exception to free trade. As A. C. Pigou (1906, 13), one of Marshall's prize students, declared, "Of the formal validity of List's [infant industry] argument there is no longer any dispute among economists," despite the fact that since Mill's statement there had really been no deeper examination of the precise theoretical issues involved.

Over the first half of the twentieth century, the infant industry argument remained a universally acknowledged theoretical exception to free trade, despite the continued skepticism among economists about such protection in practice. Over these fifty years, however, the theory behind the argument remained vaguely formulated. Not only was it difficult to lay down general rules for ascertaining the likelihood of infant industry protection being successful, it was not even clear what specific market failures and other underlying conditions gave rise to the infant industries in the first place. What was the specific barrier that necessitated government intervention: the lack of a domestic supply of skilled labor? insufficient accumulated production experience? failures in the capital market? Depending upon the particular factors that prevented infant industries from arising and maturing on their own, the implications for trade policy could be quite different.

When economists finally began to put more economic structure on the argument, the case for protection appeared more limited than previously thought. Because the argument was for temporary (rather than permanent) protection, the infant industry case was inherently dynamic and involved some irreversibilities, such as accumulated dynamic scale economies resulting from learning by doing. In this context, the focus turned to identifying the precise point of market failure because that determined which method of government intervention was best suited to improving upon a *laissez-faire* outcome. James Meade (1955, 255–57) described the infant industry argument as follows: if a firm tries to enter a market it will initially incur a loss, but "after a time experience would bring with it the necessary skills and know-how and the industry would turn out to be an economic one for the country to undertake." However, Meade pointed out, "infancy as such provides no argument even for temporary State support." If the firm can eventually earn a suitable rate of return, then private enterprise in the capital markets will have an incentive to provide these funds and "there will be no case for a State subsidy." Thus, if capital markets were efficient there would be no need for government action. And even if capital markets were not efficient, one would be hard pressed to explain why the government should not attempt to remedy the particular deficiency in the capital market rather than impose trade restrictions (which would fail to solve the underlying problem).

An alternative market failure could lie in the acquisition of technical knowledge by the firm. Meade pointed out that "it may be difficult for one infant to learn without thereby affecting the knowledge of other infants." In other words, an initial investment by one firm could affect the production conditions for all subsequent firms if that knowledge is easily transferable. If the knowledge generated by learning by doing or research and development expenditures spill over costlessly to other firms, then it is conceivable that no firm will undertake the initial investment. "In such a case the temporary subsidization of the first firm may be socially desirable; but this would be so not because infants have to learn but because infants teach each other." The further qualification here is that spillovers must be geographically local or national in scope; if such knowledge spillovers were worldwide in nature, there would be no special barrier to domestic firms in acquiring that knowledge from firms in exporting countries.

The principle of policy targeting implicit in Meade's analysis suggests that the most efficient government intervention addresses the failure of marginal conditions between price and cost to hold at the precise source of their divergence.[16] In this vein, Robert Baldwin's (1969) classic critique of the infant industry argument for protection stresses that, even if the precise market failure associated with infant industries has been specified, a trade policy intervention does not necessarily provide a remedy that will ensure the maturation of the infant. Baldwin noted that import protection alone fails to provide the right incentives for an infant firm to make additional investments in acquiring technological knowledge. Nor does it necessarily improve the firm's ability to retain the benefits of its investments in knowledge, but does serve to make old production techniques profitable. The appropriate policy actions should focus on correcting the specific, underlying problems thought to be associated with acquiring new technologies and investments in new techniques.[17] As Baldwin (1969, 303) justly concluded, "If the infant industry argument for tariff protection is worthy of its reputation as the major exception to the free trade case, it should be

[16] This is the underlying logic of the theory of domestic divergences, discussed in chapter 10.

[17] As Harry Johnson (1965, 28) explained, "Once knowledge of production technique is acquired, it can be applied by others than those who have assumed the cost of acquiring it; the social benefit at least potentially exceeds the private benefit of investment in learning industrial production techniques, and the social use of the results of such learning may even reduce the private reward for undertaking the investment. Where the social benefits of the learning process exceed the private benefits, the most appropriate governmental policy would be to subsidize the learning process itself, through such techniques as financing or sponsoring pilot enterprises on condition that the experience acquired and techniques developed be made available to all would-be producers."

possible to present a clear analytical case, based upon well-known and generally accepted empirical relationships unique to infant industries, for the general desirability and effectiveness of protective duties in these industries." Nearly a century and a half since Mill lent his support to the infant industry argument for protection, the case has still not achieved this level of intellectual coherence.

.   .   .

Despite the intuitively appealing metaphor of "infant" industries, analytical progress in assessing this argument for protection has come extremely slowly since Mill's qualified endorsement. Although hampered by a lingering sense of vagueness, the infant industry argument in modern treatments now relates to hurdles faced by new firms in acquiring knowledge or capital. To the extent that government intervention is called for it is to improve upon the existing conditions of appropriability of knowledge investments or improving the functioning of capital markets. Trade interventions are not directly appropriate because those improvements may be desirable regardless of whether the industry in question is involved in international trade. As a result, this particular argument for protection is not nearly as prevalent or supportable today as it was several decades ago. Still, the infant industry argument has been difficult to dismiss altogether and it continues to occupy an uneasy place in the theory of commercial policy.

Chapter Nine

GRAHAM AND THE
INCREASING RETURNS ARGUMENT

THE INFANT INDUSTRY argument for protection held that temporary protection might enable a domestic industry to reach a degree of efficiency such that it could, at some point, export without assistance at world prices. In the 1920s, Frank Graham, an economics professor at Princeton University, sought to describe conditions under which *permanent* protection could benefit a country. If manufacturing was subject to increasing returns to scale and agriculture was subject to decreasing returns to scale, then a country specializing in agriculture and importing manufactured goods could be depriving itself of production in a high productivity sector. Graham described the disadvantages of this situation and argued that a permanent tariff on manufactures could prove superior to free trade. As with previous arguments for protection, his case provoked sharp debate, but it foundered on the following criticism: increasing returns that are internal to the firm are incompatible with market competition. Still, Graham succeeded in bringing attention to the potential effects of external economies in generating arbitrary patterns of specialization and trade.

．　．　．

The classical theory of comparative advantage, which achieved prominence in chapter 7 of Ricardo's *Principles*, assumed one factor of production (labor) and constant costs of production: if the quantity of labor employed in the production of a good doubled, output would also double. Yet trade was often described in the context of several factors and different cost relationships. In 1815, Thomas Malthus, David Ricardo, and Edward West all independently applied the notion of diminishing returns to scale in the context of agricultural production: as more labor was applied to a fixed amount of land, the less each additional laborer was able to produce. Ricardo's famous critique of the Corn Laws skillfully used diminishing returns (or, alternatively, increasing costs of production) in agriculture to describe how rents, profits, and wages were determined and to assess the impact of trade policy on income distribution. Unlike Ricardo and Malthus, West also called attention to the possibility of increasing returns in manufacturing, in which the costs of production might decline as the scale of production increased. West (1815, 25) suggested that "the division of labor and application of machinery renders labor more and more productive in manufactures, in the progress of improvement." This effect was also present in agriculture, but was more than counterbalanced by recourse to inferior land, a nonaugmentable factor of production, which gave rise to diminishing returns. West's distinction between diminishing returns in agriculture and increasing returns in manufacturing was adopted by other classical economists and became established as a theme in economics that continues to the present day.[1] However, the implications of increasing returns for trade and commercial policy were not, at this point, drawn out.

Unlike the terms of trade and the infant industry arguments, the debate about increasing returns was the first in which the main participants were American economists rather than their British counterparts. Economists in the United States had long contended with or even advanced the casual argument made by protectionists there that import tariffs on manufactures were desirable to promote greater output in increasing returns industries. American economists also confronted the related belief that, when a domestic industry is characterized by increasing returns, an import tariff might not result in higher domestic prices. Rather, the popular argument reasoned, a tariff might actually reduce prices because domestic output could expand and serve the market at a lower cost. Francis Walker (1903) attempted with little success to illustrate that argument more formally. He used numerical examples loosely based on increasing returns and ostensibly designed to demonstrate the potential gain from tariffs if prices of traded commodities fell as a result.[2]

Thomas Carver (1902) did not reject the possibility of lower prices altogether, but at least recognized that if increasing returns at the firm level continued indefinitely the industry would be driven toward a one-firm monopoly. In this case, a tariff would simply strengthen this monopoly power and allow a higher price to be exacted from domestic consumers.[3] But most economists were surprisingly lax about recognizing the potential difficulties that increasing returns might create for the theoretical case in favor of free trade. Frank Taussig (1927, 83), for example, agreed that increasing returns "may alter conditions under which international trade is carried on," but nonchalantly dismissed them as "not of a novel kind, and therefore call for no new analysis."

It took a British economist, J. S. Nicholson (1897, 308–9), a professor of political economy at the University of Edinburgh, to point out that increasing returns might create problems for the theory of comparative advantage.

---

[1] Nassau Senior (1826, 86), for example, proposed the following economic law, that "every increase in the number of manufacturing labourers is accompanied not merely by a corresponding, but by an increased productive power," and asserted that if employment in the textile sector doubled, output would more than double.

[2] Jacob Viner's (1937, 475) harsh but reliable judgment is that "his procedure is defective in almost every conceivable particular . . . [and] his results are totally devoid of significance."

[3] See also Alfred Marshall's ([1890] 1925, 261–62) related discussion.

Nicholson envisioned the following scenario: suppose wheat production was subject to diminishing returns to scale (wherein the marginal product of labor declined as more labor was employed), while cloth production was subject to increasing returns to scale (wherein the average product of labor increased with employment). Specialization and trade would imply sharply different outcomes for two countries. The country having a comparative advantage in the production of cloth would enjoy both a rise in the average product of labor in cloth (as output increased) and in the marginal product of labor in wheat (as output contracted). This would lead to an increase in the wage rate; Nicholson, as others of his era were prone to do, implied that anything that increased labor's share in national income was inherently desirable.

The opposite occurs in the country having a comparative advantage in wheat: the marginal product of labor in wheat would fall as output expands, while the withdrawal of labor from cloth would decrease the average product of labor in that sector. If cloth sells at the same price per yard as wheat per bushel, then this process would usually stop when the labor used to produce 1,000 yards of cloth could be used to produce 1,000 bushels of wheat. However, with different returns to scale a country might use resources to produce less than 1,000 bushels of wheat because the standard analysis "takes no account of the reduction of the average yield to labour in cloth as the production is diminished." In this case, the extra labour in wheat could yield less than 1,000 bushels and the country "will obtain less cloth than before and the total national income will be less." For this country, which would completely specialize in wheat, Nicholson argued that the "only compensation would be in obtaining more cloth than before for the wheat exported," that is, a sufficiently large improvement in the terms of trade.

Nicholson's early but insightful analysis came just short of clinching his case because he neglected to illustrate directly the loss suffered by the country specializing in the diminishing returns sector; he only indirectly addressed the gains-from-trade issue and his argument about reduced national income was incomplete by itself. His awkward use of marginal analysis in agriculture and average analysis in manufactures signaled a potential problem in examining the international trade equilibrium with this sort of increasing returns. Marginal analysis in agriculture was standard: output would expand until a competitive equilibrium was established at which the (increasing) marginal cost of producing the good was equal to its price. This would not suffice in considering manufacturing: if marginal cost was a decreasing function of output, there would be no profits on the earlier, higher cost units of output when marginal cost was set equal to price. Thus, Nicholson was forced to couch his discussion of manufacturing in terms of average productivity (or costs): as output increased, the average cost of production over *all* units of output would fall. This situation was potentially compatible with competitive equilibrium.

Curiously, Nicholson's example drew little contemporary comment or debate.[4] In 1923, however, Frank Graham constructed a very similar example that appeared to demonstrate the loss suffered by the country that did not specialize in the increasing returns industry. Holding that comparative advantage is not an "infallible criterion" of the best commercial policy, Graham (1923, 200) argued that when manufacturing is subject to increasing returns to scale, "protection to manufactures may advantageously be continued much longer than would seem adequate to cover the infant stage, whether or not the industry could maintain itself without such aid." Proponents of temporary infant industry protection conceded too much, in Graham's view, because "it may be to a country's economic advantage to protect an industry which could not grow up or survive without protection and which never will be able to survive without it, an industry which has not comparative advantage when the protective duty is first levied nor ever attains one under it" (202–3).

To illustrate his point, Graham introduced a numerical example of comparative costs and trade in watches (subject to increasing returns) and wheat (subject to decreasing returns). Suppose in the absence of trade a country can use a unit of labor to produce 40 units of wheat or 30 watches. If the international ratio of exchange is 40 units of wheat for 35 watches, the country has comparative advantage in wheat: with trade and two units of labor, it could consume 40 units of wheat and 35 watches, 5 more watches than it could without trade. But the labor costs of production, under Graham's assumptions, are not invariant to the movement of labor between the two sectors. As labor shifts into wheat production and confronts diminishing returns, output becomes more costly to obtain and the marginal product of labor falls to 35 units of wheat; as labor leaves the increasing returns watch industry, output there also becomes more costly to obtain and labor can only produce 20 watches. If the international exchange ratio remains 40 units of wheat for 35 watches, the country at that particular point still benefits from trade. Without trade at that point the country could have 35 units of wheat and 20 watches; with trade it could have 30 units of wheat and 35 watches and, as 5 extra watches are worth more than 5 units of extra wheat, the country has a higher real income.

But that is an incorrect comparison, Graham noted. The correct comparison, he pointed out, is no trade (with labor producing 40 units of wheat or 30 watches) versus trade (with labor producing 35 units of wheat or 20

---

[4] L. L. Price's (1898, 63) review of Nicholson's book merely noted that the author "shows the importance of the possible effects of the two laws (of returns) on the terms of exchange . . . his judgment on the theoretical foundation of protection is expressed with far more caution and discrimination than older advocates of free trade would have exhibited."

watches). With trade, the country gets 10 fewer units of wheat and 5 more watches than without trade, but this is a net loss because 10 units of wheat are worth more than 5 watches. Thus, Graham concluded, "At any given moment . . . it will pay [for the country] to specialize in wheat, but the final result of the specialization is to bring about a situation in which the citizens of [the country] get less reward for their efforts than if they had never carried on international trade at all" (207).

Graham recognized that if the costs he had assumed were marginal costs, then the harmful effects of specialization were not inevitable. In this case, the higher cost of producing wheat applies to the final unit of output, not to the previous (infra-marginal) units to the same degree.[5] (In other words, the average product of labor is higher than the marginal product of labor, so simply multiplying the total amount of labor by its marginal product would understate total output.) But if the costs were average costs, then the probability of loss would depend upon the extent to which output expands and the rapidity with which costs rise as a result of trade. In the specific example considered by Graham, "the conclusion that [the] country under the conditions assumed must lose by free trade is inevitable." This result provides the basis for "advantageous permanent protection": because the country is better off in autarky or with less trade, it is "economically benefited by protection and may do well to keep it indefinitely" (208).

Although the country with comparative advantage in the decreasing returns sector would suffer losses, Graham also showed that free trade would increase overall world output. For the other country (or countries) specializing in the increasing returns industry, the amount of labor needed to produce both wheat and watches would fall with the opening of trade and they would reap an unambiguous gain. In producing watches, Graham repeated Nicholson's use of average cost analysis. Once again, the cost decline could not be at the margin because that would imply no profits on the initial, higher cost units. Instead, the lower unit cost must pertain to the entire output; as Graham put it, "An extension of output will be reflected here in a lower unit cost for the whole product and not for the new increment merely, and all producers must have approximately equal costs or be put out of business by their competitors" (208–9).

Graham concluded that "it may well be disadvantageous for a nation to concentrate in production of commodities of increasing cost despite a comparative advantage in those lines; it will the more probably be disadvantageous to do so if the world demand for goods produced at decreasing cost is growing in volume more rapidly than that for goods produced at increasing cost" (210). He dismissed the idea that the terms of trade would im-

---

[5] Of course, income distribution, in the form of higher rent to owners of land, would change in this case.

prove for the country specializing in the decreasing returns industry; that is, the price of wheat would rise relative to the price of watches because of the scarcity of resources used in the production of wheat and increasing returns in the watch industry. "There is no reason for supposing that this would happen," he maintained without explanation.

Implicit in these early analyses by Nicholson and Graham were two distinct problems with free trade under increasing returns. First, increasing returns implied multiple equilibria. Because the marginal product of labor was increasing with the amount of labor in the manufacturing sector, one could imagine one equilibrium in which no labor was devoted to manufacturing (and output in that sector would be zero) and another equilibrium in which all labor was devoted to manufacturing. Any allocation of labor in between these two positions could not result in a stable equilibrium because an additional unit of labor would contribute more in output than the previous unit of labor. A ranking of the desirability of these alternative equilibria remained outside of standard comparative-static exercise of showing the effect of protection on national income.

Second, although average cost analysis allowed a given intermediate allocation of labor to be a stable equilibrium, an economic inefficiency was also introduced. At any such equilibrium, average cost pricing implied that wages would be set equal to the average product of labor, not its marginal product as under perfect competition. In this case, too little labor would be employed in manufacturing (where the marginal product of labor exceeds the average product of labor) and output would be distorted from its optimum level, introducing a potential corrective role for protection.

But Graham's stunning contentions were swiftly challenged by Frank Knight, later a leading economist at the University of Chicago. Knight's (1924) counterattack to Graham's "fallacious" but "ingenious argument" rested on the compatibility of increasing returns and competitive analysis. Knight took issue with the following assumption that Graham (1923, 204n) had made in a footnote: "The reasoning in the text simply assumes that a decreasing unit cost is obtained by an expansion of the production of watches; whether the cause of it be external or internal economies is immaterial to the theory, tho it would, of course, affect the degree of its applicability."

The distinction between internal and external economies, casually dismissed by Graham, in fact proved critical to this debate. Internal and external economies, both forms of increasing returns, were introduced into economic analysis by Alfred Marshall in the late nineteenth century. Increasing returns are internal to the firm when the production costs of a particular firm decline as its own output expands. Increasing returns are external to the firm when the production costs of a particular firm decline as industry output expands, while its costs of production increase when its

own output expands. As Marshall (1920, 220–21) put it, internal economies (also known as economies of scale) are "dependent on the resources
of individual houses of business engaged in [the industry], on their organization and the efficiency of their management." External economies, by
contrast, are "dependent on the general development of the industry," some
of which "depend on the aggregate volume of production of the kind in
the neighborhood while others again, especially those connected with the
growth of knowledge and the progress of the arts, depend chiefly on the
aggregate volume of production in the whole civilized world."

Knight's first point was that increasing returns internal to the firm are not
strictly compatible with competition in the industry.[6] If a firm's decline in
costs was a continuous function of its own output, then one firm could
serve the entire market at the lowest cost and the industry would become a
monopoly. As he (1924, 597) put it, "If competition is effective, the size of
the productive unit will tend to grow until *either* no further economies are
obtainable, *or* there is only one establishment left and the industry is a
monopoly. . . . When all establishments have been brought to the most
efficient size, variation in total output is a matter of changing their *number*,
in which no technical economies are involved." Thus, Knight concluded,
an "increase in the output of a commodity must increase its cost of production unless the industry is, or becomes, a monopoly."

"The rejoinder to the above argument," Knight continued, "is the doctrine of 'external economies.'" But this "surely rests upon a misconcep-
tion," he added. "External economies in one business unit are internal
economies in some other, within the industry," Knight argued, a point to be
discussed shortly. "Any branch or stage in the creation of a product which
offers continuously a chance for technical economies with increase in the
scale of operations," Knight insisted, "must eventuate either in monopoly
or in leaving the tendency behind and establishing the normal relation of
increasing cost with increasing size."

Knight also pointed out what proved to be a minor error in Graham's
two-country example. He correctly noted that, in the example given above,
at least one of the countries would be completely specialized in one of the
commodities, bringing to a halt any change in the marginal productivities
of labor. If one country was still producing both goods, then the specialized
country would trade at an exchange ratio equal to the cost ratio of the diversified country. In his reply, Graham (1925) conceded his mistake about the
exchange and cost ratio and specialization and went on to demonstrate that
it did not materially affect his results. But on Knight's main contention,
Graham missed the point and essentially restated that the distinction between internal and external increasing returns was unimportant.

[6] This was recognized by Augustin Cournot in 1838 and by Alfred Marshall and others
later, but was apparently overlooked by Graham.

In his own reply, Knight (1925, 331–33) reiterated what Graham had ignored: "What Professor Graham has to do to establish his theoretical position is to show that . . . industry really operates under decreasing cost, *without tending toward monopoly*." Knight agreed that "if one can make his assumptions in regard to decreasing cost, [Graham's] conclusion is correct." However, "to vindicate decreasing costs in the sense required, it must be shown that there are, or may be, industries, in a condition of stable competition, in which no producer already engaged could decrease his real costs by expanding his output at the expense of other producers, and yet in which real costs would be decreased all around by new producers entering the industry in competition with those already there." But new entrants had to bid factors of production away from other uses and perhaps had to employ factors of lower quality: "These inevitable sources of increasing cost must be more than offset by some kind of purely 'external' economies in organization," Knight argued. "In spite of the weight of authority which may be cited for such economies, I have never succeeded in picturing them in my mind, or finding any convincing reason to believe they exist; and the hypothetical examples cited by Professor Graham in his reply has not assisted me in doing so." Even if he could, "I cannot believe such conditions general enough to justify a special law in economic theory, or a special provision in tariff legislation."

Despite these and other criticisms, Graham never recanted his case for protection. In a short book on tariffs published a decade later, Graham (1934, 81) continued to maintain (in a chapter entitled "Rational Protection") that if a country did not specialize in an increasing returns industry it "might steadily be losing opportunities to improve its *per capita* general productivity and might even suffer an absolute decline therein." For this reason, "protection for comparatively incompetent industries of declining cost per unit of output might then be warranted." But by disputing the compatibility of (internal) increasing returns and market competition, Knight had undercut a big part of Graham's case. As John Chipman (1965, 741) later wrote, "As long as Knight's objection stood, Graham's entire argument—whatever other defects it had, and there were several—was vitiated by having this as its premise."

Taking their cue from Knight, other leading economists were equally skeptical of Graham's argument. Like Knight, Gottfried Haberler (1936, 198–208) granted that "Graham's conclusion follows, provided that one accepts his assumptions," but he viewed those assumptions as "highly precarious." Jacob Viner accused Graham of making the same mistake Nicholson had, that is, confounding marginal and average analysis. Viner (1937, 480) argued, "Had Graham dealt with his problem in terms of marginal costs and marginal returns for both industries, he could not have obtained results unfavorable to free trade." This is because, Viner pointed out, and Graham had partially acknowledged, "specialization in accordance with *marginal cost to the industry of the country* must be to the advantage of the country, in so far as costs are made the criterion of advantage" (474).

Jan Tinbergen (1945, 182–99) picked up this issue and noted another error in Graham's analysis. Graham purported to show that the effect of trade is to obtain a smaller number of watches for the same effort as originally produced a larger number of watches via domestic production. But Tinbergen pointed out that the larger number of watches was calculated on the basis of the average (not the marginal) product of labor, whereas wheat production was computed on the basis of the marginal product of labor (which is lower than the average product). Graham had thus employed a bogus measure of foregone output and, as Tinbergen illustrated geometrically, if the correct marginal calculation had been made there was no loss from trade.

But Knight's strictures had far less force if one accepted the concept of external economies. What precisely were these economies? As already noted, Alfred Marshall described external economies simply as cost reductions of an individual firm that are "dependent on the general development of the industry," that is, on the scale of industry output. The relevant industry output could vary anywhere from local to national to world output; to repeat Marshall's words, "some depend on the aggregate volume of production of the kind in the neighborhood while others again, especially those connected with the growth of knowledge and the progress of the arts, depend chiefly on the aggregate volume of production in the whole civilized world."[7] F. Y. Edgeworth (1905) first succeeded in rendering the concept of external economies compatible with competitive equilibrium, something that could not be done with internal economies. Under external economies, according to Edgeworth's formulation, the marginal cost of an individual firm was increasing in its own output, but its cost curve would shift down with an increase in industry output. Because each firm was small relative to the industry, industry output was taken as given and the contribution of the firm's own output to industry output was imperceptible. In this way, each firm alone would operate under increasing costs, but the industry supply curve might be downward sloped.[8]

[7] For a discussion of Marshall's ideas on increasing returns, see Renee Prendergast (1992).

[8] An extensive debate during the 1920s and 1930s about the nature of these cost curves and the relevance of external economies (and diseconomies) takes us too far from the field of trade policy to merit review here. See the excellent discussion in John Chipman (1965, 736–49). In the end, a consensus was apparently reached that accepted external economies as compatible with competitive equilibrium. The social optimality of that competitive equilibrium, however, was disputed. Believing that the market-determined output in such industries would be too low, Alfred Marshall and A. C. Pigou argued that government subsidies were necessary to raise industry output to the social optimum. Pigou later recanted this recommendation in the case of internal economies after the attacks by Knight and Dennis Robertson, but did not disavow subsidies in the case of external economies.

As Knight's skeptical remarks indicated, the entire concept of external economies was never uncritically accepted, let alone its policy implications, partly because of Marshall's (and his followers') vague formulation of the idea. Dennis Robertson (1924, 24) expressed the confusion this way: an external economy really "only means that, given time and the progress of organisation, a larger output can be produced at a lower cost per unit than a smaller output used to be." But, he added, "we used not to dare conceive of falling cost per unit as a determinant of increased output, but only as resulting from it, or at the rashest as 'being associated with it.'" Robertson also noted that by mixing a discussion of static external economies with that of the dynamic elements of industry evolution and technological progress, Marshall's treatment was an invitation for further confusion. He questioned whether a subsidy or tariff was necessary to promote the development of external economies, inquiring, "is not the body (whether a private monopolist or State) which seeks to improve substantially on competitive output in such cases [of 'decreasing cost'] seeking to voyage *pennis non homini datis*, and not merely to penetrate the secrets of Time, but to do that leisurely old gentleman's work for him?"

The policy implications, of course, hinged specifically on what one had in mind as generating the external economies. As early as the 1870s, Marshall described three types of external economies: knowledge spillovers between firms, subsidiary supplier industries, and local pools of skilled labor. Knowledge spillovers, in which firms are thought not to appropriate fully the benefits of their investments in knowledge-generating activities, result in an unpaid side effect of one firm's activity on others and possibly the underprovision of that activity relative to the social optimum.[9] Pigou interpreted this as an externality in which the marginal social benefit of knowledge production exceeds the marginal private benefit of this activity, calling for, in principle, a government subsidy to close this divergence (and thereby increase national income). However, knowledge spillovers are not necessarily related to static external economies because they need not be linked to the scale of current output.

The last two examples, by contrast, are more consistent with what are viewed today as external economies: namely, market-size effects, wherein

---

[9] Marshall (1920, 225) described knowledge spillovers this way: "Inventions and improvements in machinery, in processes and the general organization of the business have their merits promptly discussed: if one man starts a new idea, it is taken up by others and combined with suggestions of their own; and thus it becomes a source of further new ideas." He also implied that distance was becoming less important a factor in localizing knowledge. "For External economies are constantly growing in importance relative to Internal economies in all matters of Trade-knowledge: newspapers, and trade and technical publications of all kinds are perpetually scouting for him and bringing him much of the knowledge he wants—knowledge which a little while ago would have been beyond the reach of anyone who could not afford to have well-paid agents in many distance places" (237).

the larger the size of the market, the greater the productivity of the firms in the industry. For example, a large industry is better able to support more specialized suppliers of producer services, which in turn reduce the industry's costs and increase industry output. Marshall and his followers construed these to be external economies in the following sense: if a firm decides to enter an industry or increase its output, that firm does not take into account the fact that this entry and additional output will lower the cost of production for all other firms in the industry.

Yet Marshall's (1920, 264) description of this phenomena was characteristically vague: "The most important of these [external economies] result from the growth of correlated branches of industry which mutually assist one another, perhaps being concentrated in the same localities, but anyhow availing themselves of the modern facilities for communication offered by steam transport, by the telegraph and by the printing-press." Unfortunately, Marshall's followers were no more successful in coming up with compelling instances of such economies. Thus, it was never entirely clear whether such "obvious" instances of such economies ("transport developments, the telephone and the trade journal, the shop of the club and the market price, subsidiary industries, a skilled labour supply,—we have all at some time tried to memorise and to reproduce the formidable list," Robertson [1924, 26] remarked) were just descriptions of market interdependencies and evolution rather than true examples of market failures requiring some form of government action.

In some cases, such as transport developments, Knight's statement that external economies in one industry were internal economies to another rang true. In other cases, the external economy could be internalized through market mechanisms such as vertical integration or other pricing arrangements. But the whole concept of external economies still remained elusive. As E.A.G. Robinson (1931, 138) seemed to lament: "And so we chase this will-o'-the-wisp of external economy through industry after industry, and we find it vanishing in the end or absorbed in the economies of firms or organisations below their optimum capacity." And Robertson's quip, that policy action to exploit external economies would have the state merely trying to accelerate what time and progress of organization would naturally bring about, hardly made the case more compelling.

The elusive nature of external economies ensured that suspicions about the concept were never completely dispelled. Even more slippery were the implications for government policy, let alone free trade. Depending on one's interpretation, external economies could be so rare as to be essentially a *curiosa*, or could reflect a pervasive interdependence that is rife through every sector of the economy. This greatly confused the issue in terms of its ramifications for free trade. A particular external economy might indeed call for a government subsidy to encourage the underprovided activity, and international trade might reinforce an undesirable direction of specialization. But the implications for commercial policy were still not obvious. Haberler (1936, 207), for instance, complained that external economies were so "vague and indeterminate in nature" and so "difficult to estimate [as to] their extent or value" that "it is not really practicable to base a policy of Protection" on their possible existence. The standard examples of external economies given in the 1920s and 1930s were described years later by Chipman (1965, 746) as being "so far-fetched that it is difficult to understand how an entire theory of commercial policy can be based upon them."

Yet even if one accepted uncritically the possible existence of external economies, Graham's case did not go unchallenged. Another critic pointed to the importance of reversibility of costs. Graham's position was that protection had to be permanent because, if protection were to be removed, the increasing returns sector (being one of comparative disadvantage) would contract and costs would begin to rise again. Unlike the dynamic infant industry argument, in which the cost reductions are irreversible once the infant has grown up and protection has been removed, Graham's case is static and therefore a permanent policy action is required to hold the economy in a particular equilibrium. Karl Anderson (1936, 167) believed that Graham's argument was weakened if "the sources of decreasing costs when once discovered and utilized are not to be lost again." Stating flatly that "nonreversibility is clearly the case with genuine external economies" because their presumed source, once in place, was not likely to be dislodged, Anderson concluded that "the basis for the kind of protection defended by Graham is all but completely destroyed." Yet this conclusion is simply an assertion; durability remains a debatable issue. Even if it were true, he neglected to mention that Graham's case then essentially reverts to the dynamic infant industry case.

But it was Viner (1937, 475–82) who delivered the key qualifications to the use of trade policies to take advantage of external economies. First, the implications for trade policy depended critically upon whether the external economies were a function of world output or domestic output. If the economies depended upon the size of the world market, then domestic firms would not be especially handicapped if some domestic firms reduced their output. For example, if the size of the world watch industry was affected by some special attributes of the world watch machinery industry, and such machinery were freely traded, there was no particular problem for domestic firms.[10] If part of the domestic watch machinery industry contracts, all watch firms in the world are affected symmetrically by

---

[10] In Viner's (1937, 480) words, "If there is free trade in machinery, this economy in machinery costs will not be lost to the watch industry in a particular country merely because it is shrinking in size, if there is no shrinkage in the size of the watch industry as a whole."

the lost economies, not just domestic ones specifically. This weakens the potential case for promoting domestic firms and directs attention to the tradeability of intermediate goods, a key point in modern treatments of external economies.

Second, Viner (1937, 480) took the position that, if the external economies were pecuniary, "then they are not real national economies and nothing is lost to the country when they disappear." To clarify this comment, Viner's (1931) distinction between "technological" and "pecuniary" external economies needs to be understood. Technological external economies described the interdependence of firms in a particular market in which the production function of individual firms was affected directly by the output of the industry as a whole; pecuniary external economies were those in which the profits of a firm were directly affected by the activities of other (upstream or downstream) producers. Tibor Scitovsky (1954, 145) later clarified these concepts and drew the implication that "technological external economies are the only external economies that can arise because of direct interdependence among producers and within the framework of general equilibrium theory." However, Scitovsky spoke of the "scarcity of technological external economies" because "it is not easy to find examples from industry" of them. It is difficult to consider changes in the organization of production as technical externalities, for example.[11]

Viner (1937, 480–81) concluded in this way:

> A conceivable case for protection on the basis of the existence of external economies in an industry which from the individual producer's point of view is at a comparative disadvantage in costs can be made out, therefore, only where these external economies are (*a*) dependent on the size of the national and not the world industry and (*b*) are technological rather than pecuniary, or, if pecuniary, are not at the expense of domestic sellers or services or materials to the industry. The scope for the application of the argument is extremely limited, especially as it seems difficult even to suggest plausible hypothetical cases of the existence of genuine technological external economies.

This reduced Graham's example to, in his words, "little more than a theoretical curiosity."

The decades after Alfred Marshall's first exposition on external economies revealed that economists did not really understand how to think clearly about such effects, let alone draw out the implications for trade policy. At the same time it did not seem worthwhile to abandon the concept entirely because it appeared keenly relevant to the seemingly arbitrary na-

---

[11] According to Scitovsky (1954, 136), "pecuniary external economies clearly have no place in equilibrium theory" because such "all-pervading" interdependence through the market mechanism cannot be held to lead both to an optimal allocation of resources and to a failure to lead to that optimum.

ture of comparative advantage in certain instances. An oft used example from R.C.O. Matthews (1949–50) asks, why is it that Germany specializes in cameras and Switzerland in watches? What is the role played by initial advantages in the past that cumulate to the present? Do scale economies or external economies account for this concentration and localization? If so, could not the location of the two industries be reversed and does this not illustrate the potential (as discussed earlier) for multiple equilibria?

Although the debate over external economies and comparative advantage was never satisfactorily resolved in the immediate aftermath of Graham's article, the study of the trade-related aspects of external economies nearly evaporated until the early 1980s. By this time, analysis suggested that Graham's case, taken on his own assumptions about external economies, was largely correct. Arvind Panagariya (1981) described a small open economy with a decreasing returns and an increasing returns industry (via constant-returns-to-scale firms with economies external to the firm but internal to the industry, thereby consistent with perfect competition and average cost pricing). Under these assumptions, a permanent subsidy to expand output in the increasing returns industry (or conversely a tax to discourage output in the decreasing returns industry) is required to maximize national income. A country completely specialized in the decreasing returns industry may suffer a welfare loss after the opening to trade, although that depended upon whether the terms of trade moved in a favorable enough direction. As in the infant industry case, the optimal policy is an appropriately chosen subsidy and not a tariff which engenders the additional distortion to consumption choices. Related work by Wilfred Ethier (1982b) pointed out the implicit importance of country size in Graham's argument; the country specializing in the decreasing returns sector was less likely to lose by trade the smaller the country is and (paradoxically) the greater the degree of increasing returns.

But this work, and others like it, just assumed the existence of external economies. In the absence of more concrete evidence about such economies, or whether they arose inherently from a certain, plausible market structure, the practical importance of external economies for free trade remained open to question. Ethier (1982a) later provided a possible theoretical foundation for external economies in which each firm operates under constant returns to scale but the industry overall exhibits increasing returns. The example drew upon Marshall's suggestion that a larger industry can support a greater variety of specialized inputs to production at lower cost. Ethier showed the following: if there are economies of scale within each firm that produces a differentiated intermediate good (that is, monopolistic competition), then the aggregate production function of the industry that assembles these components exhibits the features of external economies.

The key issue again revolves around Viner's point about whether the intermediates are tradeable or not. If the intermediate goods are tradeable, then the external economy depends on international production of the final good, not domestic production, and there is no strong case for government action. If the intermediates are nontradeable, then the external economy is strictly national in scope and depends on the extent of domestic production. In the latter case, the size of the domestic market can determine comparative advantage; a larger market will support larger industries and hence have lower costs than those in smaller markets. Under this Ethier specification, as James Markusen (1990) has pointed out, external scale economies lead to several potential distortions, including multiple equilibria (with a high and a low level of output of the industry with external economies), average cost pricing, and inefficient factor combinations. A one-time production subsidy could be used to establish the right equilibria, and then a permanent factor subsidy could be used to correct for the inefficient factor combination. But the desirability of Graham's permanent protection is not so obvious.

.   .   .

Increasing returns in the form of external economies of scale still prove to be somewhat vexing: their effects seem potentially important and difficult to dismiss, yet our ignorance about them is still vast after a century of debate. With small differences in initial market size, trade could potentially reinforce a certain pattern of international specialization. But until the underlying factors giving rise to external economies are better understood, the case for a trade remedy of import protection as the obvious, first-best policy response has not been made. Our understanding of the determinants and effects of external economies is so weak, both conceptually and practically, that it has yet to be established whether they offer a reasonably clear case in which protection could enhance economic wealth. A greater division of labor may come about as a result of extending the market, but extending the market by artificial means does not necessarily generate a greater division of labor that results in scale advantages.

Chapter Ten

MANOÏLESCU AND THE
WAGE DIFFERENTIAL ARGUMENT

THE RELATIONSHIP between trade and wages has been a perennial source of debate. Mercantilists saw wage differences between countries as a key factor in international competition. They believed that poor, low-wage countries could "undersell" rich, high-wage countries and usurp their trade, thereby bringing into question the wisdom of free trade for developed countries. The classical economists effectively laid this concern to rest in the 1830s by working out the wage implications of the theory of comparative costs, but not before David Hume, Josiah Tucker, and others had pondered the issue at length. A more substantive debate, in terms of its implications for free trade, concerned whether wage differentials within a country could generate a valid argument for protection. Mihaïl Manoïlescu, a one-time government minister in Romania, argued that developing countries were justified on economic grounds in using protection to shift labor from low-productivity (low-wage) agriculture to high-productivity (high-wage) industry. This contention was resolved by clarifying the case for free trade under conditions of possible market failures and, in the process, helped divorce it from its long-standing association with the *laissez-faire* doctrine.

· · ·

The argument that high-wage countries should fear imports from low-wage competitors dates back at least to the mercantilist period. Throughout the seventeenth and eighteenth centuries, the export price of domestic manufactures was assumed to be determined largely by the wage costs of production. This led to many complaints in England about the adverse effect of high domestic wages on exports. High wage rates made exporting more difficult because other countries with lower wages could afford to "undersell" them in trade. Thomas Manly (1669, 20) doubted that high wages necessarily made for a rich and thriving commonwealth and lamented that the "vent for our manufactures [is] daily lessened through the excessive wages of our artificers." The anonymous author of *The Grand Concern of England Explained* (1673, 54) pronounced that the "handicraft tradesmen's high wages, which they exact for their work, is greatly mischievous, not only to every man that hath occasion to use them . . . but it is destructive to trade, and hinders the consumption of our manufactures by foreigners,

and the exportation of those vast quantities that used to be transported."
Many mercantilists advocated measures that would diminish domestic
wages, such as reducing the costs of subsistence goods or adding to the
labor stock via immigration, to improve the competitive position of exporting manufacturers.

These views were repeated well into the eighteenth century. "The first
and great disadvantage [of high wages] is that of being undersold by the
French and Dutch in our principal manufactured goods," complained one
writer. "This is a terrible wound to our commerce, and without a remedy is
speedily applied to the same, it must in the end prove fatal . . . the price of
labour is so extravagant in this kingdom . . . if too long neglected, may be
our ruin. . . . The high price of labour is a fatal stab to the trade and manufactures of this country; and without the greatest care taken, it will in time
be attended with very dreadful consequences."[1] John Powell (1772, 281)
protested that the "balance of trade is against us in almost every country in
Europe, because those countries who rival us in manufacture and commerce by living cheaper and paying smaller wages, undersell us in most
foreign markets."

As the eighteenth century wore on, an increasing number of dissents to
this position was registered.[2] These observers viewed high wages as reflecting the wealth and prosperity of the nation rather than as something
hindering its development. The apparent contradiction between high wages
and a low price for manufactures was resolved in terms of the productivity
of labor (a resolution proposed, of course, by Henry Martyn in 1701). If
labor was highly productive, employers could afford to pay high wages
even though the price per unit of output was low.

The principals of the Scottish enlightenment considered the implications
of this broad question in what came to be known as the Hume-Tucker "rich
country-poor country" debate.[3] Controversy over the role of luxury and
excess, corruption and virtue in the decline of nations raged at the time, a
theme pursued and popularized by Edward Gibbon's *Decline and Fall of
the Roman Empire*, for example. The question of whether rich England was
destined to endure a similar fate was widely discussed at the time. Hume
touched on the issue of high wages in his essay "Of Commerce," where he
(1752, 17–19) noted that "'tis true, the English feel some disadvantages in
foreign trade by the high price of labour, which is in part the effect of the
riches of their artisans, as well as of the plenty of money." But Hume was
optimistic: once a country has reached a certain extension of its commerce,

---

[1] *Propositions for Improving the Manufactures, Agriculture, and Commerce of Great
Britain* (1763, 11–12, 21).

[2] See A. W. Coats (1958).

[3] For a more detailed discussion of this debate, see J. M. Low (1952), Bernard Semmel
(1965), and especially Istvan Hont (1983).

"a nation may lose most of its foreign trade, and yet continue to be a great and powerful people." For example, "If strangers will not take any particular commodity of ours, we must cease to labour in it." That labor will turn "towards some refinement in other commodities, which may be wanted at home," thereby ensuring that commerce and wealth would flourish. "As foreign trade is not the most material circumstance," Hume argued, "it is not to be put in competition with the happiness of so many millions."

A passage in his essay "Of Money," however, triggered a great controversy. In attacking the mercantilist preoccupation with acquiring specie, Hume contended that money is simply a veil over real economic activity. After mentioning that having plenty of money was not necessarily an advantage to a country in foreign trade, Hume (1752, 43) then remarked:

> There seems to be a happy concurrence of causes in human affairs, which checks the growth of trade and riches, and hinders them from being confined entirely to one people; as might naturally at first be dreaded from the advantages of an established commerce. Where one nation has gotten the start of another in trade, it is very difficult for the latter to regain the ground it has lost; because of the superior industry and skill of the former, and the greater stocks, of which its merchants are possessed, and which enable them to trade on so much small profits. But these advantages are compensated, in some measure, by the low price of labour in every nation which has not an extensive commerce, and does not much abound in gold and silver. Manufactures, therefore gradually shift their places, leaving those countries and provinces which they have already enriched, and flying to others, whither they are allured by the cheapness of provisions and labour; till they have enriched these also, and are again banished by the same causes. And, in general, we may observe, that the dearness of every thing, from plenty of money, is a disadvantage, which attends an established commerce, and sets bounds to it in every country, by enabling the poorer states to undersell the richer in all foreign markets.

Hume clearly states that advanced countries have many advantages which are counterbalanced, "in some measure," by low wage rates elsewhere. But, in writing of manufactures "flying to others" because wages were lower elsewhere, he drew critical comment from his friend, James Oswald, and later from Josiah Tucker, among others. Unfortunately, much of the debate was semantic and rested on either a misunderstanding or an exaggeration of Hume's position. In a letter to Hume in October 1749, Oswald commented on the essay prior to its publication and took issue with whether poor countries could exploit their low-wage advantages to undersell the rich.[4] "The advantages of a rich country in this respect, compared with the disadvantages of a poor one, are almost infinite," Oswald stated.

---

[4] These letters are reproduced in Hume (1955, 190ff).

"Poor countries with cheap necessaries, some cheap materials, and even cheap labour in some things, do not always, nay, seldom do, and but in a few cases, work up manufactures so cheaply as in the provinces of a rich country, and, what is even more surprising, as even in its capital." Raw materials were frequently more expensive in poorer countries, Oswald argued, and the lack of strong domestic demand for such manufactures was an additional hindrance.

Hume replied nearly a year later in November 1750. "Your enumeration of the advantages of rich countries above poor, in point of trade, is very just and curious," he (1955, 198) wrote, "but I cannot agree with you that, barring ill policy or accidents, the former might proceed gaining upon the latter for ever" because such growth naturally "checks itself." "The rich countries would acquire and retain all the manufactures, that require great stock or great skill; but the poor country would gain from it all the simpler and more laborious." Stating this simple point earlier—that there would be a division of labor between the rich and poor countries in the production of manufactures, without using the evocative phrase "flying to others"— would have perhaps avoided the subsequent controversy with Tucker and others since he later had to repeat this clarification.

But Hume's passage made implications that several others found objectionable and came in for more criticism when finally published. Josiah Tucker (1774, 9) disputed the "universally received" notion that "trade and manufactures, if left at *full liberty*, will always descend from a richer to a poorer state" and Hume's insinuation that "every poor country is the natural and unavoidable enemy of the rich one." Tucker posed the question: "Which of these two nations can afford to raise provisions, and sell their manufacturers on the cheapest terms?" His answer was, without any question, the richer country. The richer country "hath acquired its superior wealth by a general application, and long habits of industry, it is therefore in actual possession of an established trade and credit . . . a great variety of the best tools and implements in the various kinds of manufactures, and engines for abridging labour;—add to these, good roads, canals, and other artificial communications; . . . Whereas the poor country has, for the most part, all these things to seek after and procure" (21–22). Thus, the rich country's "superior skill and knowledge" more than compensated for any advantages the poor country had.

Hume (1955, 200–201) replied to Tucker in a letter to a mutual friend, Lord Kames (Henry Home), in March 1758:

> All of the advantages which the author insists upon as belonging to a nation of extensive commerce, are undoubtedly real: great capital, extensive correspondence, skilful expedients of facilitating labour, dexterity, industry, &c., these circumstances give them an undisputed superiority over poor nations, who are ignorant and unexperienced. The question is, whether these advantages can go

on, increasing trade *in infinitum*, or whether they do not at last come to a *ne plus ultra*, and check themselves, by begetting disadvantages, which at first retard, and at last finally stop their progress. Among these disadvantages, we may reckon the dear price of provisions and labour, which enables the poorer country to rival them, first in the coarser manufactures, and then in those which are more elaborate.

Were it otherwise, Hume continued, "one spot of the globe would engross the art and industry of the whole." Turning Tucker's argument on its head, he stated that "it was never surely the intention of Providence, that any one nation should be a monopolizer of wealth." That a rich country could not perpetually accumulate industries followed "not from accidental events, but necessary principles." Hume (1955, 200–201) then took up the case of Scotland:

> I am pleased when I find the author insist on the advantages of England. . . , but I still indulge myself in the hopes that we in Scotland possess also some advantages, which may enable us to share with them in wealth and industry. It is certain that the simpler kind of industry ought first to be attempted in a country like ours. The finest arts will flourish best in the capital: those of next value in the more opulent provinces: the coarser in the remote countries . . . tho a rich country, by its other advantages, may long maintain its ground against a poorer, which makes attempts towards commerce, it will not be able entirely to annihilate or oppress it.

As in his letter to Oswald, Hume makes it clear that rich and poor countries would specialize in different types of manufactures, not that the poor country would undermine all of the rich country's industries. But these points were never made public.

In a July 1758 reply to Kames, Tucker bristled at the term *in infinitum* and asserted simply "that the progress would be indefinite."[5] On the potential monopoly of the rich country, that "fact must be acknowledged," he stated, although later he (1774, 39) admitted that it was "contradicted by fact and experience." Continuing, Tucker argued:

> True it is, that *caeteris paribus*, the rich industrious country would always undersell the poor one; and by that means attract the trade of all poorer countries to itself;—but it is equally true, that if either of these poor countries hath any *peculiar* produce of its own, it may prohibit its exportation till it be wrought up into a complete manufacture. It is true likewise, that all of them have it in their power to load the manufactures of the rich country upon entering their territories, with such high duties as shall turn the scale in favour of their own manufactures. [Quoted in Hume (1955, 203)]

---

[5] Quoted in Hume (1955, 202ff).

Thus, protectionist tariffs in developing countries were a way in which "the rich may be prevented from swallowing up the poor" as well as a means of stimulating the poor to emulate the rich.

Tucker disputed what he took as Hume's proposition that "the poor country, by having wages and raw materials cheaper, would certainly undersell the rich one in the coarse and more imperfect manufactures, so likewise it would from thence gradually ascend to others, till at last it equaled, and perhaps exceeded the rich country in every thing." As the poor country started producing more and more sophisticated goods, he argued, the prices of labor and materials would correspondingly rise and thereby eliminate this advantage. "In short," Tucker concluded, "though both countries may still go on in their respective improvements, the poor country, according to my apprehension, can never overtake the rich, unless it be through the fault and mismanagement of the latter."[6]

To the extent that Hume acknowledged these points, it is in the later essay "Of the Jealousy of Trade," published around 1758. Hume argued against viewing the economic success of other countries with an invidious eye because, as he put it, an increase in the riches and commerce of any one country commonly promotes that of others. Noting that Great Britain had adopted innumerable technical improvements from other countries over the past two centuries, Hume (1955, 78) maintained that "where an open communication is preserved among nations, it is impossible but the domestic industry of every one must receive an increase from the improvements of others." No state need "entertain apprehensions, that their neighbours will improve to such a degree in every art and manufacture, as to have no demand from them. Nature, by giving a diversity of geniuses, climates, and soils, to different nations, has secured their mutual intercourse and commerce, as long as they all remain industrious and civilized" (79). Furthermore, if a country "has some peculiar and natural advantages" for producing a certain commodity, "and if, notwithstanding these advantages, they lose such a manufacture [to foreign competition], they ought to blame their own idleness, or bad government, not the industry of their neighbors."

Adam Smith's only direct comment on this debate came in his lectures on jurisprudence and in parts of an early draft of the *Wealth of Nations* that did not survive into publication. In the draft, Smith (1978, 567) makes the point (made by Henry Martyn earlier) that the advance of productivity occasioned by the division of labor could reduce the price of output and increase the price of labor. "It is in this manner that in an opulent and commercial society labour becomes dear and work cheap, and those two events,

---

[6] This position was also taken by others, such as Robert Wallace (1758, 40ff): "Trade is, indeed, limited because the earth and everything in it is limited. Our nation can never extend its trade *in infinitum*, or over all the earth. But a richer nation, by a proper management, may always maintain its superiority in trade over the poorer."

which vulgar prejudices and superficial reflection are apt to consider as altogether incompatible, are found by experience to be perfectly consistent." Indeed, Smith argues, the high price of labor is not just proof of the general opulence of society, "it is to be regarded as what constitutes the essence of public opulence."

How does this relate to the Hume-Tucker controversy? "The more opulent therefore the society, labour will always be so much the dearer and work so much the cheaper, and if some opulent countries have lost several of their manufactures and some branches of their commerce by having been undersold in foreign markets by the traders and artisans of poorer countries, who were contented with less profit and smaller wages, this will rarely be found to have been merely the effect of the opulence of the one country and the poverty of the other." "Some other cause," Smith insisted, "must have concurred" and "the rich country must have been guilty of some great error" of policy, such as suppressing that commerce or manufacture with taxes or increasing the price of subsistence goods and thereby inflating wages artificially. Smith agreed with Tucker: "Where no error of this kind has been committed, as among individuals a rich merchant can always undersell and a rich manufacturer underwork a poor one, so among great societies a rich nation must always in every competition of commerce and manufactures have an equal or superior advantage over a poor one."[7]

Even into the early nineteenth century writers sought to reassure their readers that Hume had underestimated the advantages of a rich country.[8] But such broadly ranging debates in political economy was giving way to the narrow but more precise logic of the classical economists. These economists resolved any concerns about trade and wages through the theory of comparative advantage. Wages were strictly tied to the productivity of labor, and even if that productivity differed between countries (that is, wages were uniformly lower in one country owing to the lower level of productivity) they could still engage in mutually advantageous trade. In the context of the Ricardian theory of comparative advantage, Nassau Senior (1830, 26–28) demonstrated how wage rates were determined by the productivity of labor in the export sector and attacked "the absurdity of the opinion that the generally high rate of wages in England unfits us for

[7] A very similar passage can be found in reports of Smith's Lectures on Jurisprudence from 1762–63. See Smith (1978, 343–44).

[8] James Maitland (1804, 299) argued that Hume "did not sufficiently attend to the unlimited resources that are to be found in the ingenuity of man in inventing means of supplanting labour by capital; for any possible augmentation of wages that increased opulence can occasion, is but a trifling drawback on the great advantages a country derives, not only from the ingenuity of man in supplanting labour by machinery, but from capital laid out in roads, canals, bridges, inclosures, shipping; and employed in the conduct of home and foreign trade, all of which is alike engaged in supplanting the necessity of paying the wages of labour."

competition with foreign producers." "Our power of competing with foreigners depends on the efficiency of our labour, and it has appeared that a
high rate of wages is a necessary consequence of that efficiency." In his
words, "to complain of our high wages is to complain that our labour is
productive—to complain that our workpeople are diligent and skilful."[9]

This effectively ended the "rich country-poor country" debate and sealed
the fate of attempts to build a case for protection in high-wage developed
countries.[10] But the relationship between trade and wages soon attracted
attention again in a somewhat different context. The classical economists
generally believed that rich countries need not fear a flight of its manufactures to poor, low-wage countries, but at the same time held out the pros-
pect that poor countries could gradually develop and acquire advantage in
the production of certain types of manufactures.[11] But would not comparative advantage in (say) raw produce and agriculture dictate and then perpet-
uate their existing specialization in low-wage, low-productivity sectors and
thereby prevent them from ever becoming rich by specializing in high-
wage, high-productivity sectors?

Thus, rather than wage differences between countries, wage differences
between sectors within a country became the issue; specifically, the use of
protection to shift labor into the high-wage manufacturing sector. The argument that countries specializing in agricultural products and importing
manufactures were depriving themselves of greater output in high-wage,
high-productivity sectors was not only as compelling as the more narrow
concept of infant industries, but it even proved (initially) to be a stronger
broadside into the free trade argument.[12] Early on it was recognized that a
troubling disconnect between wages, prices, and real labor costs could
exist. The theory of comparative advantage was originally set out in terms
of real labor costs, wherein a country could specialize in the goods in which
it had comparative labor cost advantages and, with trade, could acquire

[9] Montiford Longfield (1835, 55–56) developed similar ideas in stating: "The proportion
which the general rate of wages in one country bears to the general rate of wages in another
country, depends upon the proportion which the general productiveness of labour in the former bears to the general productiveness of labour in the other, and the course of trade is quite
independent of this proportion. . . . Neither high wages nor low productiveness of labour, can
render commerce disadvantageous to a country, or can place its industry in need of protection."

[10] This is only to say that, in general, high wages in developed countries do not constitute
an economic rationale for protection, not that popular debates over the issue will ever end. For
example, the argument that protection is required to maintain high wages continued to be
extremely popular in the nineteenth-century United States.

[11] For a discussion of classical views on economic development, see Hla Myint (1958).

[12] Friedrich List neglected the issue of wage differentials between sectors within a country,
despite its similarities to the infant industry argument. Rather, classical and neoclassical economists recognized that intersectoral wage differences might create problems for comparative
advantage.

more of all goods than without trade. But specialization was proximately ruled by relative prices, and though relative prices might be proportional to wages, those wages might not be proportional to real labor costs. Consequently, relative prices might not bear the proper relationship to real labor costs as to ensure that specialization would be along the lines of comparative advantage and that there would be gains from trade.

Montiford Longfield (1835, 57), for example, noted that in "two circumstances all commerce may be said to originate—namely, a difference in the proportion of the productiveness of labor of different kinds, in different countries; and the different scales by which the relative wages of labor vary in different countries." The first was a classic source of comparative advantage, the second was not. Longfield argued that the structure of wages could differ across countries owing to different institutional practices. But in analyzing trade, Longfield only examined a case in which a country's relative wages were proportional to real labor costs. Later in the century, John E. Cairnes (1874, 322–24, 375–406) emphasized that "non-competing groups" of labor could be responsible for different wage rates within a country. In this case, Cairnes simply noted that prices would not necessarily be proportional to real labor costs. But he too did not pursue this issue further and either ignored or missed its implications for specialization and free trade. In discussing trade, Cairnes (like Longfield) assumed that wage costs and real labor costs were proportionate.

Soon thereafter, J. S. Nicholson (1897, 315–17) made an ambitious attempt to show how a segmented labor market could make a country worse off as a result of opening to trade. Nicholson considered a country in which, in the absence of trade, the wage rate of labor in manufactures was twice that of labor in agriculture, but whose labor was divided equally into the two sectors. If the world price of manufactures was half the original domestic price, then labor will be driven from the high-wage manufacturing sector into the low-wage agricultural sector as a result of opening to trade. With diminishing returns to labor in agriculture, the country could acquire in money terms less than half of the manufactures it could before, even though their price was now lower. Nicholson deserves credit for pursuing what Longfield and Cairnes had neglected and he has the kernel of a correct argument. But Nicholson's short and confusing example failed to bring out fully the problem presented for comparative advantage and free trade. By expressing his example in terms of the nominal prices of goods and wages of labor, a tempting strategy that can often lead to erroneous conclusions, he did not clearly demonstrate that the actual quantity of goods commanded by the country would fall as a result of trade, or that protection could improve matters.[13]

---

[13] Charles Bastable (1900, 181–84) chided Nicholson for departing "from the established mode of exposition," namely, using nominal prices rather than focusing on the exchange of

Frank Taussig (1906) examined a multitude of cases in which differences in domestic wage rates due to noncompeting groups could alter relative prices such that specialization would not take place in the industries which had comparative labor cost advantages. If specialization did not take place along these lines, Taussig recognized that trade may fail to bring about an economic gain. Thus, a potential problem was acknowledged but, like his predecessors, he did not pursue it to a logical conclusion. Taussig denied that there was a major problem for free trade by asserting (in a very weak defense) that wage differences between industries were the same across industrialized economies and would not therefore affect the gains from specialization according to comparative advantage. As he (1927, 47–48) put it, "The existence of non-competing groups within a country affects its international trade only so far as the situation thus engendered is peculiar to that country."

The problem was finally exposed in a way that triggered a serious debate in a book first published in 1929 by Mihaïl Manoïlescu, a former Romanian Minister of Industry and Trade. Manoïlescu based his analysis on an empirical regularity that he purported to document: the value productivity (value added) of labor and capital is substantially greater in manufacturing than in agriculture. He then argued that, although classical comparative cost theory needed a simple modification to take account of this fact, this modification destroyed the free-trade implications of that theory. In particular, the classical gains from trade may not hold if a country specialized in agriculture. As he (1931, 106) stated, "For international trade to outweigh home production, for it to be advantageous for an agricultural country not to produce an industrial article but to buy it abroad, paying for it with agricultural produce, it is necessary that the comparative superiority of agriculture in the agricultural country should be greater than the intrinsic (qualitative) superiority of industry over agriculture."

Manoïlescu's complicated and confused exposition, both written and algebraic, did not serve to convey his major insight very well. By comparative superiority he meant comparative costs of production in terms of quantities of labor. By intrinsic (qualitative) superiority he can be taken to mean the relative exchange ratio of the two goods that embodied the value productivity of labor. In other words, there was a divergence between the real labor costs of two goods and the ratio of their exchange. The implication is that a country may not wish to specialize in producing an agricultural good when "industry has an intrinsic (qualitative) superiority over agriculture in any country of the world." In such a case, "we have proved . . . that the solution of direct production nearly always outweighs the commercial solution" (110).

---

physical quantities of goods across countries. This made the analysis "more troublesome" and "tend[ed] to distract attention from the essential points."

To express the idea more intuitively, Manoïlescu used the following example:

> In Roumania a truck of foreign coal can be obtained for 6,000 lei, although Roumanian coal of the same quality costs 7,500 lei per truck. On the other hand, the productivity of coal production is 75,000 lei per producer per annum, while the average productivity of the country is about 30,000 lei per year. In these circumstances it is more advantageous for Roumania to produce coal than to import it. Indeed, in order to produce 100 trucks in the country, worth 750,000 lei, the productivity being 75,000 lei per producer per annum, ten producers are required per year. At the same time, in order to pay for 100 trucks of imported coal, worth 60,000 lei, national goods of an average production of 30,000 lei per producer per annum have to be exported—so twenty producers are required per year. . . . In importing them, it is with the labour of twenty producers during a year that we get 100 trucks of coal, while in producing them directly in the country, with the same labour, we get 200 trucks of coal. (116)

In other words, although a comparison of the domestic and foreign price of coal indicated that Romania should import that product, the divergence in the value of labor's productivity in the two sectors indicated otherwise.

The clearest exposition of Manoïlescu's main idea was made perceptively in a few sentences by Gottfried Haberler (1936, 196–98), who accepted it with due qualification. Suppose one unit of labor is required to produce a unit of an agricultural and a manufactured good, but that the domestic price of the manufactured good is twice that of the agricultural good (so two agricultural goods buy one manufactured good, and vice versa). In this situation, the (market) exchange ratio of the two goods differs from the (production) substitution ratio of the two goods. The exchange value of manufactures is greater than its real labor content suggests, with the difference arising presumably because labor is more productive in manufacturing and therefore earns a higher wage.

Suppose the country then opens to trade and that the international exchange ratio is such that three agricultural goods buy two manufactured goods. In this case, comparing the domestic and international exchange ratios of the two goods, the country has comparative advantage in, and thus would specialize in and export, the agricultural good. If the domestic exchange and substitution ratios were originally identical, trade would bring about a clear gain. But the divergence in the domestic exchange ratio (which is compared with the international exchange ratio to determine the industry of specialization) from the domestic substitution ratio alters this conclusion. Specializing in agriculture along the substitution ratio, only two units of the agricultural good are produced at the expense of two units of manufactures. Through trade, however, those two manufactures could have been exported to acquire three units of the agricultural good. A tariff to prevent such specialization, Haberler concluded, would "undoubtedly benefit" the country.

Although his exposition left much to be desired, Manoïlescu's methodological approach, though expressed in an extreme way at times, was unreproachably economic. He harshly criticized all previous attempts of continental (mainly German) economists to show the advantages of protection because they did not rest on a satisfactory scientific criteria: that protection could actually increase economic wealth. "Not having a scientific theory, protection exists and develops itself empirically and arbitrarily *without a guiding principle*," he (1931, xxiii) declared. "Its force is not reason, but instinct." Despite their similar interest in industrialization, Manoïlescu took List severely to task for not putting protection on a proper theoretical basis.[14] Such a proper basis would "permit the application of protection, *according to certain scientific criteria*, fixing objective rules without arbitrary and selfish suggestions." It would also "give us precise indications as to the branches of production which we ought *and ought not* to protect" and "would enable us to establish the degree of protection which should be granted to every article in commerce."

Since differences in value productivity across industries were measurable in principle, Manoïlescu believed that such a scientific specificity could emerge from his approach, something no other theory of protection (with the possible exception of the terms of trade argument) could promise. He was proud of his accomplishment: no previous attempt, he argued, directly challenged the comparative advantage foundation of free trade. Manoïlescu did precisely this because he succeeded in showing that trade could reduce real national income for a distorted domestic economy. This was an intellectual achievement not to be belittled, although it hinged on a posited configuration of prices and costs which needed further scrutiny. Under this scrutiny, the apparent damage suffered by the free trade doctrine diminished almost entirely.

Manoïlescu's argument quickly drew the attention of the most eminent international economists of the day. A prescient review by the Swedish economist Bertil Ohlin in 1931, by cutting through Manoïlescu's complexities and focusing on the key elements of his analysis, anticipated much of the later discussion of this case. Ohlin's main criticism was the assumption that protection brings a benefit in shifting labor from low-productivity to high-productivity industries. But Ohlin (1931, 36–37) asked an obvious question:

[14] As Manoïlescu (1931, xxii) put it, "[H]is system adopts the *provisional* (educational) protection only *for industries* and *for certain countries* which are passing through a certain phase of their economic and social evolution. List's system, far from strengthening the *general principle* of protection, weakens it. He presents protection as the exception, and *grants the character of general validity* to the free trade system."

Why then does not a transfer take place without protection? If a worker obtains a much higher wage in the Roumanian coal industry than in most other Roumanian industries, why do not those employed in the latter offer themselves to the coal industry at somewhat lower wage rates than the present ones? If they did, the Roumanian coal industry would be remunerative without import duties. . . . Why does such a transfer take place only when the state puts on import duties or gives other aid and not otherwise?"

Because efficiency considerations dictate that the marginal product of labor should be equal across sectors, Ohlin agreed that true wage differentials were "undesirable, if one wants a high national income in terms of goods." Such differentials reduced national income because "the high-wage industry, where the marginal productivity of labour is relatively great, is kept back, while the low-wage industry develops more than it would have done under conditions of uniform wage rates." But Ohlin seriously doubted the existence of significant real differences in wages and productivity across industries. Productivity as measured by output per worker was inadequate because it ignored the contribution of capital, and nominal wage differences between agriculture and manufacturing were more apparent than real because of differences in the quality and the educational attainment of labor and in the cost of living between urban and rural areas. To the extent that there were real wage differentials, he attributed these to trade unions, which artificially divided workers into "non-competing groups."

Ohlin then posed the another key question: "Can protection reduce the losses which follow from the existence of noncompeting groups, i.e., bring about a use of the factors of production which resembles what it would have been in the absence of such groups?" "The answer," he continued, "is under certain conditions in the affirmative." Ohlin's reasoning is worth fully reproducing:

If a certain country has artificial non-competing groups, duties might aim at bringing about the same combination of industries as would have existed if labour had been freely mobile. An industry which produces for the home market, and gets its competitive power reduced through the forcing up of wages by trade unions, will see this power reduced by means of an import duty. . . . It goes without saying that the situation will not be exactly what it would have been under other labour conditions. A cash bonus corresponding to the extra labour costs would bring the situation more close to a 'normal' one, than a system of duties can do. The import duty will raise the commodity prices, reduce the sales and the number of workers employed, compared with the 'normal' situation. Thus, the wage level in other parts of the labour market will tend to be depressed, and some industries will develop more than they would otherwise have done. Yet, the fact remains that a combination of non-competing groups and duties make the line of industries more like the 'normal' one than if wage discrepancies exist but not duties. It does not follow that the existence of artificial non-competing groups is a sufficient argument for protection. The more natural remedy is, of course, to increase the labour mobility and do away with the watertight labour compartment. (44)

Jacob Viner's (1932, 122–25) harsher review agreed that the author "follows the Ricardian assumptions faithfully enough with the one exception on which he rests his case, . . . that the value product per unit of labor and the wages of labor are assumed to vary substantially from industry to industry under equilibrium condition." Manoïlescu, however, "makes his analysis highly unsatisfactory by keeping prices and wages constant in the face of substantial changes in trade relations." According to Viner, "weight can be given to specific prices and wage rates, in determining whether a given allocation of resources is desirable or not from the national point of view, only after examination of the reason why these prices and wage rates are what they are." If the wage differential reflects "equalizing differences," such as the greater disutility of work or higher cost of living or worker skill levels, then the wage difference is illusory and specialization in agriculture is beneficial even if wages appear to be lower there. If there are noncompeting groups, with labor in manufacturing being somehow different than labor in agriculture, then "there would be no shift of labor in either country from the high-productivity to the low-productivity occupation, the basis of the author's attack on free trade, since by hypothesis such a shift is impossible."

Yet suppose there was labor mobility and a real wage differential, "through trade union influence or custom." Then "protection to the cloth [manufacturing] industry, instead of resulting in a diversion of labor from a more productive to a less productive occupation, will operate to reduce the extent of such diversion." This, Viner stated, was the "very tiny" grain of truth "embedded—but not displayed—in the author's exhaustive argument." But, he added, "it is a very tiny grain, indeed." If free trade were permitted, labor in manufacturing "would face the alternatives of either abandoning their monopoly wage or abandoning the hope of obtaining employment." "As soon as they accepted a wage rate at which they could obtain full employment under free trade," the price of the clothing manufacturers would fall sufficiently to undersell that of others, and "labor would be employed in the industry in which it had a comparative advantage," to the overall national benefit, "even if to the possible loss of those cloth-makers who under protection could have found employment at their monopoly wage rate." Viner, perhaps too dismissingly, concluded that "the task of finding an intellectually satisfactory economic defense of protection still awaits achievement, and has not been carried forward by this attempt."

Like Ohlin, Gottfried Haberler (1936, 196–98) conceded that a tariff could potentially benefit a country under the strict circumstances laid out by Manoïlescu. But he concurred with both Ohlin and Viner that, as a practical matter, those circumstances could exist "only if the monopolistic groups of workers are strong enough to maintain their wage rates after they are faced with foreign competition—only, that is, if they prefer a reduction, and quite possibly a heavy reduction, in the amount of employment available in these high-paid occupations, to a reduction in wages." In this case, free trade proves beneficial: "International trade will merely be a means of breaking the monopoly power of such groups and thus of ending their exploitation of the rest of the community."

Manoïlescu was subjected to other less prominent and less insightful reviews. In reply to his critics, Manoïlescu (1935) was unrepentant. He rejected their skepticism about whether labor productivity differences between sectors represented a real failure of the market and argued again that protection would prove beneficial. But nothing he said diminished Ohlin's incisive critique of pointing out the difficulties of simply positing (without explaining the source of) a wage distortion and the superiority of a labor employment subsidy over an import tariff as a means of rectifying the situation.

The theme around which Manoïlescu had centered his analysis, sectoral wage differentials in developing countries reflecting productivity differences, became a major part of the literature on international trade and economic development in the 1940s and 1950s. Most development economists had a pervasive sense that factor and product markets failed to allocate resources properly in developing countries. Real or imagined misalignments between prices and costs, private and social benefits, bred a deep mistrust of the market mechanism. With such mistrust came the strong belief that the whole case for free trade was brought into serious doubt, that it was a relic of a bygone era of *laissez-faire*, incapable of addressing the manifold market failures in economies. Pointing to the various theoretical assumptions made by international economists, Thomas Balogh (1949), among others, argued that free trade conclusions were unwarranted because the assumptions made by theory did not hold in the real world.

In response to these criticisms, Haberler (1950) addressed the implications for free trade of departing from standard assumptions, using once again the powerfully illuminating tool of comparing the exchange ratio of goods (relative prices) with the transformation ratio of goods (production trade-offs). Haberler's main conclusion was that it was not automatically the case that relaxing the assumptions of standard trade theory undermined the case for free trade. If there was complete factor immobility between sectors, for example, then—given this state of affairs—free trade was still better than any alternative policy. If there was complete immobility of factors and complete rigidity of factor prices, however, free trade could generate unemployment and protection could possibly, but not necessarily, prove beneficial.

Haberler's keenly insightful contribution was further clarified in a seminal book by James Meade (1955). Meade's analysis centered around the optimal conditions of domestic production and trade as summarized by a series of marginal conditions between value (price) and cost. In chapter 14, he (1955, 226) inquired about the impact of an "initial and fixed divergence between marginal values and costs within the domestic economy" of a trading country. The purpose was to discover "whether in these circumstances the damage to economic welfare caused by the domestic divergence between marginal values and costs might not be in part offset by a departure from free trade."

Without direct reference to the Manoïlescu argument, Meade considered an externality relating to the employment of labor in a particular industry, such that the social value of employment exceeds the private cost. (This is nearly equivalent to a Manoïlescu-type situation in which the marginal product of labor is higher, and hence too little labor is employed, in an industry compared to elsewhere in the economy.) Meade noted that "the thing which it is desirable to encourage in this case is not an expansion of the output [to close the divergence between value and cost in the industry and thereby increase economic efficiency] . . . but an expansion of the employment of labour" (232). Like Ohlin, he proposed an employment subsidy to the industry as the most appropriate method of accomplishing this goal. By reducing the cost of hiring labor, the subsidy would expand labor employment both through the substitution of labor for other factors of production and through the increased domestic production resulting from lower costs of production.

Alternatively, import protection "will increase the employment of labour in the industry only by expanding the demand for and so the output of" the industry and, "as compared with a subsidy of the employment of labor . . . will therefore be a most uneconomic method of adjustment if there is considerable substitutability between labour and the other factors of production in the industry" (234). Thus, protection is neither the most obvious nor the most direct remedy for this particular market failure.[15] An additional problem with protection, Meade noted earlier in the chapter but not directly in this context, is that by raising the price to consumers the policy introduced a new distortion unrelated to the original divergence.

Meade's crisp economic logic carried the analysis of the problem, and the role of trade protection as a remedy for domestic market failures, an

[15] As Meade put it, "The argument for some element of protection is strong only when the divergence between marginal value and cost in the competing domestic industry is associated with the total output of that industry rather than with a particular way of producing it."

important step beyond Ohlin. Shortly thereafter, Jagdish Bhagwati and V. K. Ramaswami (1963), responding in part to the reconsideration of Manoïlescu's argument for protection by Everett Hagen (1958), further clarified the underlying policy implications. They first distinguished between wage divergences and wage distortions, the former a compensation for an economic phenomena (such as cost of living difference or skill difference) and the latter a genuine labor market failure. They assumed in their analysis that "the wage differential represents a genuine distortion while remaining skeptical about the degree to which such distortions obtain in the actual world." In terms of maximizing national income, Bhagwati and Ramaswami established the following policy hierarchy: the first-best policy is an appropriately chosen (optimal) employment subsidy to manufacturing, which is capable of yielding a higher real income than an optimal production subsidy, which in turn was capable of yielding a higher real income than an optimal import tariff on manufactures.

The logic behind this ranking hinges on the fact that the factor market distortion produces a less desirable mix of goods (thereby adversely affecting allocative efficiency) and reduces the technical efficiency (in terms of factor proportions) with which this mix of goods is produced (thereby restricting the set of production possibilities). An employment subsidy corrects the factor market distortion directly to bring about the optimal use of labor between the sectors, thereby rectifying both the problems of allocative and technical efficiency. A production subsidy, however, though changing the relative prices of the goods and thereby improving allocative efficiency, would leave the suboptimal factor useage (the technical inefficiency) undisturbed. Import protection would do likewise, but is even less adequate because it further distorts the consumption choices made in the economy.

Meade's insights and the Bhagwati-Ramaswami analysis led to the theory of domestic divergences (or distortions, as it became known), a landmark in the history of free trade ideas. The theory proposed a hierarchy of policies, ranked in terms of the efficiency with which they corrected a given divergence between relative prices and relative costs.[16] For a given market failure, the first-best policy intervention can improve economic efficiency (and hence increase real national income) by correcting the divergence directly at its source. If the divergence is wholly domestic in nature, afflicting domestic product and factor markets regardless of whether the

---

[16] The classic references are Harry Johnson (1965) and Jagdish Bhagwati (1971), the latter making the important distinction between exogenous distortions and policy-dependent distortions (those arising because of government restrictions on market competition). The earlier paper by W. M. Corden (1957) provided an improved, concise version of Meade's approach to evaluating a production subsidy and an import tariff as a form of protecting a domestic industry.

economy is engaged in any international trade, trade interventions (such as import tariffs or export subsidies) will not be the ideal remedy. Other policies, including trade interventions, may be second- and third-best in that they can also mitigate the divergence to some degree and raise real income, but only indirectly and inefficiently at the cost of introducing other "by-product" distortions that offset some of the efficiency attainable under the first-best policy.

The theory of domestic divergences constitutes such an important landmark because it established general, powerful principles that limited the damage suffered by free trade from any number of imaginable market failures. For example, the case for free trade is often based on the argument that competitive markets enable a society to allocate its scarce resources efficiently in taking advantage of the opportunity to engage in international trade. Opponents of free trade often concluded that, if the market could be shown as failing to produce an efficient allocation of resources, the case for free trade would necessarily be compromised. (Alternatively, critics would state that because the theory behind free trade was based on theoretical assumptions that obviously did not hold in the real world, any partiality toward free trade must be abandoned in favor of protection.) The theory of domestic divergences demonstrated that such conclusions were not correct.

The Manoïlescu argument is a case in point and provides a clear example of their application. Standard theory held that economic efficiency is achieved through the mobility of labor between sectors to equalize its marginal product, and hence its wage. Manoïlescu argued that this assumption was absurd, that markets (for whatever reason) are not efficient in this regard, and that therefore the case for free trade was not viable under the circumstances. But the theory of domestic divergences indicates that domestic market failures, if they are shown to exist, are best handled by policies that address them at their specific source. Trade interventions such as protection are quite unlikely to be first-best.[17] Accepting for the sake of argument Manoïlescu's contention that labor is inefficiently allocated with underemployment in manufacturing, the first-best policy response is to subsidize employment in manufacturing; the second-best policy, a production subsidy, indirectly expands employment by expanding output; the third-best policy, an import tariff, indirectly expands employment by expanding output but creates a by-product distortion relating to domestic consumption.[18] As one goes down the hierarchy, there is a decline in the effi-

---

[17] The most robust first-best case for a trade intervention is for a country that has the ability to affect its terms of trade through import or export taxes, the terms of trade argument for protection considered in chapter 7. The trade intervention helps ensure the attainment of the first-best conditions for economic efficiency by establishing an equality between domestic rate of transformation between goods in production and the foreign rate of transformation.

[18] The numerous variations on the factor market divergences case are considered in

ciency with which the optimal policy intervention corrects the underlying divergence, and thus a decline in the attainable level of national income.

The broader consequence of the theory of domestic divergences was sweeping: once and for all the case for free trade was delinked from the case for *laissez-faire*. Because the rise of the free trade doctrine in the early nineteenth century was so closely intertwined with sentiment in favor of *laissez-faire*, it was often thought that the concepts rose and fell together. This no longer was the case, and one could accept the existence of market failures and accept a governmental role in rectifying them, but still rule out deviations from free trade.

Of course, free trade did not emerge completely unscathed because trade interventions could remain a second- or third-best policy option over no corrective response whatsoever. But the theory of domestic divergences served to insulate the case for free trade from the claim that market failures no longer made that policy desirable. Other policy actions dominate import protection, and if protection is proposed to remedy a presumed market failure, the burden is not only to establish that a market failure indeed exists, but to justify the particular constraints (political or otherwise) that make it necessary to go down the policy hierarchy toward less efficient and more costly policy instruments. In terms of achieving economic efficiency, domestic market failures can undermine the case for *laissez-faire*, but the case for free trade is compromised to a much lesser extent.

· · ·

The ever controversial relationship between trade and wages has created ongoing issues for economic theory to address. In terms of wage differences between countries, high-wage countries have often feared competition from low-wage countries, though classical analysis suggests that wage differences are due to differences in labor productivity across countries and do not make free trade any less appealing. Wage differences between sectors within a country, to the extent they reflect a true divergence, is just one example of any number of possible market failures that is best dealt with through domestic policies rather than trade protection. Free trade remains desirable because other government policies dominate protection as a means of correcting domestic market failures.

Stephen Magee (1973). Perhaps the most interesting case is that considered by John Harris and Michael Todaro (1970), which suggests that if manufacturing (or the "urban" sector) is subject to a high minimum wage (such that the marginal product of labor in manufacturing exceeds that in agriculture), then policies to promote manufacturing may exacerbate unemployment more than they correct for the underlying factor market divergence.

Chapter Eleven

THE AUSTRALIAN CASE FOR PROTECTION

NINETEENTH-CENTURY economic thought in the United States, Germany, and elsewhere was, on the whole, strongly protectionist in orientation. According to the prevailing view there, free trade may have been an appropriate policy for Britain but it was inappropriate to the economic circumstances of the newly industrializing countries. One reason for the alleged unsuitability of free trade was that factor endowments and the pattern of trade in these countries were unlike those in Britain. Ricardo and the classical school favored free trade as a means of relieving diminishing returns in agriculture by substituting imported goods for domestic production, while shifting factors of production to manufacturing where output could be more easily expanded. But what about other countries that also faced diminishing returns in agriculture, but which instead *exported* those goods? Would free trade under these conditions prove to be just as advantageous as in Britain's case? Several economists have thought not, and in the 1920s these ideas crystallized in a debate over what came to be known as the "Australian" case for protection. The debate mainly addressed rather technical and subtle points of theory and came far short of a direct assault on free trade. But it proved useful in clarifying legitimate from illegitimate claims for free trade and focused attention on the impact of trade on income distribution.

· · ·

The "Australian" case for protection takes its name from the policy-oriented debate in that country in the 1920s over the effects of its import tariff. Two closely related but conceptually distinct ideas about tariffs and trade, both associated with the economist James Bristock Brigden, constitute the heart of the Australian argument.[1] The first, set forth in the famous semi-official Brigden Report of 1929, actually had much older origins going back to Robert Torrens. Long before he developed the terms of trade argument for protection, Torrens (1821, 276ff) was a staunch free trader who imagined "one case in which a free foreign trade might impoverish and depopulate a country." Consider various countries which are diversified in production but where no additional factors could be profitably employed in

---

[1] Gary Manger (1981) and Paul Samuelson (1981) revisit and clarify various issues in this debate.

the primary sector.[2] Should one country suddenly achieve a technological advantage in producing manufactures, Torrens hypothesized, "the free importation of such articles into the other countries would dislodge a great portion of their capital without presenting any possible opening for reinvestment, and would cause their manufacturing population to emigrate or perish." In this case, "the labour and capital dislodged from domestic manufactures shall be unable to extract from the soil an additional supply of food and material equal to that which is sent out in exchange for foreign fabric." Free trade in such circumstances "would be the greatest calamity which could befall the country," although Torrens believed that centuries would elapse before such diminishing returns would become a real concern for most countries around the world.

Over half a century later, Henry Sidgwick independently considered an analogous situation that entailed diminishing, but not zero, marginal returns in the primary sector. Sidgwick (1883, 494–95) described the following "extreme hypothetical" if not "implausible" example:

Suppose a country (A) so thickly populated that additional agricultural produce could not be obtained from the soil except at a rapidly increasing expense. . . . Suppose that the country having been strictly protected adopts Free Trade, and that consequently the manufactures in question are obtained at half the price from another country (B) in exchange for corn. . . . What then are the manufacturing labourers thrown out of work by the change to do? The course most obviously suggested by circumstances is that they should emigrate and supply the labour required in the extended manufactures of B. . . . If they do not do this, there seems no general ground for assuming that they will all be able to find employment in A, as remunerative as that withdrawn from them. No doubt as the cost of production in agriculture may be assumed to increase continuously, a certain amount of additional labour may now be employed in agriculture which will be more productive on the whole than some of the labour employed before the trade opened—the diminution in the amount of corn produced by each new labourer being more than balanced by the increased power of the corn to purchase manufacture. But if the additional labour is only applicable at a rapidly increasing cost, the point will very soon come at which this balance will be reversed: and it is theoretically quite possible that a portion of the labourers thrown out of manufacturing employment could not . . . be so employed at all; so that the natural result of Free Trade may be that A will only support a smaller, though wealthier, population—the economic gain resulting from it to the community as a whole being a gain which it would

_____

[2] Or more realistically, Torrens (1821, 277) suggested, the marginal product of capital in the primary sector is driven down to 2 percent, "the lowest rate of profit for the sake of which the capitalist will engage in production."

require violent government interference to distribute so as to retain the labourers thrown out of work.

Sidgwick (1901, 498) later concluded that "the natural result of free trade may be that [country] A will only support a smaller population and that its aggregate wealth may be diminished by the change," although per capita wealth would be greater.

Though startlingly contrary in appearance to classical doctrine, Sidgwick's analysis went remarkably uncontested: J. S. Nicholson (1897, 315ff) accepted it without much comment and F. Y. Edgeworth (1894, 622) called it "especially masterly." Charles Bastable (1887, 104ff) alone questioned the conclusions Sidgwick drew from his example. Bastable accepted that free trade could have sharp income distributional consequences even though the community as a whole benefited from free trade. With agricultural goods exported under conditions of diminishing returns, labor and capital could suffer (and landowners prosper) under free trade and prompt "severe" conflicts of interest over trade policy, although this loss would be mitigated by increasing returns to scale in foreign manufacturing that enabled agricultural exporting countries to reap ever improving terms of trade over time.[3]

But he also argued that simple comparative cost reasoning implied that "the effect of free trade in reducing population cannot be established on theoretical grounds." A country's import rather than export sector was generally much more subject to diminishing returns, Bastable (1890, 123) asserted, and increasing costs of agricultural exports would eventually eliminate or reverse comparative cost differences between nations and either cause trade to cease or prompt the country to export manufactures. This last contention triggered a response from Edgeworth, who exposed Bastable's erroneous reasoning by noting that the increasing costs in the primary sector are incurred precisely because the relative price of those goods had increased.[4]

---

[3] Bastable suggested that the circumstances envisioned by Sidgwick may be applicable to Ireland, but not to other land-abundant countries where property was widely distributed and freely traded.

[4] See F. Y. Edgeworth's (1897, 1900) reviews of several editions of Bastable's book, and Bastable's (1901) confused reply. Bastable was unwittingly put in the awkward position of asserting that a given decline in the price of manufactures would cause an exporter of primary commodities to reverse its trade pattern and become an exporter of manufactures. Bastable (1903, 187–97) continued to maintain that Sidgwick was in error and criticized his artificial introduction of international factor mobility, saying that wages could fall without entailing emigration or starvation. The support for Bastable lent by Achille Loria (1901) was flawed in employing a Ricardian constant cost example with no diminishing returns, as Edgeworth (1901) pointed out.

Several other economic writers latched onto ideas about diminishing returns in a country's export sector to support calls for protection, but they contributed few insights into the economic theory underlying the Torrens-Sidgwick example. Many of them drew weakly on the analogy that free trade was detrimental in new countries for expanding primary sector production, just as protection was detrimental in England for the same reason. In the United States, for example, Simon Patten (1890), in the tradition of the Henry Carey's Philadelphia School of Protection, argued that free trade fostered natural monopolies that enriched landowners at the expense of labor. Stating that even if diminishing returns reduced the gains from trade a country was still better off than under protection, Frank Taussig (1893, 174) responsed crisply: "If the distribution of wealth so ensuing needs to be corrected, the method should not be one that involves a diminution of the productive powers of the community as a whole."

These general ideas were resurrected in a report prepared for the Australian government in 1929 on the economic effects of the tariff. Written by a distinguished group of Australian economists headed by J. B. Brigden, the report drew heavily on and added little to Sidgwick's ideas (without mentioning him), arguing that Australia was situated in circumstances as envisioned by Sidgwick: an exporter of agricultural and primary commodities operating under diminishing marginal returns. In steering resources toward the primary sector, free trade would raise the return to a few landowners, but not generate many employment opportunities and thereby shrink the wages of laborers. The Brigden (1929, 1) report concluded that "the evidence available does not support the contention that Australia could have maintained its present population at a higher standard of living under free trade." The report took "as fundamental to the whole inquiry the necessity of maintaining at least our present [European] population at the present standard of living," and found that a protective tariff was "an effective means" of achieving this end (70). Indeed, the report noted that "we are satisfied that the same average income *for the same population* could not have been obtained without protection" (5).

The report succeeded in generating more controversy among economists than previous debates over Sidgwick's example. But the report failed to marshall an effective indictment of free trade on theoretical grounds because it did not claim that protection would increase aggregate national income: "It is quite certain that without the tariff it would have been possible to have obtained a larger national income per head—but for a considerably smaller population." The primary purpose of the tariff was to redistribute income; with the tariff, "employment has been subsidized at the expense of land values, enabling the standard of living to be maintained with a rapidly increasing population" (70).

These two points formed the basis of Jacob Viner's (1929) incisive review of the report. Viner noted that the Australians defined "standard of living" as the wage income of labor alone, not including the capital and land income that accrues to others in the economy. Viner conceded that a tariff might increase wages, but said that he could not muster enthusiasm for a policy that reduced landowners' income to transfer a lesser amount to workers, arguing that more efficient means to achieve the same end should have been explored. He dismissed the Australian argument as a noneconomic case for protection because its objective was not to maximize national income but redistribute that income along certain lines. As D. B. Copeland (1931, 291), one of the authors of the report, later wrote: "The committee in no way denies the free trade position that the development of 'natural production' without tariff assistance would have given a greater income per head for a smaller population. On *economic* grounds there is, of course, no special virtue in a large population, but for political reasons it is essential that Australia should absorb population as quickly as her resources will allow."

A second, more clever version of the Australian case for protection had actually been developed by Brigden (1925) alone. He again began with the idea that diminishing returns was a feature of the primary sector in Australia and that devoting more resources to production in that sector would lower output per capita. To this point was added not the loss of population through emigration, but the notion that Australia had market power in primary products—any increase in exports would depress world prices of primary products. Consequently, a natural increase in population or immigration would press against diminishing returns in the export industry and lower output per capita, while the additional output would further aggravate the situation by adversely affecting Australia's terms of trade. These two effects would combine to reduce both wage income relatively and aggregate income overall in Australia and in any similarly situated country. A tariff provided an escape from the dilemma and brought an actual economic gain—the improved terms of trade induced by the tariff would not only increase aggregate income, but redistribute it in what was deemed a desirable way.

Adding the standard terms of trade effect, even if not new in itself, contributed to the novelty of the Australian case and appeared to make it impervious to criticism. But would labor really benefit from protection? Although Bastable admitted labor could be injured from free trade under certain circumstances, many economists resisted such a conclusion. Gottfried Haberler (1936, 194–95) argued that while specific factors such as land could be harmed, factors of production that were mobile between sectors (such as labor, at least beyond the short run) would not lose from free trade. This hypothesis provided great reassurance to those sympathetic to the free trade doctrine, but was not well established.

The inability to determine precisely the response of factor prices to a change in domestic prices brought about by changes in the terms of trade and commercial policy revealed much about the imperfect state of the theory of international trade in the 1920s and 1930s, which was in the midst of a transition from a classical (essentially Ricardian) to a neoclassical (Heckscher-Ohlin-Samuelson) basis.[5] This transition accelerated when at least one critic made false claims on behalf of free trade. In rejecting the Australian case for protection, Karl Anderson (1938) denied that tariffs could increase national income via improved terms of trade (unless foreign demand was inelastic) and claimed that free trade maximized not only total income but also each factor's income. Marion C. Samuelson (1939) quickly demonstrated that both assertions were false: the terms-of-trade motive for tariffs always exists in some degree unless foreign (reciprocal) demand is infinitely elastic, and the equalization of a factor's marginal products between sectors did not imply that the return to each factor was maximized.[6]

But she did not explicitly show how factor rewards varied with goods prices, leaving an opening for a rigorous description of the relationship by Wolfgang Stolper and Paul Samuelson (1941) in the context of what became known as the standard Heckscher-Ohlin-Samuelson model, wherein two perfectly mobile factors of production (capital and labor, for example) are used in different proportions to produce two different goods. This model implies that the country with a relative abundance in a particular factor compared with other countries (such that its capital-labor ratio is higher than in other countries, for example) will tend to export the good that uses intensively that factor of production (the capital-intensive good in this example). Stolper and Samuelson showed that when protection brings about an increase in the domestic price of the imported good, this would unambiguously increase the real return (measured in terms of any good) to the scarce factor of production used intensively in its production, and conversely reduce the real return to the abundant factor of production used intensively in the exported good. The implication was clear: if the import-

---

[5] The classical theory developed by Ricardo and others developed around the real costs of production in terms of one factor of production (labor). Neoclassical theory (associated with the Swedish economists Eli Heckscher and Bertil Ohlin and the American Paul Samuelson) focused more on different factor endowments and opportunity costs between countries as driving international trade.

[6] The foreign demand referred to is, strictly speaking, the foreign reciprocal demand as developed by John Stuart Mill in the context of the tariff and terms of trade debate discussed in chapter 7.

competing sector produced a labor-intensive good, an import tariff could without question raise the real income of labor and reduce the real income of capital. No longer could free trade advocates argue that protection would reduce a factor's absolute income even if it increased its share of total income.[7] Furthermore, if all land (as the factor in relative abundance) were owned by just a handful of individuals, free trade might reduce the real income of the mass of population.

The Stolper-Samuelson theorem starkly illuminated the income distributional consequences of either free trade or protection. Of course, abstracting from terms of trade effects, free trade would still lead to the highest national income because under protection the gain to the scarce factor is exceeded by the loss to the abundant factor. Brigden seemingly avoided this problem with protection by introducing the terms of trade effect. In this case, a tariff could achieve both a desirable change in income redistribution (toward the wage earnings of labor) and a higher level of national income without any trade-off between them.

Yet the irony is that, the closer were the circumstances to those Brigden envisioned, the greater the chance this outcome would fail to arise. The surprising conclusion to the Australian debate emerged over twenty years after Brigden's original article had appeared. The development that qualified Brigden's theory was Lloyd Metzler's (1949) analysis of a tariff's impact on the terms of trade and on the distribution of income. Metzler discovered that if foreign demand (again in terms of the foreign reciprocal demand) was inelastic, a tariff could increase national income as expected, but the real return to the scarce factor would not rise but *fall*. In this case, by a strange twist, Bridgen's dual objectives were incompatible. The intuition for Metzler's result hinged on distinguishing between the internal relative prices of goods and the external terms of trade. For a country that could affect its terms of trade, a tariff would normally have the effect of raising the (relative) price of exports in world markets while raising the (relative) price of imports in the protected market. With inelastic foreign demand, however, the external price effect would dominate the internal price effect and the domestic relative price of imports would also fall. Thus, in the end, a tariff would not provide any protection for the import-competing industry. Brigden had not stated the degree to which foreign demand for Australian goods was inelastic, but the Metzler paradox suggested that the greater

[7] A model in which certain factors of production are specific to a sector (and not mobile) might be more appropriate to the Australian debate than the Heckscher-Ohlin-Samuelson model. If labor is mobile between the primary and manufacturing sectors, and land is specific to the primary sector as capital is to the manufacturing sector, then the effect of protection on wages is ambiguous and depends upon the consumption patterns of labor. Roy Ruffin and Ronald Jones (1977) establish a reasonable presumption that protection will reduce real wages, lending some support to the contentions of Haberler and others.

market power Australia had in primary products, the more improving its terms of trade through a tariff conflicted with the objective of increasing the real wage of labor.

. . .

The Australian case for protection never constituted a direct indictment of free trade, but showed that not all groups in an economy are necessarily positioned to benefit from free trade. Though Ricardo's discussion of the Corn Laws centered around its sharp income distributional consequences, theoretical analysis of such distributional effects was neglected for many decades until the Australian debate. While recognized as an interesting noneconomic argument for protection, the Australian case prompted a more important question: if some individuals or economic classes are worse off under free trade, can economists really argue that free trade is superior to protection on a scientific basis without making an implicit value judgment about income distribution? This question, considered in the next chapter, came to the forefront of academic discussions in the 1930s.

Chapter Twelve

THE WELFARE ECONOMICS OF FREE TRADE

THE Australian debate, which indirectly led to the Stolper-Samuelson theorem, was closely followed by a discussion about this question: if some individuals or groups were made worse off under free trade, how could economists advocate that policy without making an implicit value judgment about the desirability of a particular distribution of income? The deeper issue behind this query was the thorny methodological problem of whether economic theory can be employed to reach conclusions about the welfare effects of economic policy.

. . .

The classical economists, if not Adam Smith, took as given the economic objective of achieving the greatest possible material wealth of a country.[1] However, they never argued that material wealth should be always and everywhere the solitary goal of economic policy. They recognized that economic analysis was silent about what society's preferences should be and could scarcely object if society wished to sacrifice some material wealth to achieve other objectives. (Smith's belief that defense is more important than opulence reflected this position.) But to the extent that material considerations were thought to be important (as they almost always are, at least to some extent), the classical economists strongly believed that economic analysis could greatly inform economic policy and thereby contribute to improved material circumstances.

Smith and the classicals defined the wealth of a nation roughly as its aggregate material wealth in terms of production possibilities, or the overall amount of goods an economy could command through the productivity of its primary factors of production (land, labor, and capital). Smith's term for a country's aggregate wealth was its annual produce or real revenue, otherwise known today as real national income. This definition of material wealth implicitly involves the weighting (at competitive market prices) of all commodities produced in an economy. Smith and the classicals saw international trade as an important means of increasing the effective pro-

---

[1] As John Stuart Mill (1836, 12–13) put it in reference to individuals, political economy "is concerned with [man] solely as a being who desires to possess wealth. . . . It makes entire abstraction of every other human passion or motive; . . . Not that any political economist was ever so absurd as to suppose that mankind are really thus constituted, but because this is the mode in which science must necessarily proceed."

ductivity of a country's resources and thereby advancing the material wealth (or real national income) of a country. Smith hailed the "great and important services" performed by the division of labor and trade, which served to "augment [a country's] annual produce to the utmost, and thereby to increase the real revenue and wealth of the society."[2] The theory of comparative advantage convinced the classical economists that the opportunity to trade was akin to a productivity advance and could potentially increase the quantities of all goods available to the community. As John Stuart Mill ([1848] 1909, 579) stated, a country by trade "obtains a more ample supplement of the commodities it wants, for the same labour and capital."[3]

With few exceptions, Adam Smith and the classical economists thought that a free trade policy was the best way to capitalize on these gains from trade and thereby increase real national income to its utmost. Of course, material wealth via productive efficiency was not an end unto itself. "Consumption is the sole end and purpose of all production," Smith declared.[4] And Mill ([1848] 1909, 45) put it only slightly differently in stating that the ultimate aim of production is to produce utility for those who purchase and consume such goods.

But in terms of evaluating free trade or any other policy, the conceptual leap from considering production to consumption was far from slight. Although largely successful in arguing that free trade would augment material wealth, the classical analysis fell short of the more ambitious task of showing how that additional material wealth necessarily translated into the greater economic well-being of society as a whole. The distinction between economic "wealth" and "welfare" clarifies this issue.[5] Wealth means material wealth in terms of the overall quantities of goods (valued at competitive prices) that are available to society. Welfare is a more nebulous concept that evokes Jeremy Bentham's idea of an individual's utility, meaning happiness or satisfaction. To conceptualize the economic welfare of the nation, the individual utilities of all in society must somehow be combined through some aggregation scheme.

Classical economics focused much more on the forces behind material wealth (productive efficiency) than on the determinants of economic welfare, which depended partly upon the distribution and consumption of that wealth in society.[6] Of course, the classical economists postulated that eco-

---

[2] *WN* (IV.i.31).

[3] John E. Cairnes (1874, 418) wrote that "the true criterion of the gain on foreign trade [is] the degree in which it cheapens commodities, and renders them more abundant."

[4] *WN* (IV.viii.49).

[5] Among modern economists, J. R. Hicks (1940) was among the first to draw the distinction between real income as a measure of productive capacity and real income as a measure of economic welfare and to suggest that they were quite different things. For a detailed discussion of these issues, see A. K. Sen (1979).

[6] As John Stuart Mill (1836, 9) wrote, "We contend that Political Economy . . . has nothing

nomic wealth (quantities of goods either produced directly or indirectly via trade) and economic welfare (consumer satisfaction derived from consuming those goods) were closely linked with no basic conflict between them. An increase in wealth was frequently taken to imply an increase in welfare, as when Ricardo ([1817] 1951, 128) stated that trade "will very powerfully contribute to increase the mass of commodities, and therefore the sum of enjoyments."

But taking wealth and welfare as synonymous created a bit of a methodological problem for two reasons. First, wealth and welfare were always understood to be conceptually distinct, and it was only for the sake of convenience that they were confounded. Second, the classical economists clearly appreciated the distributional effects of free trade: even if a larger real national income meant that more goods were available to the nation as a whole, some individuals or groups probably would be worse off under free trade. (That was the main point of Ricardo's description of agricultural protection—the Corn Laws—as an income transfer from capitalists to landlords via the higher price of corn.) The classical economists often equated wealth and welfare simply to avoid the issue of income distribution. Their position seemed to be that the government should pursue various policies to maximize economic wealth, and then concerns about income distribution could be addressed at the end of the day. If each and every policy action also had to correct for any resulting, undesirable change in income distribution, they feared that economic policy reforms would become too cumbersome to implement.

But simply positing that economic welfare (by some measure) would increase because the availability of all goods was potentially enlarged by trade did not make it so, and Nassau Senior (1836, 2–4) sharply criticized claims that it would. He insisted that "the subject treated by the Political Economist, using that term in the limited sense in which we apply it, is not Happiness, but Wealth." Despite his free trade views, Senior argued that economists could not give policy advice based on their scientific knowledge: "An author who, having stated that a given conduct is productive of Wealth, should, on that account alone, recommend it, or assume that, on that account alone, it ought to be pursued, would be guilty of the absurdity of implying that Happiness and the possession of Wealth are identical." The author's error would not be "in confining his attention to Wealth, but in confounding Wealth with Happiness." Senior argued that the economist's conclusions, "whatever be their generality and their truth,

---

to do with the consumption of wealth, further than as the consideration of it is inseparable from that of production, or from that of distribution. We know not of any *laws* of the *consumption* of wealth as the subject of a distinct science: they can be no other than the laws of human enjoyment."

do not authorize him in adding a single syllable of advice" regarding economic policy since wealth is just one of the constituent items that leads to happiness.[7]

While Senior's strictures were considered too severe by other economists, the question he was raising was unavoidable: can economic science make ethically neutral statements about the impact of government policy on economic welfare? In what sense could a situation in which capitalists gain two dollars for every dollar lost by landlords be said to constitute an improvement in overall economic welfare? To make such a statement requires that money be an adequate metric of utility and that the marginal utility of income be constant and identical for the two groups. For example, if the marginal utility of income of the landlords is greater than that of the capitalist, then society may wish to weigh the (smaller) losses of the landlords greater than the (larger) gains of the capitalist.

To avoid this problem and bridge the gap between wealth and welfare, John Stuart Mill (1825, 399) formulated what became known as the compensation principle in the context of the Corn Law debate:

> If . . . there were nothing in the whole process but a transfer; if whatever is lost by the consumer and by the capitalist were gained by the landlord; there might be robbery, but there would not be waste; there might be a worse distribution of the national wealth, but there would be no positive diminution of its aggregate wealth. The evil of the Corn Laws admits not even of this alleviation: they occasion in all cases an absolute loss, greatly exceeding the gain which can be derived from them by the receivers of rent; and for every pound which finds its way into the pockets of the landlords, in consequence of the Corn Laws, the community is robbed of several.

"It would be better," Mill concluded, "to have a repeal of the Corn Laws, even clogged by compensation, than not to have it at all; and if this were our only alternative, no one could complain of a change, by which, though an enormous amount of evil would be prevented, no one would lose." Mill's proposal seemed to resolve the conflict: if compensation is paid to those whose incomes would fall under free trade, no one would be worse off and everyone could potentially be better off. In this case, free trade would prove best not just for national wealth, but for national welfare as well.

Despite Mill's insightful comments, the issue remained largely dormant until European general equilibrium theorists made the utility concept more operational at the end of the nineteenth century. In response to pleas from

---

[7] As Senior (1860, 183–84) put it, once the economist "gives a *percept*, whenever he advises his reader to do anything, or abstain from doing anything, he wanders from science into art, generally into the art of morality, or the art of government. . . . We cease to be scientific as soon as we advise or dissuade, or even approve or censure."

his colleagues to avoid interpersonal comparisons of utility, and thereby avoid implicit value judgments about particular distributions of income, the Italian economist Vilfredo Pareto devised a criterion (quite related to the one Mill proposed) for comparing welfare in two different situations where goods have been allocated differently. An efficient allocation, Pareto (1894) argued, is one in which no individual can be made better off unless another is made worse off. By this standard, one allocation of goods (e.g., that under free trade) is said to constitute an improvement over another (e.g., under protection) if no one is worse off and at least one person is better off. While any welfare criterion such as this is arbitrary and involves a value judgment, Pareto's guideline has achieved broad acceptance because its underlying principle—a change is desirable if no one is made worse off and at least one person is made better off—is relatively unobjectionable.

On these terms, free trade could not be said to constitute a Pareto-improvement over protection because some individuals may be worse off. But free trade with compensation might satisfy that stringent standard. Pareto (1895) himself made a flawed attempt to use the principle to validate the optimality (in terms of welfare) of free trade on these grounds. As John Chipman (1987, 1: 526) points out, however, this effort failed because "he assumed trade to be balanced in domestic prices and thus he failed to take account of the improvement in the terms of trade and the beneficial effect of the tariff revenues."[8]

Armed with the compensation principle and Pareto's welfare criterion, economists were poised to establish more rigorous propositions about free trade and economic welfare. Ruling out both distributional issues (by viewing a country as composed of any number of identical individuals, producers and consumers) and terms of trade effects (such that a country could trade as many goods as desirable at an arbitrarily chosen vector of international prices), Paul Samuelson (1939) produced what modern economists would accept as the first clear step toward a rigorous demonstration of the gains from trade. Using the concept of revealed preference, Samuelson illustrated how a country under free trade could have afforded to purchase the bundle of goods it had under autarky, and therefore was no worse off with trade. But all Samuelson showed was that, while it is not possible to demonstrate that free trade is best for a country, some trade is better than no trade.

The two key assumptions, of course, were identical consumers and no terms of trade effects. Murray Kemp (1962) and Paul Samuleson (1962) used the compensation principle to relax the strong assumption about identical consumers, as did the later more technical work by Jean Grandmont

---

[8] See also John Chipman (1976) and Andrea Maneschi (1993). Mention should be made of Enrico Barone's pathbreaking (but ignored) graphical depiction of the gains from trade in 1908, as reproduced in Andrea Maneschi and William Thweatt (1987).

and Daniel McFadden (1972). Conditional on an acceptance of the Pareto criterion, the actual payment of compensation to those made worse off, and the assumption of fixed terms of trade, free trade could be ranked as Pareto-superior to autarky and even to any tariff-inclusive equilibrium. The welfare status of free trade when countries could affect their terms of trade, as discussed in chapter 7, proved more problematic. J. de V. Graaf (1949) pointed out that, under the optimal tariff, the beneficiaries of protection could compensate those who would otherwise benefit from free trade.

Thus, the compensation principle proved necessary to ensure that no one is made worse off as a result of free trade, as required by Pareto's criterion. The question of whether it was possible to support free trade *without* compensation being paid arose in a controversy during the 1930s. This controversy led to a rediscovery of the compensation principle and to the discovery of consistency problems with hypothetical compensation tests. At the time, theoretical welfare economics in Britain still relied on interpersonal comparisons of (supposedly measurable) utility. In a famous book published in 1932, Lionel Robbins sought to remind economists of the weaknesses of this approach: any interpersonal comparisons of utility were inherently based on implicit value judgments that could not be supported as a feature of economic science. Roy Harrod, for one, found such a view much too restrictive for economists who wished to say something about economic policy. In defending the treatment of all persons equally by assuming the same marginal utility of income across individuals, Harrod (1938, 396–97) posed this rhetorical question:

> Consider the Repeal of the Corn Laws. This tended to reduce the value of a specific factor of production—land. It can no doubt be shown that the gain to the community as a whole exceeded the loss to the landlords—but only if individuals are treated in some sense as equal. Otherwise how can the loss to some—and that there was a loss can hardly be denied—be compared with the general gain? If the incomparability of utility to different individuals is strictly pressed, not only are the prescriptions of the welfare school ruled out, but all prescriptions whatever. The economist as an adviser is completely stultified, and unless his speculations be regarded as of paramount aesthetic value, he had better be suppressed completely.

No, Harrod stated, "some sort of postulate has to be assumed" to allow such policy prescriptions to be made.

In reply, Robbins (1938, 638) did not dispute that treating all individuals equally was widely acceptable, but insisted that that particular standard came outside of economics. Indeed, all "prescriptions regarding policy were conditional upon the acceptance of norms lying outside of economics." Robbins did not wish to inhibit economists from discussing economic policy, but simply argued for recognizing that such discussions invariably involved a leap outside of economic science. Economic science could evaluate how certain courses of action differed in terms of achieving a desired end, but economic science could not judge those ends themselves. In taking up the case of the repeal of the Corn Laws, Robbins argued that "it was not possible to say that economic science showed that free trade was justifiable" because there was an "arbitrary element" to the economist's advocacy of free trade, the arbitrary element being that free trade brought about a new distribution of income that required a comparison of welfare between different individuals or groups.

Nicholas Kaldor (1939, 550) entered the controversy and unwittingly reproposed Pareto's (and Mill's) criterion as a resolution, contending that "in the classical argument for free trade no such arbitrary element is involved at all." The previous distribution of income could always be maintained "by compensating the 'landlords' for any loss of income and by providing the funds for such compensation by an extra tax on those whose incomes have been augmented." In this way, Kaldor continued, "everybody is left as well off as before in his capacity as an income recipient; while everybody is better off than before in his capacity as a consumer" because the price of corn has fallen. This, of course, is merely a restatement of Mill's compensation doctrine.

But Kaldor went further in stating the following:

> In all cases, therefore, where a certain policy leads to an increase in physical productivity, and thus of aggregate real income, the economist's case for the policy is quite unaffected by the question of the comparability of individual satisfactions; since in all such cases it is *possible* to make everybody better off without making anybody worse off. There is no need for the economist to prove—as indeed he never could prove—that as a result of the adoption of a certain measure nobody in the community is going to suffer. In order to establish his case, it is quite sufficient for him to show that even if all those who suffer as a result are fully compensated for their loss, the rest of the community will still be better off than before. Whether the landlords, in the free-trade case, should in fact be given compensation or not, is a political question on the economist, *qua* economist, could hardly pronounce an opinion. The important fact is that, in the argument in favour of free trade, the fate of the landlords is wholly irrelevant: since the benefits of free trade are by no means destroyed even if the landlords are fully reimbursed for their losses. (550–51)

Thus, Kaldor's position was that a policy change could be deemed desirable simply if compensation could be *feasibly* paid to reach a Pareto-improvement, even if compensation were not *actually* paid. This "potential" Pareto-improvement criterion is, in some sense, equivalent to the classical view that an increase in aggregate economic wealth is a sufficient grounds for presuming that an improvement in economic welfare would or could take place.

Fearing the "shirking of live issues" and the "euthanasia of our science" if policy analysis was put in jeopardy, John R. Hicks (1939, 697) quickly endorsed Kaldor's general position and then proposed an alternative test. Hicks (1940) suggested that free trade would constitute a "potential" Pareto improvement if the landlords could not bribe the capitalists into opposing that policy. The reason for advancing this alternative is that it put the burden on those adversely affected by a proposed policy to develop a compensation scheme to stop it. Thus, the repeal of the Corn Laws was said to constitute a "potential" Pareto-improvement in welfare either if capitalists could pay the landlords for supporting free trade (Kaldor's criteria), or if the landlords could not pay the capitalists for opposing free trade (Hicks's criteria).

The aim of what was grandly called the "New Welfare Economics" was to provide an objective basis for making welfare propositions about economic policy. But the Kaldor-Hicks argument that free trade need only pass a hypothetical compensation test for it to constitute a "potential" Pareto improvement quickly ran into two problems. First, the goal of achieving a value-free assessment of economic policy was lost if one was indifferent as to whether compensation was paid or not. The hypothetical (and not actual) nature of compensation is the crucial feature of both tests. As John Chipman (1987, 524) noted, "The most important and controversial way in which value judgements enter into the compensation principle is in the conflict between potentiality and actuality: one situation is judged better than another if everybody *could* be made better off in the new situation even though some in fact become worse off." To be content with hypothetical compensation tests, one was essentially back to arguing about economic wealth (as Kaldor explicitly did) or back to making interpersonal comparisons. And the whole point of the exercise was to free the theory of economic policy from such judgments while also addressing questions of economic welfare.

A second problem arose when Tibor Scitovsky (1941) showed that a logical consistency problem plagued the hypothetical compensation tests. He demonstrated that even if the capitalists could compensate the landlords to secure the enactment of free trade (passing Kaldor's test), it might also be possible that the landlords could compensate the capitalists into enacting protection (passing Hicks's test). This became known as the Scitovsky "reversal" paradox: free trade could dominate protection (by Kaldor's test) *and* protection could dominate free trade (by Hicks's test). As a result, neither the Kaldor nor the Hicks criterion alone was necessarily sufficient to rank order economic policies. As Scitovsky put it,

> We must first see whether it is possible in the new situation so to redistribute income as to make everybody better off than he was in the initial situation; secondly, we must see whether starting from the initial situation it is not

possible by a mere redistribution of income to reach a position superior to the new situation, again from everybody's point of view. If the first is possible and the second impossible, we shall say that the new situation is better than the old was. If the first is impossible but the second possible, we shall say that the new situation is worse; whereas if both are possible or both are impossible, we shall refrain from making a welfare proposition. (86–87)

Hence, the resulting Scitovsky "double" criteria required that a policy pass *both* the Kaldor and the Hicks tests. This undermined the hope that a single and unique metric could be employed to evaluate the economic welfare effects of various policies.[9]

·   ·   ·

The New Welfare Economics is generally considered to have been a failure because one could not rely on hypothetical compensation tests to make strong Pareto statements. Because discussions of economic welfare quickly get into deep and thorny methodological territory, propositions about economic wealth, rather than economic welfare, are much easier to make. One is led back to the classical proposition that free trade leads to the maximization of national wealth and creates the opportunity to make available more of all goods. Yet the distributional difficulties remain an important practical argument against the claim that free trade is "best" since some groups will be made worse off and compensation may not be made.

Of course, the Pareto criterion is a very strict one that puts exacting, stringent standards on any proposed policy. The criterion is biased in favor of the status quo, which itself need not be equitable by some standard. The criterion is troublesome to opponents of free trade as well since making a case for protection (or *any* economic policy for that matter) encounters equally daunting distributional considerations. Still, the debate over trade policy and economic welfare helped define the limits to the case for free trade and helped clarify the relationship between economic theory and economic policy.

[9] For an overview of the manifold problems that have plagued assorted proposed welfare criteria in the subsequent literature, see John Chipman and James Moore (1978).

Chapter Thirteen

KEYNES AND THE
MACROECONOMICS OF PROTECTION

JOHN MAYNARD KEYNES ranks among the most influential economists of the twentieth century, if not all time. His writings, particularly *The General Theory of Employment, Interest and Money* (1936), reoriented the discipline of economics toward thinking in macroeconomic terms: aggregate income and output, the price level, and total employment. In the debate over how to deal with a persistently high unemployment rate in the late 1920s and early 1930s, Keynes argued that free trade should be abandoned in favor of protection in light of Britain's particular circumstances. These circumstances included three key elements: downwardly inflexible wages, a government commitment to maintain a fixed exchange rate, and a large pool of unemployed labor. Under these conditions, Keynes proposed, and with his stature (like Mill and infant industries) legitimized, using tariffs to help expand output and increase employment. Despite the specific conditions under which his advocacy of tariffs had been made, Keynes's views had a profound impact on economic theory and policy and were perceived as weakening the case for free trade for decades.[1]

. . .

Keynes began his career as a staunch proponent of free trade. As an undergraduate he served as secretary of the Cambridge University Free Trade Association and argued for free trade in several debates. In 1923, already established as a leading economist, he endorsed free trade in no uncertain terms:

> We must hold to Free Trade, in its widest interpretation, as an inflexible dogma, to which no exception is admitted, wherever the decision rests with us. We must hold to this even where we receive no reciprocity of treatment and even in those rare cases where by infringing it we could in fact obtain a direct economic advantage. We should hold to Free Trade as a principle of international morals, and not merely as a doctrine of economic advantage.[2]

---

[1] For overviews of Keynes's views on free trade and protection, see Randall Hinshaw (1947), Barry Eichengreen (1984), Bernard Wolf and Nicholas Smook (1988), Hugo Radice (1988), and Peter Clark (1988, 197–225).

[2] *JMK*, XVII, 451. The direct economic advantage Keynes speaks of is a terms of trade improvement. Citation to Keynes's writings are from the *Collected Writings of John Maynard*

Keynes also employed strong language to attack the frequent claim that tariffs could alleviate unemployment: "If there is one thing that protection can *not* do, it is to cure unemployment. . . . There are some arguments for protection, based upon its securing possible but improbable advantages, to which there is no simple answer. But the claim to cure unemployment involves the protectionist fallacy in its grossest and crudest form. . . . The proposal to cure the present unemployment by a tariff on manufactured goods . . . is a gigantic fraud."[3]

By 1928, however, Keynes had softened his position by suggesting that "the free trade case must be based in the future, not on abstract principles of *laissez-faire*, which few now accept, but on the actual expediency and advantages of such a policy."[4] This retreat to a more pragmatic free trade stance gave way to a decisive breach in 1930 based on new circumstances which prompted changes to his theoretical framework. With the backdrop of unrelentingly high rates of British unemployment in the 1920s, Keynes came to argue that import tariffs could help to boost aggregate output and employment. The younger Keynes would have agreed that tariffs could increase employment in protected sectors, but at the offsetting loss of employment in other (probably export) industries. Keynes now held that tariffs could expand total employment when all labor was not fully utilized.[5]

Hints of Keynes's modified views appeared in a section of *A Treatise on Money* (1930) that analyzed Britain's return to the gold standard in 1925 at the pre–World War I parity.[6] Keynes had been sharply critical of the decision to fix the pound sterling at its prewar price vis-à-vis gold, arguing that wartime inflation had diminished the value of sterling. According to Keynes, returning sterling to its prewar peg resulted in an overvaluation of sterling relative to other currencies. This tended to increase Britain's investments abroad (as the sterling price of foreign assets fell) while shrinking its balance of trade surplus (as domestic wages and prices rose relative to those abroad, harming the competitive position of British exporters and

---

Keynes, London: Macmillan for the Royal Economics Society, 1971–89, cited as *JMK* with the volume and page number.

[3] *JMK*, XIX, 151–52, 156. Keynes accepted as legitimate four exceptions to free trade: to achieve noneconomic objectives (such as protection to agriculture), to insure against excessive dependence on other countries in "key" industries, to promote infant industries, and to prevent predatory dumping.

[4] *JMK*, XIX, 729–30.

[5] The claim that the case for free trade does not hold under conditions of less-than-full resource utilization is an old one, dating back at least to the mercantilists. Richard Schüller (1905) tried to make the case for protection under these circumstances, but not in a macroeconomic context like Keynes and his argument lacked satisfactory theoretical underpinnings. For an English translation of Schüller, see Frank Taussig (1921, 371–91); for critical assessments, see C. F. Bickerdike (1905) and Gottfried Haberler (1936, 253–59).

[6] *JMK*, VI, 162–69.

import-competing producers). If an equivalence between foreign lending and the foreign balance, to use his terminology, was not maintained, an outflow of gold would be required to finance the gap in the balance of payments (the excess of foreign lending over the foreign balance). Because the British government's gold reserves were finite, the outflow of gold ultimately had to be stopped either by reducing foreign investment or by increasing the export surplus.

A devaluation of sterling against gold would correct the underlying exchange rate misalignment, restore equilibrium to the balance of payments, and end the gold outflow, but Keynes took as given the government's commitment to keeping sterling on the gold standard at the current rate. Instead, the Bank of England had to implement a deflationary monetary policy, with interest rates set higher than they otherwise would be, to restrain foreign investment and reduce import demand and thereby stop the gold outflow. But this tight monetary stance also tended to depress domestic output and employment. In a world free of economic frictions, the loss of output and employment would prove temporary. The Hume price-specie-flow mechanism (described briefly in chapter 3) provided the classical means by which the full-employment level of output and the balance of payments equilibrium would be restored. Deflationary pressures brought about by the gold outflow would reduce the nominal sterling value of domestic wages and other production costs. As the price of British goods fell, exports (and output and employment) would increase until the balance of trade improved enough to restore external balance and eliminate the gold outflow.

Unfortunately, Keynes believed, modern conditions prevented the smooth operation of this adjustment mechanism. As he wrote in the *Treatise*: "I believe that the resistances to a severe income deflation . . . have always been very great. But in the modern world of organized trade unions and a proletarian electorate they are overwhelmingly strong. The attempt by the entrepreneurs to bring this expedient into operation culminated in the general strike of 1926. But political and social considerations stood in the way of allowing the advantages won by the defeat of the strike to be pushed home."[7] Because trade unions and the electorate would fight a reduction in nominal wages, a deflationary monetary policy would reduce prices but not wage costs, leading to business losses and unemployment. Indeed, Keynes had charged in 1925 that such a monetary policy constituted a *"deliberate intensification of unemployment."*[8] Eventually, of course, severe unemployment could overcome the resistance to a reduction in wages, but he argued in the *Treatise* (1930) that "social and political forces stand in the way" of tolerating such a situation and alternative

---

[7] *JMK*, VI, 164.

[8] *JMK*, IX, 218, from his famous articles on "The Economic Consequences of Mr. Churchill."

policies were required to address Britain's predicament. Keynes's preferred escape from the dilemma was to subsidize home investment, which would reduce the incentive for foreign investment (and thus the need to have a large export surplus to maintain balance of payments equilibrium) as well as expand the domestic economy. But he admitted "coming round to the view that there is also room for applying usefully some method of establishing differential prices for home and foreign goods."[9]

In private evidence given in 1930 before the Macmillan Committee on Finance and Industry, set up to offer economic advice to the British government at the onset of the Great Depression, Keynes elaborated on proposed solutions to the deepening economic crisis. The fundamental problem was worsening unemployment, caused in his view by the overvalued exchange rate which required the Bank of England to maintain a deflationary monetary policy. In his February testimony, Keynes considered seven possible remedies to restore business profitability so that output and employment could expand once again. First, Britain could change the price at which sterling was pegged to gold (devaluing sterling and revaluing gold) and thereby pursue a more expansionary monetary policy. For political reasons, he commented, "there is no likelihood of such a remedy being adopted in present circumstances."[10] Second, there could be a general agreement to reduce money wages, facilitating the operation of the classical adjustment mechanism. Keynes believed that this was "in some respects the ideal remedy," but was probably impractical if not "chimerical" under the circumstances.[11] Third, industry could be subsidized in order to restore business profitability without entailing any cut in money wages, but this encountered practical (mainly fiscal) difficulties and its adoption was "very unlikely."[12] Fourth, industry could enhance its productivity (rationalize production), producing more output at the same wage costs, but this uncertain method operated too slowly and could actually exacerbate unemployment in the short run. Keynes noted that these four remedies were "all variations of the same tune"; they were designed to bring into balance the money costs of production at home and abroad, thereby increasing Britain's export surplus and restoring balance of payments equilibrium, and thus allowing the Bank of England to reduce interest rates and expediting an economic recovery.

Keynes also pointed to three other remedies of a different class. Fifth, as suggested in the *Treatise*, import tariffs could be imposed in an effort to increase domestic output and employment while improving the trade balance. Protection would reduce real wages and increase prices, he stated, something that was desirable under the circumstances. Sixth, domestic in-

---

[9] *JMK*, VI, 169.

[11] *JMK*, XX, 102, 106.

[10] *JMK*, XX, 100.

[12] *JMK*, XX, 108.

vestment could be indirectly subsidized to increase domestic output and reduce foreign lending. Keynes called this "my own favourite remedy," which could be accomplished by a tax on foreign bonds, by changes in the banking system to increase domestic lending, or even by direct capital expenditures by the government.[13] Seventh, major central banks could act jointly to pursue a more inflationary monetary policy, thereby expanding their economies and relieving unemployment without violating balance of payments constraints or requiring exchange rate adjustments. This was deemed problematic because of ignorance at the Bank of France and the narrowly domestic orientation of the Federal Reserve System.[14]

As most remedies could be ruled out as impractical for whatever reason, the choice essentially came down to either import tariffs or home investment incentives. When asked whether abandoning free trade was worth the potential ameliorative effects of protection, Keynes replied, "I have not reached a clear-cut opinion as to where the balance of advantage lies," indicating that his preferred remedy was still a policy of increasing home investment. Keynes saw the merits of tariffs as an alleviation rather than a solution to the slump, but was reluctant to endorse them. "I am frightfully afraid of protection as a long-term policy," he testified, "but we cannot afford always to take long views . . . the question, in my opinion, is how far I am prepared to risk long-period disadvantages in order to get some help to the immediate position." He also added, "It is extremely difficult for anyone of free trade origin, so to speak, at this juncture to speak in a way that he himself believes to be quite truthful and candid without laying himself open to misrepresentation and to being supposed to advocate very much more than he really does."[15]

By July 1930, as the economic situation worsened and no government action was forthcoming, the benefits of a general tariff became much more apparent to him. In response to questions from the prime minister, Keynes indicated that he had "become reluctantly convinced that some protectionist measures should be introduced."[16] While additional employment could be had either by increasing exports or decreasing imports, the latter was easier to arrange through policy action and had the advantage of generating fiscal revenue and improving the terms of trade. Throughout his private and public advocacy of a tariff, however, Keynes made clear that his conviction arose from "a question of a *choice* between alternatives, none of which are attractive in themselves."[17]

Having gravitated toward protection, Keynes began to press his views more strongly. In a memorandum prepared in September for the Committee of Economists of the Economic Advisory Council, Keynes elaborated

---

[13] *JMK*, XX, 126, 138, 140. [14] *JMK*, XX, 150, 154. [15] *JMK*, XX, 120.
[16] *JMK*, XX, 378. [17] *JMK*, XX, 494.

on the benefits of a tariff, which he now described as "simply enormous."[18] These benefits included solving the basic problem of the misalignment of money costs and the exchange rate: a tariff would raise domestic prices and reduce real wages toward their equilibrium value, while avoiding a disruptive fall in nominal wages. A tariff would also restore business confidence and create a favorable climate for new investment, he stated, but would not (unless poorly designed) trigger demands by trade unions for higher pay or have adverse employment effects.[19]

In another paper prepared for committee discussion, Keynes proposed a uniform 10 percent tariff on imports and an equal bounty for exports. As an alternative to reducing money wages, he argued, such a plan would effectively restore the conditions which would exist under free trade if money costs of production were reduced 10 percent. It would also be economically equivalent to a 10 percent devaluation, except the value of sterling obligations would be left unchanged in terms of gold.[20] Despite disputes and dissension among several of its members, the Committee of Economists issued a report in October which set out these options and reached a majority support for protection, as long as it was tied to industry efforts at rationalization. Keynes's proposal for a system of matching export bounties was rejected because it might provoke foreign countries to implement offsetting antidumping measures. The report also called for the tariff scheme to be removed either when unemployment had been sufficiently reduced or when prices had been restored to their 1925–28 level.[21]

Up to this point, Keynes's views had been expressed only in the privacy of quasi-governmental committees and advisory groups. In March 1931, he unveiled his position to the public in a newspaper article which, according to the editor of his *Collected Writings*, "as the recantation of an avowed free trader, it caused a sensation."[22] Keynes saw three feasible policy options to increase employment and rejuvenate business activity: devaluation, nominal wage reductions, and import tariffs. Despite opposing the return to the gold standard in 1925, he rejected devaluation on grounds that it would undermine already weak confidence in the London financial markets. Indeed, Keynes now thought that "our exchange position should be relentlessly defended today, in order, above all, that we may resume the

[18] *JMK*, XIII, 191.

[19] Keynes couched his exposition in terms of the theoretical relationships between savings, investment, and the terms of trade as developed in the *Treatise*. No increase in primary employment was possible without an increase in total investment (home and foreign, as Keynes defined them) relative to savings. An increase in the foreign balance, which a tariff could bring about, was equivalent in its impact on output and employment as an increase in investment.

[20] *JMK*, XX, 416–19.

[21] The Committee's report appears in Susan Howson and Donald Winch (1977, 180–227).

[22] *JMK*, XX, 231.

vacant financial leadership of the world." Wage reductions "would certainly lead to social injustice and violent resistance. . . . For these reasons a policy of contraction sufficiently drastic to do any real good may be quite impractical."[23] Instead, Keynes proposed "import duties of 15 per cent on all manufactured and semi-manufactured goods without exception, and of 5 percent on all foodstuffs and certain raw materials, whilst other raw materials would be exempt." "In so far as it leads to the substitution of home-produced goods for goods previously imported," he stated flatly, "it will increase the employment of this country."[24]

In another newspaper article in September 1931, Keynes repeated the three basic policy options: devaluation, wage reductions, and import tariffs. In the intervening months, he warmed to the idea of a devaluation—"I personally now believe [it] to be the right remedy"—but ruled it out because "the decision to maintain the gold standard at all costs has been taken" by political authorities and devaluation "is not yet the policy of any organized party in the state." Hopes for wage cuts adequate to restore equilibrium "would involve so drastic a reduction of wages and such appallingly difficult, probably insoluble, problems, both of social justice and practical method, that it would be crazy not to try first the effects of the alternative, and much milder, measure of restricting imports."[25] So Keynes once again fell back upon the tariff, not as the best method but simply a method of promoting economic recovery.

In various statements and writings, Keynes argued that the unequivocal case for free trade was undermined by the failure of wage flexibility to operate effectively as an equilibrating mechanism. "Free trade, combined with great mobility of wage rates, is a tenable intellectual position," he readily acknowledged, but "it presents a problem of justice so long as many types of money [wages] income are protected by contract and cannot be made mobile."[26] Keynes rejected the standard view that tariffs just shuffled labor from employment in one industry to another without affecting aggregate employment. "When a free trader argues that a tariff cannot increase employment but can only divert employment from one industry to another, he is tacitly assuming that a man who loses his employment in one direction will lower the wage rate which he is willing to accept until he finds employment in another direction . . . in present circumstances [this] is sheer nonsense." The trouble with free trade, Keynes suggested, was the

[23] *JMK*, IX, 235.   [24] *JMK*, IX, 231, 237.   [25] *JMK*, IX, 241, 242.

[26] *JMK*, XX, 490, 496. An addendum to the Macmillan report signed by Keynes stated: "The fundamental argument for unrestricted free trade does not apply without qualification to an economic system which is neither in equilibrium nor in sight of equilibrium . . . if this condition of full employment is neither fulfilled nor likely to be fulfilled for some time, then . . . a tariff may bring about a net increase of production and not merely a diversion" (*JMK*, XX, 298).

assumption "that if you throw men out of work in one direction you re-employ them in another. As soon as that link in the chain is broken the whole of the free trade argument breaks down."[27]

Keynes's heretical views on the tariff sparked opposition and debate within government policy circles and then in the public realm with the appearance of his newspaper articles. Lionel Robbins, also a member of the Economic Advisory Council, sharply disputed Keynes's tariff recommendations and refused to sign the final report. A tariff would not alleviate the depression in economic activity, he maintained, but would have adverse international consequences by inciting foreign protectionists and provoking retaliation. Robbins (1971, 155–56) argued (he later recalled) for a principled adherence to free trade, because "once the taboo of abstention from the obstruction of imports had been broken, there was small hope that the process would stop there." According to Robbins, Keynes "showed extraordinary naïveté" in believing that import duties could be easily removed once they had served their purpose.[28]

Other prominent economists responded to Keynes's proposals with deep skepticism if not outright hostility.[29] Under the guidance of William Beveridge, several prominent economists then at the London School of Economics, including Robbins, T. E. Gregory, Arnold Plant, J. R. Hicks, and others, collaborated on the book *Tariffs: The Case Examined*, a restatement of standard arguments against tariffs.[30] The economists were particularly insistent that protection was not a remedy for unemployment, noting that

[27] *JMK*, XX, 117. Keynes argued that free trade would be fine under conditions of full employment or if the economy functioned in a fluid manner. But "supposing we get jammed at the point of unemployment . . . it may be that the free trade method leaves us for the moment in a worse position, because the choice is not between making one article and something else for which we are not so well suited, the choice is between making something for which we are not so well suited and making nothing" (*JMK*, XX, 115).

[28] See also Lionel Robbins (1931). Robbins's dissent from the Committee's report appears in Howson and Winch (1977, 227–31). Robbins (1971, 154, 156) later regretted opposing Keynes's proposals for expansionary measures ("the greatest mistake of my professional career"), but believed he was right in resisting the tariff ("I am as glad to have opposed Keynes on commercial restriction as I am sorry to have opposed him on financial reflation"). Robbins proved to be right on the tariff. As Donald Moggridge (1992, 514) comments, "By refusing openly to advocate devaluation and by lending his public support to protection, largely as a result of an understandably mistaken comparison of the costs and benefits of the two courses of action and of the possibility of sterling being pushed from gold in any case, Keynes helped to create the climate of opinion in which, after Britain left gold and did not need protection on Keynes's grounds, she got a highly protective tariff system anyway."

[29] For example, while Ralph Hawtrey (1931, 59–60) admitted that a tariff has "*some* efficacy as an emergency measure against trade depression, . . . in reality the benefit it offers is very modest, perhaps almost insignificant, and for a great exporting country almost any measure which threatens to retard a world revival is injurious."

[30] Robbins (1971, 158) later admitted that "the statement is mediocre" and "has far too much of the popular and vulnerable traditional free-trade argument to satisfy the fastidious."

other countries with high tariff barriers were suffering from even higher rates of unemployment than Britain. They refused to concede that classical trade theory was inoperative under conditions of unemployment: it is never optimal to maximize employment of labor, land, or capital, they argued, and free trade remained the best policy, whatever the degree of resource utilization. If imports of manufactures were blocked to stimulate domestic output and employment, either exports must decrease equivalently or foreign investment must increase. It was a "pure gamble," the Beveridge (1931, 58) report stated, to assume that investment would increase and thereby avoid employment losses in export industries. However, the economists did concede that higher total employment could be brought about in the unlikely situation that a tariff shifted imports toward goods not produced at home, thereby keeping the import bill constant and not diminishing foreign demand for British exports.

Responding to his critics, Keynes acknowledged Robbins's point that reversing the tariff policy could prove difficult, but argued that the risk was overstated and "it is a risk which circumstances demand that we should take."[31] As he once put it, by using tariffs "you may also have got into bad habits and ten years hence you might be a trifle worse off than if you had been able to grin and bear it," but you also may "have avoided a social catastrophe."[32] In a letter to Beveridge, Keynes noted his agreement with much in the *Tariffs: The Case Examined* collection, but he dismissed chapter 6 on tariffs and unemployment as addressing a serious issue in an amateurish way.[33] Keynes strongly rejected the claim by Beveridge and other free traders that a reduction of imports would not generate a net stimulus because of an offsetting reduction in exports. Keynes vigorously denied that there was any simple and direct relationship between the volume of imports and exports. Stating that Beveridge's "defense of free trade is, I submit, the result of pure intellectual error, due to a complete misunderstanding of the theory of equilibrium in international trade," Keynes posed the following question: "Does he believe that it makes no difference to the amount of employment in this country if I decide to buy a British car instead of an American car?"[34]

Keynes did not have an extended opportunity to respond to critics because the tariff debate was soon cut short and rendered moot by events. He had endorsed tariffs under the assumption that an alternative option, devaluation, had been ruled out. As it happened, just days after his September 1931 newspaper article repeating his call for tariffs, the British government abandoned its commitment to the gold standard and sterling depreciated sharply on foreign exchange markets. In a letter to the *Times* shortly

---

[31] *JMK*, XX, 495.
[33] *JMK*, XX, 513–14.

[32] *JMK*, XIII, 199.
[34] *JMK*, XX, 508, 509.

thereafter, Keynes promptly dropped his call for a tariff and proposed moving on to discuss other policies that would stimulate economic recovery: "Until recently I was urging on Liberals and others the importance of accepting a general tariff as a means of mitigating the effects of the obvious dis-equilibrium between money costs at home and abroad . . . [now] proposals for high protection have ceased to be urgent." He spoke as one who rejoiced "at the breaking of our gold fetters" since it now freed monetary policy to pursue domestic economic objectives, such as stimulating the economy through lower interest rates, rather than the exchange rate objective.[35]

The year 1931 was a tumultuous one of intellectual crossfire over the tariff issue. The tariff debate subsided after Britain abandoned the gold standard in September and passed a general tariff in February 1932. But as Keynes was (and is) such a commanding figure in economics, even his *obiter dicta* regarding free trade and protection are of interest as they became part of the intellectual milieu of the period. In an address in 1932, Keynes stated that "the free trader starts with an enormous presumption in his favour" because of the demonstrable gains from trade.[36] But "the free trade argument against the use of a tariff for drawing workers into an industry for which they are relatively ill-suited fundamentally assumes that, in the absence of a tariff, they will be employed in some other more suitable industry, and does not allow for the contingency that they may not be employed at all." A worldwide system of tariffs would, of course, increase unemployment worldwide, but a country employing its tariffs alone might be able to shift some of the burden of its unemployment onto others.[37] The Keynes of this period also often trivialized the gains from the international division of labor and implied that the costs of protection were negligible.[38]

Revealing a deep-seated conservative streak, Keynes wrote favorably of inward-looking policies that, though economically costly, were worth the price of avoiding external entanglements. He endorsed protection to a new

[35] *JMK*, IX, 243, 245.

[36] One passage reveals his skills in the art of rhetorical flourish: "Nine times out of ten [the free trader] is speaking forth the words of wisdom and simple truth—of peace and of goodwill also—against some little fellow who is trying by sophistry and sometimes by corruption to sneak an advantage for himself at the expense of his neighbour and his country. The free trader walks erect in the light of day, speaking all passers-by fair and friendly, while the protectionist is snarling in his corner" (*JMK*, XXI, 205).

[37] *JMK*, XXI, 207–8.

[38] "In the case of most manufactured articles I doubt whether today there is any great advantage to be gained by a high degree of specialization between different countries," he once opined. "Any manufacturing country is probably just about as well fitted as any other to manufacture the great majority of articles." "I am no longer a free trader . . . to the extent of believing in a very high degree of national specialisation and in abandoning any industry which is unable for the time being to hold its own" (*JMK*, XX, 379; XII, 193).

industry (motor cars), an old industry (iron and steel), and agriculture, all out of a sense of England's heritage and an image of what the country should be. As he put it: "Neither free trade nor protection can present a theoretical case which entitled it to claim superiority in practice. Protection is a dangerous and expensive method of redressing a want of balance and security in a nation's economic life. But there are times when we cannot safely trust ourselves to the blindness of economic forces; and when no alternative weapons as efficacious as tariffs lie ready to hand."[39] In a famous 1933 article entitled "National Self-Sufficiency," Keynes continued on this theme, writing of his sympathy "with those who would minimise, rather than with those who would maximize, economic entanglements between nations. Ideas, knowledge, art, hospitality, travel—these are things which should of their nature be international. But let goods be homespun whenever it is reasonable and conveniently possible; and, above all, let finance be primarily national."[40]

The political debate over Britain's tariff policy abated with events, but the economic debate continued. In attacking the economic basis and the desirability of free trade under conditions of unemployment, Keynes had presented a real challenge to free trade and a wide gulf separated his views from those of traditional free traders. But in his major works on economic theory, as opposed to his policy advocacy in newspapers and elsewhere, Keynes was cautious about the generality of his case for tariffs for purposes of promoting employment. Chapter 23 of his *General Theory*, for example, is famous for its rehabilitation of mercantilist doctrine. Although approving of the mercantilists' attention to the balance of trade, Keynes argued not in favor of systematic restrictions on trade, but against the theoretical foundations of *laissez-faire*, particularly "the notion that the rate of interest and the volume of investment are self-adjusting at the optimum level." Indeed, he wrote that "there are strong presumptions of a general character against trade restrictions unless they can be justified on special grounds. The advantages of the international division of labour are real and substantial, even though the classical school greatly overstressed them." Trade restrictions, he added, are "a treacherous instrument even for the attainment of its ostensible object since private interest, administrative incompetence and the intrinsic difficulty of the task may divert it into producing results directly opposite to those intended."[41]

While a favorable balance of trade helped promote domestic employment, this benefit came only at the expense of other countries: just as not every country can improve its terms of trade against one another, not all countries could improve their trade balance against one another. Keynes concluded that domestic policies were best suited for ensuring full employ-

---

[39] *JMK*, XXI, 210.   [40] *JMK*, XXI, 235.   [41] *JMK*, VII, 338–39.

ment and efforts to contrive a more favorable trade balance should be avoided.

> If nations can learn to provide themselves with full employment by their do-
> mestic policy, . . . there would no longer be a pressing motive why one country
> need force its wares on another or repulse the offerings of its neighbour. . . .
> International trade would cease to be what it is, namely, a desperate expedient
> to maintain employment at home by forcing sales on foreign markets and re-
> stricting purchases, which, if successful, will merely shift the problem of
> unemployment to the neighbour which is worsted in the struggle, but a will-
> ing and unimpeded exchange of goods and services in conditions of mutual
> advantage.[42]

What is one to conclude about Keynes's views on free trade? Despite occasional remarks deprecating the gains from trade, the Keynes of the early 1930s clearly appreciated the benefits of free trade. But in the midst of an economic catastrophe and constrained by political considerations from advancing the best remedy for Britain's economic ills, he embraced the tariff as an expedient if desperate measure to promote recovery. (In terms of his policy advice in the 1940s, however, Keynes revealed himself to be much less of a friend to free trade.[43])

But Keynes did much more than just advocate protection under particu-larly rare and extreme circumstances. He succeeded in showing the prob-lems for free trade once key theoretical assumptions were relaxed, namely, those of factor mobility and factor price flexibility. Gottfried Haberler (1950) illustrated the problem neatly in a more traditional framework of international trade theory, in which production possibilities are the focus and trade is always in balance. Haberler first showed that if labor was not mobile between sectors but wages were flexible, then free trade was still the best policy. But in the extreme case of factor immobility and factor price rigidity, free trade might lead to unemployment and an inferior allo-cation of resources. In this case, Haberler (1950, 231, 235) noted, "trade

---

[42] Ibid.

[43] In his advisory role in international economic policymaking during World War II, Keynes frequently objected to the abolition of import quotas and expressed a preference for such quantitative restrictions over import tariffs. Abolishing quotas "does not fit in at all with that degree of planning which is likely to exist in the post-war world," as such controls were useful for excluding imports that a country could not afford. (Keynes took for granted govern-ment responsibility for the allocation of foreign exchange for purchasing imports.) In com-menting on British proposals, Keynes wrote: "I do not like the appearance of special hostility to import regulation, since it seems to me to be, not merely temporarily, but permanently much the best technique open to us for the sorts of things we are likely to want to do. I am not clear that it is yet fully appreciated how the growth of state trading and planning generally is likely to favour import regulation as the better technique compared with tariffs or subsidies" (*JMK*, XXVI, 258, 261, 284ff).

may be very detrimental" and, "at least in the short-run, [this finding] is a matter of serious practical concern."

Keynes had essentially come to the same conclusion in a novel macroeconomic framework, viewing factor immobility as a problem of insufficient aggregate demand. He also proved influential in gaining acceptance for import restrictions as a legitimate, useful tool for reducing conflict between the domestic economic objective of full employment and the external objective of balance of payments equilibrium under fixed exchange rates. Such a conflict could arise in the following way: expansionary demand policies to achieve full employment would also draw in imports under fixed exchange rates and move the balance of trade into deficit; if the expansionary policies were not to be reversed, a balance of payments adjustment was required to prevent the loss of foreign exchange reserves.

Currency devaluation perhaps would have been the solution proposed by Keynes in the 1920s and 1930s, but the Keynes of the 1940s had come to favor trade restrictions: "I have no sympathy with the idea, which . . . I regard as vestigial, that, if imports have to be restricted, it is in some way sounder to raise their prices by depreciation of the exchanges than by any other technique."[44] Keynes was skeptical of the efficacy of devaluation on grounds that the trade balance might worsen if certain elasticity conditions are not met. Devaluation, in his view, also had the tendency to deteriorate the terms of trade, a shortcoming not shared by tariffs.

Keynes irretrievably established the idea that tariffs and other import restrictions were reasonable options to be called upon in the arsenal of policies designed to maintain the full-employment level of economic activity. His more enthusiastic disciples spoke of his having "repudiated" and "demolished" the free trade doctrine by showing that classical international payments mechanisms do not work smoothly. As Joan Robinson (1946–47, 112) pronounced, "As soon as the assumption of full employment is removed, the classical model for the analysis of international trade is reduced to wreckage." "The notion of a unique natural position of equilibrium is a mirage," she stated, "and, for better or worse, international trade must be directed by conscious policy." Yet despite their rejection of classical analysis, Keynes's disciples largely heeded the call in the *General Theory* to avoid proposing the use of tariffs for domestic output and employment objectives.[45]

As a result of these developments, J. R. Hicks observed in 1951 how free trade had been called into severe question by the theoretical changes

---

[44] *JMK*, XXVI, 289.

[45] For example, Robinson (1937) concluded that exchange-rate depreciation, wage reductions, export subsidies, and import tariffs and quotas were all "beggar-thy-neighbour" remedies for unemployment and by no means endorsed tariffs as superior to other policies in this effort.

brought about by Keynes. "The doctrine which used to derive much of its strength from its association with accepted economic theory, has lost much of that strength too," Hicks (1959, 41–42) explained. "Free trade is no longer accepted by economists, even as an ideal, in the way that it used to be . . . the preponderance of economic opinion is no longer so certainly as it was on the free trade side." "The main thing which caused so much liberal opinion in England to lose its faith in free trade was the helplessness of the older liberalism in the face of massive unemployment, and the possibility of using import restrictions as an element in an active programme of fighting unemployment. . . . It was this, almost alone, which led Keynes to abandon his early belief in free trade" (48). Hicks accepted the policy trade-offs that Keynes had highlighted: "If we are unwilling to [go right over to a system of flexible exchange rates (or capital controls)], we have got to admit that there is a strong case for import restrictions, as a means of facilitating expansion without weakening the balance of payments. . . . It is this, more than anything else, which has undermined the intellectual foundations of free trade" (53). But Hicks also pointed the way out of the dilemma. One may prefer protection with full employment to free trade with unemployment, but "the question remains whether full employment with free trade . . . really is out of reach. It is not right to abandon the pursuit of the higher goal until we are assured that it really is unattainable."

In time compelling arguments emerged that, if not shattering the Keynesian case for import restrictions, at least relegated it to a narrow range of circumstances in which other, more preferable options had been ruled out. Keynes's argument for tariffs in the early 1930s hinged on two critical assumptions: fixed exchange rates and nominal wage rigidity. In the post–World War II period, as in the early 1930s, fixed exchange rates were an integral part of the international monetary system and downward wage flexibility was not thought to be a feature of modern economies. But changing views on exchange rates in particular and macroeconomic policy in general ultimately undermined the Keynesian employment case for protection and diminished the perception that the standing of free trade had been diminished.

First, economists gradually came to prefer exchange rate flexibility over import restrictions as a means of external adjustment. Keynes and his followers were willing to sacrifice free trade on the alter of exchange rate stability, a choice dictated more by circumstances and his policy preferences than for reasons having a sound grounding in economic theory.[46]

---

[46] As noted, Keynes preferred import restrictions over devaluation for the positive terms of trade effect. But Gottfried Haberler ([1952] 1985, 167–74) pointed out too that a devaluation did not necessarily lead to a deterioration in the terms of trade since both import and export prices would rise in domestic terms and fall in foreign terms.

Subsequent research comparing devaluation with tariffs weakened any inclination in favor of trade restrictions as opposed to exchange rate adjustment as a means of maintaining external balance.[47] With the development of the "absorption" approach to the balance of payments, a devaluation proved more efficient than import restrictions in improving the trade balance, which was determined by the difference between domestic production and total spending. For example, of expenditure-switching policies that shifted demand away from imported goods and toward domestic goods, a devaluation would switch both domestic and foreign expenditures toward home-produced goods, whereas import controls would shift just domestic expenditures toward home production.

A growing number of economists also came to question the desirability of fixed exchange rates. In a classic essay, Milton Friedman (1953) argued that flexible exchange rates would free monetary policy from being devoted to a particular exchange rate parity to focus on the more important economic policy goal of maintaining domestic price stability. By allowing greater flexibility in the conduct of monetary policy, the very deflationary shocks that prompted Keynes's turn to tariffs in the first place could be avoided altogether. Friedman also stressed that flexible exchange rates were the most direct and efficient means of balancing international payments, eliminating the need for government gold or foreign exchange reserves and hence for direct policy concern over external balances.

Indeed, James Meade (1955, 6) argued that "free trade and fixed exchange rates are incompatible in the modern world; and all modern free traders should be in favour of variable exchange rates." According to Meade, of the three major economic policy objectives—stable domestic prices, stable exchange rates, and free trade—just two were attainable; all three were incompatible. To avoid the deflation of the early 1930s and the accompanying contraction of economic activity, Meade argued that domestic price stability should be afforded top priority. But if monetary policy was already obligated to service another objective, a fixed exchange rate, and exchange rate changes were ruled out, then trade restrictions became the means by which the conflict between domestic price stability and exchange rate parity was resolved without sacrificing either objective. Suppose, for example, the demand for British exports fell under a fixed exchange rate regime. The resulting trade deficit would result in a loss of foreign exchange reserves, putting deflationary pressure on monetary policy. If a fall in domestic prices was deemed undesirable because of employment reasons and an exchange rate change was ruled out, then direct regulation of foreign trade transactions was the only way of restoring balance of

---

[47] Sidney Alexander (1951) made an early, uneasy case in favor of exchange rate adjustment.

payments equilibrium and also avoiding an economic downturn. If the domestic currency were allowed to depreciate on foreign exchange markets, free trade and stable domestic prices could be maintained.

Originally conceived under conditions of deflation and unemployment, the whole Keynesian framework came into question in the late 1960s when the economic problem was one of inflation and unemployment. The development of the natural-rate of unemployment theory by Milton Friedman (1968) and others began to supplant Keynesian economics as the dominant framework in macroeconomics. According to this approach, even if nominal wages were considered fixed in the short run, government policy could not permanently reduce unemployment through the use of stimulative monetary and fiscal policy, whether these policies were anticipated or not. In this framework, protection offered no solace whatsoever to the problem of unemployment.

These developments severely limited the Keynesian case for protection, but did not prevent the resurrection of the argument by Cambridge economists in the mid-1970s, this time in the context of flexible exchange rates. Assessing the depressed state of the British economy in the mid-1970s, the Cambridge Economic Policy Group (CEPG) advocated reducing the current account deficit while implementing expansionary demand policies to alleviate unemployment. Based on an explicit econometric model with real wage rigidity, the CEPG concluded that import quotas and high tariffs were the only way to reduce the external deficit without aggravating unemployment or requiring a steep devaluation of the pound.[48] According to the CEPG, devaluation would deteriorate the terms of trade and raise import prices (leading to higher inflation), both of which would reduce demand. By contrast, import quotas were assumed to increase demand and employment without rekindling inflation.

The Cambridge proposals provoked debate, but failed to capture support. Indeed, CEPG economists Wynne Godley and Robert May (1977, 32) admitted that their proposals had been "so far met with almost universal opposition, not least from professional economists." Many opponents argued that the standard case for devaluation and fiscal restraint remained intact as the best remedies for correcting the external imbalance.[49] But the structure of the Cambridge model raised serious doubts about the credibility of its results. One incongruity was the assumption that quotas and trade restrictions would not induce a rise in import prices. As a consequence, the model ruled out by assumption (one explicitly denied by Keynes) any inflationary price effect from quotas, the very point on which they based their

[48] Department of Applied Economics (1975, 9ff) and (1976, 11ff).

[49] See W. M. Corden, I.M.D. Little, M. FG. Scott (1975), who note that the CEPG model does not necessarily generate results consistent with the policy advice they offer. See also Charles Collyns (1982) and W. M. Corden (1985, 311–26).

dismissal of devaluation. The structure of the model also lacked any explicit treatment of how wage and price expectations were formed, an important feature of modern macroeconomic models. The policy choice posed by the CEPG was also odd: the exchange rate was no longer a direct policy instrument, as the term devaluation implies, because the flexible exchange rate regime made the foreign-exchange value of sterling a market-determined price, requiring a statement of the particular mechanism that generates depreciation on foreign exchange markets.

Professional skepticism was buttressed by the lack of support in economic theory for the CEPR's contentions. In a macroeconomic setting with flexible exchange rates and real wage rigidity, Barry Eichengreen (1983) showed that a tariff would actually reduce output and employment under certain plausible circumstances.[50] Robert Mundell (1961) had established a similarly surprising finding that import restrictions were contractionary, leading to lower output and employment, in the context of a standard Keynesian model with flexible exchange rates and sticky nominal wages. In Mundell's case, aggregate supply had to fall to accommodate the lower demand that came about because the tariff-induced terms of trade improvement generated additional savings. Although somewhat sensitive to how tariff revenue is redistributed, this result was later found to hold under a variety of theoretical assumptions, sufficient to establish at least a general presumption about its robustness.[51]

. . .

How should one treat Keynes's legacy for the theory of commercial policy? The evidence suggests that he was, for the most part, a free trader who was willing to use tariffs as an inferior, short-lived expedient to remedy macroeconomic ills as opposed to doing nothing at all. Handicapped by the gold standard from obtaining exchange rate (or interest rate) adjustments, Keynes sought temporary reliance on a tariff as a reasonable alternative in light of the extreme economic circumstances. His case for tariffs faltered as the benefits of exchange rate flexibility came to be appreciated, and, perhaps more fundamentally, as his macroeconomic framework—implying high equilibrium rates of unemployment—underwent critical scrutiny. Under a regime of flexible exchange rates, when the necessity of external

[50] This finding is sensitive to the assumptions made about the distribution of the tariff revenue. The maintained assumption is that the revenues are neutrally redistributed to agents in the economy. If the revenues are used to finance production subsidies, the tariff can be expansionary. In addition, a tariff could be expansionary in the short run (but not in the long run) if real wages are rigid only with an adjustment lag. See also Barry Eichengreen (1981).

[51] These Keynesian macroeconomic models of commercial policy and employment, it should be noted, are not equipped to consider economic welfare or the optimality of any policy instrument in solving the problem of unemployment.

balance as a policy objective vanishes, even Keynesian-type models often imply that tariffs can be contractionary. While it is not impossible to construct examples where tariffs increase employment and improve external balances, the theoretical basis for such tariffs has not been soundly established. Yet until these qualifications were well understood, Keynes succeeded for many years in placing the free trade doctrine in doubt and putting its advocates on the defensive.

Chapter Fourteen

STRATEGIC TRADE POLICY

IN TREATING international trade as the (barter) exchange of one good for another between nations, standard trade theory lacked any sense of the rivalry between actual firms pitted against one another in international competition. In the early 1980s, economists began to examine trade in situations where a small number of firms were competing against one another and discovered new theoretical grounds for departing from free trade. Markets which have few competitors may be characterized by a strategic interdependence among firms (in that the pricing, investment, and output decisions of one firm affect those of the others) and imperfect competition (in that the rivalry among existing firms or the threat of new entrants is insufficient to drive profits down to a normal level). In such markets, government promotion of a domestic firm could potentially affect the behavior of foreign firms to the national advantage, such as by shifting profits to the domestic firm and thereby increasing national wealth. While theoretical reasoning along these lines initially bred skepticism about the desirability of free trade under imperfect competition, further research demonstrated that the policy implications of this analysis were fragile and hinged on a number of crucial assumptions. In the end, the theory of strategic trade policy clarified many aspects of international competition under various market conditions, but failed to provide a robust and unqualified case against free trade.

. . .

Because the classical theory of trade addressed the exchange of goods between nations as a whole and left little room for examining the competitive rivalries between firms, the argument for strategic trade policies does not have a long intellectual lineage. Prompted by the prevalence of (and the fierce rivalries between) state-chartered monopoly trading companies during the seventeenth century, mercantilist writers occasionally discussed the competitive interaction of two or more firms in lucrative foreign markets. As discussed briefly in chapter 2, one theme in mercantilist thought was that the volume of world trade was fixed and set to be divided among the few large trading countries (represented by the monopoly companies) of the period. The idea that "there is but a certain proportion of trade in the world" led easily to William Petty's conclusion that "the wealth of every nation consist[s] chiefly in the share which they have in the foreign trade with the whole commercial world." As trade was set along "channels" that could not accommodate more traffic, entry was possible only by displacing existing merchants. This led to attitudes well expressed by Josiah Child, who argued in 1693 that trade should be managed by judicious government intervention to ensure "that other nations who are in competition with us for the same, may not wrest it from us, but that ours may continue and increase, to the diminution of theirs."[1]

Although they vaguely anticipated some of the insights arising from the contemporary discussion of strategic trade policies, mercantilist writers lacked a well-developed economic framework in which to evaluate this competition.[2] Adam Smith and the classical economists did not pursue these insights, but took a more benign view of the trading success of other nations and sharply criticized government-supported trading companies for their sloth and mismanagement.[3] The French economist Augustine Cournot ([1838] 1927) was perhaps the first to consider in detail competition among a small number of firms. Cournot provided a theory of the competitive interaction of two firms (a duopoly), although his brief consideration of international trade and the possible gains from tariffs has not been well regarded.[4]

While later theoretical analysis of commercial policy considered situations of monopoly or oligopoly on occasion, this line of research was not pursued systematically. Nor was it embedded in a theoretical framework that illustrated the interactions between firms in a way that captured the essence of competition in such markets. Theoretical advances in industrial organization and game theory during the 1970s, however, refined the analysis of competition under different market structures in which a firm's behavior depended upon the actions of its rivals. For example, if a firm could credibly commit itself to a high level of output, such as by making irreversible investments in production capacity, this action might have a strategic effect in reducing the investments of other firms or deterring the entry of potential rivals.

---

[1] For the citations to these quotes, see chapter 2 above, p. 31.

[2] For a further discussion and an illustration of the parallels between mercantilism and strategic trade policy, see Douglas Irwin (1991) and (1992).

[3] Gary Anderson and Robert Tollison (1982) study Adam Smith's views on government chartered companies.

[4] In chapter 12, Cournot ([1838] 1927) attempted to show that removing import duties can possibly result in a lower nominal and real national income. Subsequent commentators have been critical of Cournot's opaque analysis. Viner (1937, 587), for example, states that Cournot reached this conclusion "by virtue of a process of reasoning which no one has so far satisfactorily explained." In chapter 10, Cournot committed a key conceptual error in trying to illustrate how an export tax would reduce prices in both the home and foreign market. In his correspondence in 1892, the Italian economist Vilfredo Pareto considered refuting Cournot at one point, commenting: "These mathematical economists have a real mania for trying to find reasons in favor of protection." Quoted in Erich Schneider (1961, 162).

These developments naturally called for an extension to an international context. James Brander and Barbara Spencer, economists at the University of British Columbia, were among the first to explore the impact of export subsidies and import tariffs in markets with strategic interactions among firms.[5] In a novel application of Cournot's duopoly theory to an international setting, Brander and Spencer (1985) considered the simple case of a domestic and a foreign firms competing to sell a homogeneous good in a third market. If both firms produced under constant marginal costs (allowing for sunk fixed costs) and could not collude to maximize joint profits like a cartel, then noncooperative duopolistic competition would take place much as described by Cournot: each firm would choose its own output level to maximize its profits, taking as given the output of the other firm (that is, assuming that changes in its own output would not affect that of its rival). In equilibrium, neither firm could change its output and increase its profits, given the current output of the other firm. Competition in this market would be imperfect in that firms would restrict output and not drive the market price down to marginal cost; profits would be greater than had perfect competition prevailed, but less than if the firms had colluded.

Suppose, however, that the government decided to subsidize the exports of the domestic firm. If this decision was announced before each firm had decided the quantity of output to produce in a given period and was fully credible, in that both the domestic and foreign firms believed it would be implemented, the subsidy would have a strategic impact on the competition between the two firms and thereby alter the resulting market equilibrium. Because the export subsidy encourages greater production by the domestic firm, which reduces the market price, the optimal (profit-maximizing) response of the foreign firm is to reduce its output. Thus, the export subsidy (or even the credible threat of an export subsidy) would enable the domestic firm to displace (to some extent) the foreign firm from the export market. In assisting the domestic firm to capture a larger share of a profitable market, the subsidy would essentially shift profits from the foreign firm to the domestic firm. In fact, Brander and Spencer demonstrated that a properly chosen (optimal) subsidy could increase the home country's national wealth because the increase in profits to the domestic firm would exceed the cost of the subsidy.[6] This national gain arises in part because the reduced production of the foreign firm mitigates the fall in the market price that results from the additional (subsidized) domestic output.

---

[5] Brander and Spencer (1981) began their research by examining the use of import tariffs to extract profits from exporting foreign monopolists. Aside from using a different set of analytical tools, this study was similar in spirit to the use of tariffs by an importing monopsonist to improve its terms of trade, as in Stephen Enke (1944).

[6] There being no domestic consumption in this simplified situation, domestic producer welfare is the only consideration in determining national wealth. It is also assumed that there is no pronounced effect of the government subsidy on other sectors of the economy.

The benefits of such an export subsidy, however, hinged on unilateral action: a gain arose to a particular country only if that country alone implemented the subsidy and there was no foreign retaliation. If each government subsidized its own firm, both countries would be worse off. In this case, neither firm is driven from the market: the subsidies would only encourage both firms to expand output, driving down the market price such that the cost of the subsidies would exceed the profits earned by each firm. Like the optimal terms-of-trade tariff, an export subsidy augments national wealth only as a unilateral, beggar-thy-neighbor policy; profits are shifted to the domestic firm at the expense of the foreign firm, and total industry profits after the subsidy are lower than in the absence of a subsidy. (Consumers in the third market, of course, benefit from the lower price.)

The framework proposed by Brander and Spencer proved to be flexible enough to handle a variety of imperfectly competitive situations in which firms exhibit a strategic interdependence. Spencer and Brander (1983) had earlier considered a related scenario of two-stage competition between a domestic and a foreign firm. First, firms choose the amount to spend on research and development (R&D) expenditures, which were assumed to have a diminishing marginal effect in reducing the cost of producing output in the second stage. Having chosen these R&D levels, the firms would then select the profit-maximizing level of output to produce. As in the previous example, government policy can again play a role in redistributing profits from the foreign firm to the domestic firm. If a government announces an export or R&D subsidy for the domestic firm before the two firms had chosen their R&D investment level, the subsidized firm could afford to invest more in first-stage cost reduction and thereby profitably increase production in the second stage. Once again, credible government intervention would affect the strategic choices of each firm in R&D spending and output: by subsidizing the domestic firm at an early stage in the competition, thereby reducing its cost of production and increasing its output, the foreign firm would again be induced to contract its output. Once again, the increase in profits to the domestic firm (resulting from the foreign firm's retreat from the market) could exceed the cost of the government subsidy. Similarly, if both governments subsidize R&D expenditures, both countries would be worse off because both firms would expand output, driving down the market price and with it the profits of both firms.

Brander and Spencer simply but cleverly extended to an international context the notion that strategic commitments by government can, in principle, deter potential or actual competitors and increase the profits of the favored firm. Each firm, of course, has every incentive to attempt to increase its profits at the expense of its rivals on its own, but the possibilities for strategic behavior on the part of the firms are assumed to have been already exhausted as part of the existing equilibrium. Government policy is introduced as another strategic instrument outside of the market that can potentially change the market outcome. However, the government intervention must have two characteristics to affect the economic behavior of the firms. First, the government must announce its policy before the output choices of the firms have been made, otherwise it is too late to affect the final outcome. Second, the government's policy must be credible, meaning either that the government has acquired a reputation for following through on its announcements or that it is committed by some institutional mechanism (such as automatic legislation) to a certain, irreversible course of action.

Brander and Spencer's findings attracted a great deal of attention among economists and even filtered into popular discussions of trade policy. Their research triggered a surge of analysis of trade policy in imperfectly competitive markets.[7] For example, Avinash Dixit and Albert Kyle (1985) considered a situation in which internal economies of scale were so pronounced (that is, fixed costs of entry were so high) that world demand could profitably support production by only one firm. If two rival firms from different countries were considering entry into the market, a credible commitment by one government to support its firm in the market could have the strategic effect of deterring foreign entry into the market, thereby safeguarding the monopoly profits for the domestic firm. Numerous other cases were considered in which government policy could change the pattern of trade, but few of these cases were geared toward explicitly considering the impact of such policies on national economic wealth. Merely showing that government policy could alter the pattern of trade in imperfectly competitive markets, of course, fell far short of demonstrating that such a policy might be desirable on economic grounds.

Much of this research was motivated by contemporary observations that international trade in certain products (such as large aircraft) was dominated by just a few firms. The apparent existence of such imperfectly competitive market structures was thought to imply that theories of strategic trade policy had an immediate, practical relevance for commercial policy. Yet authors of the strategic approach were cautious in suggesting that their theoretical modelling be applied to economic policy. Brander (1986, 45), for example, wrote that the "case for interventionist trade policy presented here is limited and narrow," specifically adding that the new theory "does not provide a rationale for a broad-based policy of subsidization." But in pointing out that his work "demonstrates that there is a unilateral economic motive for interventionist trade policy in certain cases," he also stated that "this conclusion is in sharp contrast to the standard results and received wisdom of mainstream international trade theory."

---

[7] For a much more complete survey of these developments, see James Brander (1995).

Paul Krugman (1987, 131–32) went much further in arguing that conventional views about free trade needed to be seriously rethought in view of the new theories. Krugman claimed that "the case for free trade is currently more in doubt than at any time since the 1817 publication of Ricardo's *Principles of Political Economy* . . . because of the changes that have recently taken place in the theory of international trade," which he called "substantial and radical." Free trade, according to Krugman, "is an idea that has irretrievably lost its innocence" and "can never again be asserted as the policy that economic theory tells us is always right."

Krugman's assertions drew much critical comment. Many economists were suspicious of the strategic trade theories and sought to defend free trade by putting the recent developments into a broader perspective. Jagdish Bhagwati (1989, 19, 41) called Krugman's remarks "surely puzzling" because the theory of domestic divergences (considered in chapter 10) meant that "one cannot assert that free trade is 'the policy that economic theory tells us is always right' . . . certain developments make the case for free trade more robust whereas others make it less so . . . [and] the latter are subject to many difficulties as one passes from the classroom to the corridors of policymaking." Robert Baldwin (1992) thought that the theory of strategic trade policy could be readily incorporated into the corpus of existing theory. In constructing examples of cases in which trade intervention could generate a "beggar-thy-neighbor" gain at the expense of others, the new theories were similar to the terms-of-trade argument for tariffs, with the added dimension that the strategic interaction made an export subsidy, rather than an export tax, the appropriate policy instrument. Many also believed that the existence of a few examples in which government intervention could prove superior to free trade still did not fundamentally shatter the basic presumption in favor of free trade.

Such reactions correctly moderated any exaggerated claims about the new theories, but the most important responses tackled the theory itself head on. The Brander and Spencer framework had one great attribute: unlike some previous cases, most notably the infant industry argument, the theoretical structure used in the analysis of strategic trade policies was explicit, concrete, and transparent for all to see in a formal economic model. This had the tremendous virtue of allowing the policy implications to be checked for robustness in terms of the underlying assumptions. These policy implications, it turned out, were highly sensitive to simple changes in those assumptions. The combined impact of the many qualifications to the theory of strategic trade policy erased any belief that the theory constituted a general case for departing from free trade, confirming the views of the skeptics.

In the prototypical Brander and Spencer (1985) analysis, for example, competition was assumed to take place between two firms. If one considered situations in which there were a fixed number of firms, the optimal export subsidy varies inversely with the number of firms. With a sufficiently small number of firms (whose precise number was determined by cost and demand conditions), the case for profit-shifting export subsidies remained. But as Avinash Dixit (1984) showed, the greater the number of domestic firms, the closer the market approached perfect competition and the less an export subsidy was advisable. The fixed duopoly assumption also drew criticism for excluding the possibility of market entry. If there were no entry barriers, then new competitors would begin production and eliminate the extra profits, thereby obviating the case for profit-shifting policies.[8] Ignatius Horstmann and James Markusen (1986) pointed out that if there are increasing returns to scale in these industries targeted for export subsidies, tariff and subsidy policies could also promote inefficient entry, raising average costs of production and prices to consumers.

The Brander-Spencer results also hinged on the assumption that the two firms were Cournot competitors; that is, that each firm chooses the quantity of goods to produce in a given period. An alternative (so-called Bertrand) approach has firms choose the prices to sell at rather than quantities to produce in their competition with one another.[9] Jonathan Eaton and Gene Grossman (1986) considered the optimal trade policy under the Bertrand assumption of price competition and discovered that the Brander-Spencer results were reversed: if firms choose prices rather than quantities in order to maximize profits, then the best government policy is an export tax rather than an export subsidy. Price competition generally yields a more competitive outcome than quantity competition because there are greater incentives to undercut the price of a competitor and capture a larger share of the market. In this more competitive environment, firms fail to exploit their market power and the optimal government policy is to restrict output. An export tax reduces domestic output, raising the market price and with it the profits of the domestic firm. Unless there was a compelling reason to presume that

[8] Indeed, one had to be certain that profits were not really more apparent than real. As Gene Grossman (1986, 57) pointed out, "Often what appears to be an especially high rate of profit is just a return to some earlier, risky investment. Research and development expenses, for example, can be quite large, and many ventures end in failure. Firms will only undertake these large investments if they can expect to reap the benefits in those instances where they succeed. Once the market is in operation, we will of course only observe those companies that have succeeded. We may then be tempted to conclude that profit rates are unusually high. But industry profits should be measured inclusive of the losses of those who never make it to the marketing stage."

[9] The price-setting approach has been attributed to Joseph Bertrand's review of Cournot in 1883. However, Jean Magnan de Bornier (1992) reproduces this review and argues that this attribution is based on a misinterpretation of Bertrand's criticism. Robert Ekelund and Robert Hébert (1990, 145) suggest that Paul-Gustave Fauveau (in a 1864 review of Cournot) made the point that firms often compete in terms of price, and that noncollusive price competition between firms could lead to a competitive level of output.

the Cournot assumption about competition was more appropriate than the Bertrand assumption, the nature of the optimal policy, a tax or a subsidy, was in doubt.

Another aspect of the Brander and Spencer analysis derived from Cournot is that each firm takes as given the output of the other firm. A proposed deviation from this Cournot behavior in market conduct, known as the "conjectural variations" approach, is to assume that the firm takes into account an adjustment in its rival's output to its own output.[10] Eaton and Grossman (1986) also considered how the optimal trade policy was affected by different assumptions about the conjectural variation. If the domestic firm takes its rival as more aggressive than it actually is—that is, it anticipates that an increase in its own output will not induce much of a reduction in foreign output, when in fact it will—export subsidies can capture profits from a rival. This possibility exists because the domestic firm does not take into account the fact that the foreign firm actually will reduce its output if the domestic firm expands production. If, on the other hand, the domestic firm takes its rival as more passive than it actually is—that is, conjecturing a significant fall in foreign output in response to an increase in its own output, when it actually will not fall very much—then an export tax will be the appropriate policy. In this case, the domestic firm overstates its ability to dominate the market.[11] Consequently, whether a tax or a subsidy is the best policy depends crucially on the particular competitive interaction that is assumed to take place between the two firms. And the government must have better information than the private firms themselves about this market conduct in order to implement the correct policy.

Another consideration relates to the timing of the decisions. The early Brander and Spencer analysis assumed that the government acts first in credibly committing itself to a particular subsidy rate that is independent of the particular quantities chosen and that is set before the two firms choose the quantity of output to produce. Calum Carmichael (1987) reversed the sequence of events, such that the government announced the subsidy rate *after* the two firms had decided on output, and discovered that then the firm captures the entire subsidy for itself. In this case, the domestic firm chooses its price knowing that the subsidy depends upon its price and uses this

[10] The "conjectural variations" approach is now discredited owing to its logical difficulties. Strictly speaking, there is no opportunity for the firms to respond to one another in the static Cournot model because both firms choose their outputs simultaneously in a one-shot game. The Cournot model simply examines the final equilibrium and cannot consider the hypothetical adjustments that serve to establish that equilibrium.

[11] If each firm perfectly anticipates the response of its rival to changes in its own output, the so-called "consistent" conjecture, then no opportunity exists for profit shifting and there is no case for government intervention. But this is subject to the important caveat in the preceding footnote.

information in deciding what price to set. The subsidy ends up being a pure transfer to the firm with no change in the price charged to consumers, no change in output, and no change in domestic welfare since no profits have been shifted.

Avinash Dixit and Gene Grossman (1986) also suggested that the case for targeting strategic industries for promotion is weakened if these industries draw upon a common, critical factor of production. In the Brander and Spencer example, export subsidies increased domestic output by drawing upon resources from other sectors, where these resources are priced according to their marginal product and earn no rents themselves. However, if several strategic industries require a common resource in fixed supply, such as skilled labor or R&D scientists, then the promotion of one sector raises the price of this resource for other sectors and hence lowers output in those sectors. In this case, Dixit and Grossman showed that the gain to one industry could be more than offset by the losses to others. Unless the government had precise information on where the marginal gain from export subsidies was the greatest among many industries within a strategic sector, any intervention risked being detrimental.

The case for strategic trade policies is also qualified once the possibility of foreign ownership of the domestic firm (or international equity holdings more generally) is introduced. If ownership claims on a domestic firm are held by both domestic and foreign residents, government policies to maximize national wealth must then take into account the flow of dividend payments across countries. Sanghack Lee (1990) pointed out that the optimal subsidy is lower the greater is the share of foreign ownership in the industry targeted for export promotion. At some point before the limiting case, in which the domestic firm is wholly foreign-owned and the foreign firm is wholly owned by domestic residents, export subsidies for the domestic-producing firm harm national wealth.

Each of these critiques essentially take the basic Brander-Spencer framework as given and consider whether a plausible but slight modification of one assumption changes the implications for commercial policy. Almost every such modification did change the implications in quite remarkable and often unexpected ways. Taken together, these critiques proved devastating to any claim that strategic considerations establish a general presumption in favor of activist trade policies of a certain type. So many prerequisites and assumptions are required before a definitive policy conclusion can be reached that if uncertainties exist about any one of the prerequisites or assumptions, then the implications for commercial policy are ambiguous. This does not mean that the presumption in favor of free trade as the optimal policy survives intact. In most of these models of strategic competition, unilateral free trade is rarely optimal. But it is never entirely obvious what the optimal policy is. The sensitivity of these results qualifies, if not undermines, the practical case for strategic trade policies derived from theory and severely diminishes its operational value.

In spite of his earlier comments, Paul Krugman (1992, 432) later called the Brander and Spencer model an "admirable piece of modelling craftsmanship" that "generated intellectual and political heat out of all proportion to its long-run importance." This is because "theoretical weaknesses of the strategic trade policy argument help to dispel any notion that Brander and Spencer had discovered any fundamentally valid principle." The analysis of strategic trade policies, like the terms of trade argument, illustrated the possible unilateral advantages of deviating from free trade to exploit one's trading partners. Like the tariff and terms of trade debate, attention was focused on the potential harm foreign trade policies can have on domestic firms and domestic economic wealth.

But the real implication of the strategic trade policy models is not so much that, in certain restricted cases, trade interventions can be potentially beneficial. Rather, these theories reinforced the notion that trade is a form of economic interdependence. If each country ignored others and pursued policies that were apparently to its unilateral advantage, most countries would likely be worse off in the end. Cooperative agreements between countries, in which all agree to forgo the use of such policies, could potentially make each of them better off.

・ ・ ・

The Cournot duopoly framework provided an extremely simple, intuitive rationale for government intervention in support of domestic firms engaged in strategic international competition. If two firms are competing for a lucrative market, government assistance to one to drive the other from the market allows the favored firm to reap the profits that formerly went to its rival. This simple logic has appeal today, as it did during the mercantilist period of state-chartered monopoly trading companies. But when better economic foundations were sought for this simple logic, this proposition failed to prove as straightforward as promised, as numerous theoretical complications arose that severely qualified its implications for commercial policy.

Conclusion

THE PAST AND FUTURE OF FREE TRADE

ABOUT two hundred years ago, largely as a result of Adam Smith's *Wealth of Nations*, free trade achieved an intellectual status unrivaled by any other doctrine in the field of economics. Despite being subjected to intense scrutiny over the two centuries since that time, free trade has, by and large, succeeded in maintaining this special position.

The doctrinal strength of free trade is derived from a fundamental precept of economics: just as individuals can gain from the voluntary exchange of goods between them, countries also can gain from the exchange of goods across borders. The gains from trade, in turn, are derived from the division of labor, the specialization of individuals or countries in the production of certain goods. The division of labor, Adam Smith wrote, "is the necessary, though very slow and gradual, consequence of a certain propensity in human nature . . . the propensity to truck, barter, and exchange one thing for another . . . without the disposition to truck, barter, and exchange, every man must have procured to himself every necessary and conveniency of life which he wanted."[1] The benefits of specialization and trade apply at the level of the individual, the household, the community, the city, the region, and the nation. As individuals or groups or regions specialize in certain activities, the resulting larger output can be exchanged among these entities to their mutual advantage in allowing a greater fulfillment of their material wants and desires.

The centuries-old doctrine of universal economy, considered in chapter 1, should receive the credit for first elaborating on the basic idea that international commerce can increase the aggregate wealth of all countries undertaking such trade.[2] Subsequent economic thinkers have all acknowledged this essential insight and have generally recognized and appreciated the gains from trade. Indeed, the notion that countries, like individuals, stand to gain from specialization and exchange is so powerful and so fundamental that few have dared try to refute it directly. No major school of thought has argued that complete autarky is superior to any trade. Yet, while not disputing the gains from trade, most philosophers and intellectuals before Smith still believed that trade should not be free. Rather, the

---

[1] *WN*, I.ii.1, 5.

[2] Thus, the intellectual case for free trade by no means originated with Adam Smith, although it was never strongly established or generally accepted until he gave particular force to the economic arguments in its favor in the *Wealth of Nations*.

mercantilists, as noted in chapter 2, for example, held that appropriate restrictions on international commerce could develop an economy's resources to a greater extent than possible under free trade, and others justified such restrictions on noneconomic grounds.[3]

Opponents of trade restrictions, considered in chapter 3, responded by pointing out that international trade is a desirable consequence of the different valuation (measured by market prices) of things in different places, whereby goods in regions of abundance are transported to regions where they are scarce. They maintained that trade barriers would destroy profitable commercial relationships and were unlikely in themselves to generate additional wealth and employment. Above all others, Henry Martyn raised the fundamental issue of the efficiency of trade in using a country's labor to acquire goods more cheaply than otherwise possible and argued that protection would merely put labor to less productive uses.

Yet few writers argued that absolute free trade represented the best way of taking advantage of the opportunity to trade with others. Using a consistent and persuasive framework for describing economic behavior and analyzing commercial policy, Adam Smith finally established a strong presumption in favor of the economic benefits of free trade, as described in chapter 5. Having as compelling arguments against protection as he had for free trade, Smith made the endeavor of constructing a sound economic case for protection a difficult challenge. The classical economists solidified the case for free trade with the theory of comparative advantage, the bedrock on which the case for free trade stands even today.[4]

Just as economic thinkers before Adam Smith were not entirely protectionist in orientation, those after him did not accept free trade as an unquestioned dogma. Smith constructed powerful arguments in favor of free trade and against protection, but this did not completely settle the issue among economists. Since his time, economists have sought to understand the limits of the free trade doctrine and have therefore explored many cases in which protection might possibly be advantageous. For this reason, every

---

[3] Noneconomic arguments against free trade, of course, are relatively easy to muster: one declares the overriding importance of some objective (safety against foreigners, agricultural self-sufficiency, etc.) and argues that some material welfare must be sacrificed to attain that objective (although often the implication is left that no sacrifice is required at all). On the other hand, the modern theory of commercial policy, as detailed by Jagdish Bhagwati (1971), indicates that noneconomic objectives do not justify departures from free trade except when they specifically pertain to the trade sector.

[4] That this book ends its discussion of the gains from trade with the classical economists in chapter 6 is not intended to imply that there have been no further, substantial refinements to that proposition. Various explanations for the pattern of trade (such as differences in factor endowments) and various sources of the gains from trade (such as product differentiation) have been explored by economists over the past two centuries. But the basic message from this work is similar in spirit to that of Adam Smith and the classical economists.

serious qualification to free trade has come from economists writing *after* Smith established free trade as a central tenet of economics, perhaps because those most conversant with the case for free trade (if not blinded by it) are well situated to appreciate its weaknesses.[5]

The most obvious qualification relates to a weakness in the analogy about how an individual and a country benefit from trade. The analogy ignores the fact that countries are composed of different individuals, not all of whom may reap benefits from free trade, as chapters 11 and 12 on the Australian case for protection and the welfare economics of free trade make clear. Even if free trade maximizes economic wealth (and therefore, potentially at least, economic welfare), it still cannot be said that everyone will be better off unless compensation is paid to those whose income falls. This income distribution effect constitutes an important argument against free trade (perhaps being a weightier concern in actual policymaking than the other theoretical issues considered here) and poses a serious practical obstacle to the free trade doctrine. Of course, the issue of income distribution is not at all specific to commercial policy, but affects the analysis of almost every economic policy.

The most powerful economic objection to free trade ever developed is the terms of trade argument, considered in chapter 7. The analogy at the individual or firm level is that if one has significant market power, in the sense of being able to influence the market price of one's output, it may be worthwhile to exercise that market power by restricting one's output to raise its price. Similarly, if the ratio at which a country exchanges its products with the rest of the world depends upon the volume of a country's exports and imports, government restrictions on trade can potentially manipulate that ratio to bring about larger gains to that country than would otherwise be the case. This generates a unilateral motive for trade intervention; free trade may be undesirable for any individual country, even though its gains are achieved by inflicting an even greater loss on its trading partners. However, not all countries can gain if each of them acts upon this unilateral motive and imposes tariffs in an effort to improve its terms of trade at the expense of others. For this reason, international cooperation to establish free trade can dominate a situation in which all countries seek to influence their terms of trade through trade restrictions.

Protection has been proposed as being superior to free trade in many other instances as well, many of which rest upon the assumption of fundamental differences between agriculture and manufacturing (or between the primary sector and processing industries). From the seventeenth-century mercantilists up to the present day, manufacturing has been thought to have

---

[5] The infant industry argument has a very long intellectual lineage, but was never well formulated until the nineteenth century.

distinct advantages over agriculture (or certain manufacturing industries are believed to be superior to others) in ways that are not fully taken into account by the market (such as their not being reflected in market prices and therefore not recognized by market participants). These beliefs have led to the wage differential argument, the infant industry argument, the increasing returns argument, and the strategic trade policy argument.

Although several of these attempts to provide a valid argument for protection have proven successful in achieving some standing as a logical proposition, all are subject to a crucial qualification: in none of these cases is protection the optimal, or first-best, intervention to correct for the shortcomings of the market. While some measure of protection may, under certain circumstances, be a second- or third- or fourth-best improvement over the nonintervention (*laissez-faire*) equilibrium, other policy instruments dominate import restrictions in achieving the highest level of economic efficiency. Protection is therefore not desirable on economic grounds unless there are sound reasons for ruling out more direct and less costly alternative policies. As discussed in chapter 10, for example, the use of trade intervention to correct domestic wage distortions (if such distortions are shown to exist) is at best a third-best policy option when compared with other possible corrective actions, and may in some instances exacerbate the underlying distortion.

Not just for this important reason has each of these cases failed to overthrow the general presumption in favor of free trade. They have also foundered under the weight of manifold qualifications that narrow the range of circumstances under which the argument is valid. As noted in chapter 14, the strategic use of trade policy to shift rents between countries (if such rents are shown to exist) hinges critically upon numerous assumptions about competitive behavior and market structure. This case, along with the wage distortions argument, at least has the advantage of being clearly defined with a comprehensible, underlying economic structure. The infant industry argument (chapter 8) has gone for centuries without being well specified, and has persisted even though import protection does not necessarily correct the market failures thought to prevent infant industries from arising without government assistance. The vagueness surrounding the concept of increasing returns as external economies (chapter 9) has hampered resolution of the debate over its impact on the free trade doctrine.

Thus, in terms of having as strong an analytical foundation as the terms of trade rationale, these other arguments for protection are frail in comparison. The apparent scope and significance of these claims against free trade have been limited mainly by scrutinizing the underlying economic logic of each of these propositions. These propositions are entirely conceptual and theoretical in nature, even though most cases have drawn upon observable phenomena to motivate the issue they address. As such, they do not necessarily convey any indication about their practical importance or any explanation about how they might be implemented.

Despite some rather severe theoretical limitations, however, these cases do have some standing as examples of logical arguments that qualify the case for free trade. Protection could be a third-best remedy for wage divergences, strategic trade policies could shift rents between countries, and infant industries could be promoted through protection. But, in addition to the theoretical qualifications, each case has fundamental difficulties in its operational value that have served to keep the presumption in favor of free trade intact. How are true wage distortions to be identified? Where are rents in international markets to be uncovered? Which industries are suitable infants? Where precisely are external economies to be found? These questions are exceedingly difficult to answer, and exceedingly difficult for economic policy to exploit. For this reason, Alfred Marshall [(1903) 1926, 394] argued that free trade is an advantageous expedient because "it is *not* a device, but the absence of any device. A device contrived to deal with any set of conditions must become obsolete when they change. The simplicity and naturalness of Free Trade—that is, the absence of any device—may continue to outweigh the series of different small gains which could be obtained by any manipulation of tariffs, however scientific and astute."

Regardless of this insightful advice, one might think that empirical evidence could provide additional, perhaps crucial, information for determining just how important, in terms of practical significance or empirical magnitude, a possible exception to free trade might be. Yet appeals to empirical evidence as a way of arbitrating these free trade controversies have been almost completely absent, and what empirical evidence there is has been unhelpful in making arguments against free trade more compelling. Empirical evidence has either played virtually no role (as in the wage divergences, increasing returns, Australian, and Keynesian arguments) or played a small and unproductive role (as in the terms of trade, infant industry, and strategic trade policy arguments) in evaluating the substance of an economic argument for protection. Instead, a conceptual debate over economic logic has been used to resolve each controversy, regardless of the supposed empirical importance of the issue at hand (although its supposed empirical importance helps determine how much theoretical attention it gets).[6]

---

[6] That much of science is conceptual rather than empirical has important implications for the study of the history of science. As Larry Laudan (1977, 47) notes, "Empiricist philosophies of science (including those of Popper, Carnap, and Reichenbach) and even less strident empiricist methodologies (including those of Lakatos, Collingwood, and Feyerabend)—all of which imagine that theory choice in science should be governed exclusively by empirical

Consider the example of the most important exception to free trade, the terms of trade argument. Mill and Torrens developed the theoretical reasoning behind this case for protection, but subsequent empirical evidence has contributed little in determining the significance of this effect in terms of quantitative magnitudes. The two modern quantitative methods of assessing the impact of tariffs on the terms of trade are the general equilibrium "reciprocal demand" approach and the partial equilibrium "elasticities" approach. The general equilibrium approach has consistently generated substantial terms of trade effects from any unilateral tariff change; for example, John Whalley (1985, 182) found that any major trading region embarking upon a unilateral tariff reduction suffers a loss in national welfare because adverse terms of trade effects swamp any efficiency gain.[7] These effects have been strikingly dominant in general equilibrium simulations, even arising when smaller countries with high trade barriers undertake tariff reforms.

Subsequent research revealed that these findings were driven by the assumption that traded products are differentiated by country of origin, an assumption often required to prevent complete specialization in these computable models. This differentiation confers significant market power to countries even if they comprise a very small share of the world market in any commodity. In fact, according to Drucilla Brown (1987, 512, 523), "If the elasticity of substitution [between domestic and foreign goods] implies that the foreign demand elasticity is close to unity in the initial equilibrium, then no matter how high the initial level of protection, the model will *always* indicate that the current tariff is smaller than the optimal tariff." Furthermore, these effects are not mitigated by increasing the elasticity of substitution between domestic and foreign goods in consumption. Brown concludes that "unilateral tariff reductions will not appear to be welfare-improving even for a small country with a very high level of protection . . . alternative specifications of the import demand elasticities which retain the assumption of national product differentiation are not likely to materially alter the overwhelming importance of changes in the terms of trade for the welfare conclusions of policy analysis."

The partial equilibrium approach uses econometric estimates of the price elasticities of export and import demand and supply to calculate the optimal tariff based on standard Bickerdike-type formulae. Conventional esti-

---

considerations—simply fail to come to terms with the role of conceptual problems in science, and accordingly find themselves too impoverished to explain or reconstruct much of the actual course of science."

[7] The applied general equilibrium models calibrate equations describing an economy to a detailed benchmark data set and then, after specifying particular relationships about the substitution possibilities in production and consumption, predict the effects of tariff changes on trade and national income.

mates almost invariably find that export demand is highly inelastic (usually in the range of −0.5 to −1.0, and assumed to be constant), which in turn implies extremely high optimal tariffs (often as high as 100 percent). What is particularly incredible is that such elasticity estimates are found even for countries which almost assuredly lack any significant leverage over their terms of trade. These elasticity estimates may not, in fact, be accurate empirical representations of the international market, but may arise from a particular econometric specification of the estimated trade equations. Premachandra Athukorala and James Riedel (1991, 140) report that "conventional estimates [of trade elasticities] do not properly test the small country assumption [that a country cannot influence its terms of trade]; indeed, they preclude the small country assumption finding by the way they estimate the parameters of export demand." Alternative specifications that test for the "small country" hypothesis, in particular that variations in export volume do not affect export or world prices for a commodity, have often found that it cannot be rejected, even when the standard approach suggests inelastic foreign demand.[8]

Therefore, although many quantitative studies indicate that tariffs could have potentially significant terms of trade effects, these conclusions are based on models whose underlying structure or methods tend to generate such findings. Thus, there is reason to be skeptical about the degree to which these methods reflect true economic relationships and suspicious of whether these methods demonstrate the practical importance of the terms of trade argument, let alone how to best implement such a policy. Our conceptual and theoretical knowledge in economics, having been built up over the centuries, is vastly greater than our practical or empirical knowledge, which has matured only in recent years.

Other free trade controversies are even less amenable to empirical examination. The widely debated infant industry argument has been evaluated primarily on the basis of case studies, which usually fail to provide any information on the conditions under which infant industry policies will succeed or not or any evidence on the social rates of return to government protection of such industries. Efforts to confront the theory of strategic trade policy with data have relied almost exclusively upon calibrated simulations, the outcome of which reflect the specific structure of the model and the assumptions that are embodied in that structure, rather than documenting the existence of rents. Intersectoral wage differentials are readily observable, but as empirical phenomena are not so easily classified as a genuine market distortion or a market-generated divergence. Increasing returns to scale as a form of external economies is the subject of ongoing

---

[8] James Riedel's (1988) tests of the small country assumption for Hong Kong cannot be rejected even though conventional elasticity estimates point to an inelastic foreign demand for its exports.

conceptual debates with few empirical attempts at discerning their presence, uncovering their effects, or determining their implications for trade policy.

The absence of empirical considerations in the controversies partly reflects the only recent development of advanced tools for undertaking such studies. It also partly reflects a natural barrier to our knowledge, the extreme difficulty of reaching informed and precise judgments about these elusive economic phenomena. But although empirical considerations have yet to serve as a primary arbitrator in any of these controversies does not mean that the case for free trade is won or lost at the conceptual level alone. The economic performance of different countries operating under different trade regimes has provided some important evidence on the effects of pursuing liberal trade policies. Studies by the World Bank (1987) and others have shown (in a somewhat impressionistic way) that countries with policies more "open" to the world market perform better than others that do not, although free trade may be correlated with other market-oriented economic policies or institutions. More easily documented are the actual distortions brought about by protectionist trade policies, as the influential study by Ian Little, Tibor Scitovsky, and Maurice Scott (1970) did for developing countries.

Yet as is appropriate to a book on the conceptual aspects of free trade, one should recognize that free trade commands respect among economists largely because of its continuing theoretical attractiveness. Indeed, support for free trade among economists has waxed and waned since the time of Adam Smith much more because of changes in the perceived strength and credibility of the economic analysis behind free trade than because of any noticeable changes in the evidence from country experiences. Theoretical developments are taken seriously by economists, and the intellectual framework behind free trade matters for its vitality as an economic proposition.

In the early to mid-nineteenth century, for example, the classical economists strongly supported free trade as a theoretical proposition because the theory of comparative costs seemed to raise it to an unprecedented position of scientific verity.[9] The classical economists and early neo-classical econ-

---

[9] Frank Graham (1934, 58–59) aptly described the reasoning behind this view in explaining that comparative advantage "is the universally valid analysis underlying the argument for free trade. Time, place, and circumstance are irrelevant thereto. Whether a country is rich or poor, big or little, old or new, with or without high standards of living, agricultural, industrial, or mixed, makes no difference. It is a matter of mathematics, quite independent of environment, that there is an *inherent* gain in the specialization along the lines of *comparative* competence which unshackled trade tends to develop. There is no possible refutation of this analysis. Advocates of a restrictive commercial policy must, in logic, accept it as a fact and attempt to show that the gain may be outweighed by economic or other considerations of superior

omists took free trade as axiomatic. Writing in 1869, William Stanley Jevons (1883, 181–82) argued that

> freedom of trade may be regarded as a fundamental axiom of political economy; and though even axioms may be mistaken, and any different views concerning them must not be prohibited, yet we need not be frightened into questioning our axioms. We may welcome bonâ fide investigation into the state of trade, and the causes of the present depression, but we can no more expect to have our opinions on free trade altered by such an investigation than the Mathematical Society would expect to have the axioms of Euclid disproved during the investigation of a complex problem.[10]

Since the mid-nineteenth century, statements by economists about free trade as a logical proposition have not been so confident, but have vacillated with the reassessment of existing doctrine that naturally arises with the development and evaluation of new ideas. As the terms of trade and infant industry exceptions to free trade were identified by Torrens and Mill and gradually accepted by others, economists became more careful and cautious in considering the theoretical arguments for free trade. Henry Sidgwick (1887, 488) noted that the assurance with which economists had spoken about free trade earlier in the nineteenth century had vanished because "this old system of belief in the harmony of each industrial class with the interest of the whole community [that is, the *laissez-faire* doctrine] has lost its hold on the mind of our age: and that the need of governmental interference to promote production is admitted by economists generally." Therefore, Sidgwick argued, "the fashion which lingers of treating the protectionist as a fool who cannot see—if he is a knave who will not see—what is as plain as a proof of Euclid, is really an illogical survival of a mere fragment of what was once a coherent doctrine."

Several years later, Frank Taussig (1905, 30–31) used his presidential address before the American Economic Association to echo the view that confidence in free trade among economists had eroded. "So far as the doctrine of free trade is concerned," he noted, "enthusiasm has been supplanted by cautious weighing or open doubt. . . . Free trade would seem to be the waning doctrine . . . [and] has no more sanctity or authority than any

---

importance. . . . The *presumption* is always in favor of free trade, since the gain therefrom is certain, and the loss, if any, dependent upon incidental circumstance. This presumption is rebuttable but it is ever present; and, in this sense, the classical economists were right in insisting that free trade is a ubiquitous and timeless principle. Other things being equal, it will enable people to have more goods of every kind than would otherwise be possible."

[10] "When I was asked . . . to write something in defence of Free Trade," the English barrister T. H. Farrer (1886, 1) wrote with earnest puzzlement, "it seemed to me . . . as if I had been asked to prove Euclid."

other part of the obsolete system of natural liberty, and the advantages or disadvantages of tariff restrictions are to be coolly weighed for each country itself, in the light of specific experience."

Half a century later, reacting partly to Keynes's assault on the notion that markets function well in adjusting to preserve full employment, John Hicks ([1951] 1959, 41–42) declared that free trade

> has been called into question, not only by changes in circumstances, but also by changes in economic thinking. The doctrine which used to derive much of its strength from its association with accepted economic theory, has lost much of that strength too. Free trade is no longer accepted by economists, even as an ideal, in the way that it used to be . . . the preponderance of economic opinion is no longer so certainly as it was on the free trade side.

Nearly forty years later, reflecting the advent of strategic trade policy and the renewed appreciation of increasing returns, Paul Krugman (1987, 131–32) announced that "the case for free trade is currently more in doubt than at any time since the 1817 publication of Ricardo's *Principles of Political Economy* . . . because of changes that have recently taken place in the theory of international trade itself," changes that were "substantial and radical." "Free trade is not passé, but it is an idea that has irretrievably lost its innocence," he stated. "Its status has changed from optimum to reasonable rule of thumb . . . it can never again be asserted as the policy that economic theory tells us is always right."

Of course, one should resist viewing these statements as a linear progression in which the case for free trade has been diminishing steadily since 1776. With the advantage of hindsight, we can see that each of these rather gloomy and pessimistic statements about free trade reflects the same phenomena. Each of these commentators was reflecting in the midst of a period in which some new theories had arisen which appeared to limit the generality of the free trade doctrine. After these new insights about protection came to the forefront of economic discussion, a period of reassessment necessarily followed and free trade lost some of its shine. Yet with time, the limitations (often severe) of these objections to free trade became more apparent. Consequently, despite the abundant and repeated criticisms that have been made about the theoretical case for free trade, the broad presumption behind free trade has not been substantially undercut, but has remained intact.

None of the economists above, for example, was prepared to argue that economic analysis had changed so significantly that the economic basis for supporting free trade could no longer be considered strong. While acknowledging the several "qualifications of one sort or another" to free trade, Taussig (1905, 59, 63–65) maintained that "at best, they suggest only still further qualifications and still other possible exceptions, and they leave intact the core of the classic theory of international trade. That theory, in its essentials, holds its own without serious rival." Indeed, Taussig concluded that "the fundamental principle of free trade has been little shaken by all the discussion and all the untoward events of the past half-century," although "its application is not so easy and simple as was thought by the economists of half-a-century ago." The reason was clear:

> The essense of the doctrine of free trade is that *prima facie* international trade brings a gain and that restrictions on it presumably bring a loss. Departures from this principle, though by no means impossible of justification, need to prove their case; and if made in view of the pressure of opposing principles, they are a matter for regret. In this sense, the doctrine of free trade, however widely rejected in the world of politics, holds its own in the sphere of the intellect.

For his part, Hicks (1959, 42) cautioned that "the positive argument for Free Trade is as valid as ever; what has happened is that the exceptions have grown up and, in the minds of many, have overshadowed the positive argument. We can, I think, grant that these exceptions (many of which have long been familiar) were given too little weight in the past; but we should be wary of giving them too much weight now."

In reaffirming their support for free trade, Sidgwick and Krugman subtly shifted grounds away from an economic and toward a political argument for free trade. Sidgwick (1887, 489) argued that "the gain that protection might bring in particular cases is always likely to be more than counterbalanced by the general bad effects of encouraging producers and traders to look to government for aid in industrial crises and dangers, instead of relying on their own foresight, ingenuity and energy." And according to Krugman (1987, 143), the contemporary case for free trade is "not the old argument that free trade is optimal because markets are efficient," but rather "it is a sadder but wiser argument for free trade as a rule of thumb in a world whose politics are as imperfect as its markets. . . . To abandon the free trade principle in pursuit of the gains from sophisticated intervention could therefore open the door to adverse political consequences that would outweigh the potential gains."

These last statements illustrate another important regularity in these free trade controversies: even in accepting a theoretical rationale in which free trade does not maximize economic wealth, economists often hasten to add that this does not constitute a positive case for trade intervention. Even if a positive case for free trade cannot be established, there are strong practical arguments against protection. For decades economists have relied upon three such arguments against protection, arguments that implicitly accept that such protection could increase wealth. These arguments are somewhat analogous to those made against other policy changes and noted by Albert O. Hirschman in his book *The Rhetoric of Reaction*. Hirschman (1991, 7) observes that opponents of a political, economic, or social change (or "reform," as he puts it) tend not to oppose outright the stated objective of the reformers, but "they will endorse it, sincerely or otherwise, but then attempt to demonstrate that the action proposed or undertaken is ill conceived." He goes on to analyze three categories of argument that have been used time and time again to oppose change: perversity, futility, and jeopardy.[11] Similarly, the three lines of defense economists have developed against proposals for import protection, all of which implicitly admit that an economic case for protection exists in principle, are: circumstances, politics, and retaliation.

The first line of defense—circumstances—concedes that there may be a theoretical case for protection on certain grounds, but that such protection would be inappropriate to the particular circumstances under consideration, or that the case does not apply under current conditions. In the turn of the century British debate over reciprocity, for example, Marshall ([1890] 1925, 263n) stated that "arguments of some force can be given for the belief that some of these schemes, if they could practically be carried out under certain conditions, might on the whole do a little more good than harm to England." But, he quickly added, "there seems at present to be no probability that the proposed conditions will be realized in practice." In his discussion of infant industries, to take another example, Taussig often granted that there had been a plausible case for such protection in the early nineteenth-century United States, but that these conditions and circumstances had long since past.

The second line of defense—politics—concedes that there is a theoretical case for protection on certain grounds, and concedes that protection is appropriate to the circumstances at hand, but argues that the political process cannot be presumed to produce the right kind of intervention, and could even make things worse. Adam Smith (1987, 272) once stated that trade regulations "may, I think, be demonstrated to be in every case a complete piece of dupery, by which the interests of the State and the nation is constantly sacrificed to that of some particular class of traders." This skepticism, if not cynicism, of government's handling of trade policy has persisted to this day (for some very good reasons) and this argument has shouldered much of the burden in the public defense of free trade. Never one to dismiss an argument for protection out of hand, Sidgwick (1885,

---

[11] "According to the *perversity* thesis, any purposive action to improve some feature of the political, social, or economic order only serves to exacerbate the condition one wishes to remedy. The *futility* thesis holds that attempts at social transformation will be unavailing, that they will simply fail to 'make a dent.' Finally, the *jeopardy* thesis argues that the cost of the proposed change or reform is too high as it endangers some previous, precious accomplishment."

19–20) believed that "the decisive argument against [protection] is rather the political consideration that no actual government is competent for this difficult and delicate task."[12] Reiterating this view, F. Y. Edgeworth (1894, 48) stated what many economists a century later continued to believe, that "protection might procure economic advantage in certain cases, if there was a government wise enough to discriminate those cases, and strong enough to confine itself to them; but this condition is very unlikely to be fulfilled."[13]

The third, and final, line of defense—retaliation—concedes that there is a theoretical case for protection on certain grounds, concedes that protection is appropriate to the circumstances at hand, and concedes that there is a reasonable chance that the political process can implement the right kind of policies, but argues that such a step would risk foreign retaliation. Such foreign retaliations are suggested not only to be likely (according to Adam Smith, "nations accordingly seldom fail to retaliate in this manner"), but such reprisals would erase or undo any benefits that could be accomplished by intervention. Even if reprisals are not made in a hostile way, Sidgwick (1887, 489) argued that the demonstration effect of using protection would make it undesirable "since the wisest protection in any one country would tend in various ways to encourage unwise protection elsewhere."

Therefore, even when economists fail to make a positive case for free trade, they have a reservoir of other, noneconomic arguments against protection, some more convincing than others. Yet economists should not perhaps rest their popular case for free trade too much on "government failure" if that means they too readily ignore the deeper problems that afflict even what appear to be theoretically valid arguments for protection. A closer look at each free trade controversy reveals that there are significant shortcomings to each proposed argument against free trade. Perhaps the most glaring example is that of the infant industry argument, which economists, particularly in the nineteenth and early twentieth centuries, bent over back-

---

[12] Sidgwick (1883, 485–86) maintained that "when the matter is considered from the point of view of abstract theory, it is easy to show that protection, under certain not improbable circumstances, would yield a direct economic gain to the protecting country: but that from the difficulty of securing in any actual government sufficient wisdom, strength, and singleness of aim to introduce protection only so far as it is advantageous to the community and to withdraw it inexorably so soon as the public interests require its withdrawal, it is practically best for a statesman to adhere to the broad and simple rule of 'taxation for revenue only.'"

[13] This is especially the case because most arguments for protection are second-best arguments. As Harry Johnson (1970, 101) once noted, "The fundamental problem is that, as with all second-best arguments, determination of the conditions under which a second-best policy actually leads to an improvement in social welfare requires detailed theoretical and empirical investigation by a first-best economist. Unfortunately, policy is generally formulated by fourth-best economists and administered by third-best economists; it is therefore very unlikely that a second-best welfare optimum will result from policies based on second-best arguments."

ward to accept in an effort to be fair-minded about the possibility of a positive government role. Yet a specific theoretical rationale for infant industry protection was never worked out and sound cost-benefit analyses of such protection was not undertaken until much later.

The doctrine of free trade has been subject to deep and searching scrutiny for many decades. The debate over the economic merits of free trade is an ongoing and never ending one that exhibits the richness and subtlety that can occur in the course of the evolution of economic analysis. The doctrine of free trade will continue to experience changes as new theories and new ideas confront and challenge our understanding of the theory of commercial policy. Yet if the historical experiences described here continue, free trade will remain one of the most durable and robust propositions that economic analysis has to offer for the conduct of economic policy.

REFERENCES

Author's Note: As the subject matter of most chapters is quite distinct with little overlap (many may be read in isolation), the references in this bibliography have been arranged by chapter. This provides the reader with a consolidated list of references on each chapter topic. However, the several works listed below are referred to consistently throughout the book.

Haberler, Gottfried. *The Theory of International Trade*. London: Wm. Hodge & Co., 1936.

Schumpeter, Joseph A. *History of Economic Analysis*. New York: Oxford University Press, 1954.

Smith, Adam. *An Inquiry into the Nature and Causes of the Wealth of Nations*. Edited by R. H. Campbell and A. S. Skinner. Oxford: Clarendon Press, 1979. The Glasgow Edition of the Works and Correspondence of Adam Smith.

———. *The Correspondence of Adam Smith*. Edited by E. C. Mossner and I. S. Ross, 2d ed. Oxford: Clarendon Press, 1987. The Glasgow Edition of the Works and Correspondence of Adam Smith.

Viner, Jacob. *Studies in the Theory of International Trade*. New York: Harper Bros., 1937.

INTRODUCTION

Bhagwati, Jagdish, and T. N. Srinivasan. "Optimal Intervention to Achieve Non-Economic Objectives." *Review of Economic Studies* 36 (January 1969): 27–38.

Frey, Bruno S., W. W. Pommerehne, F. Schneider, and G. Gilbert. "Consensus and Dissension Among Economists: An Empirical Inquiry." *American Economic Review* 74 (December 1984): 986–94.

Johnson, Harry G. *Aspects of the Theory of Tariffs*. Cambridge: Harvard University Press, 1971.

Taussig, Frank W. "The Present Position of the Doctrine of Free Trade." *Publications of the American Economic Association*, 3d ser. 6 (February 1905): 29–65.

CHAPTER ONE
EARLY FOREIGN TRADE DOCTRINES

Aristotle. *The 'Art' of Rhetoric*. Leob Classical Library, 1926.

———. *Politics*. Leob Classical Library, 1932.

Calvin, John. *Commentary on the Book of the Prophet Isaiah*. Translated by W. Pringle. Grand Rapids: Eerdmans Pub., 1953.

Cicero. *De Officiis*. Leob Classical Library, 1913.

D'Arms, John H. *Commerce and Social Standing in Ancient Rome*. Cambridge: Harvard University Press, 1981.

de Roover, Raymond. "The Scholastic Attitude toward Trade and Entrepreneurship." In *Business, Banking, and Economic Thought*. Chicago: University of Chicago Press, 1974.

de Vattel, Emmerich. *Le Droit Des Gens ou Principes de la Loi Naturelle* (1758) [The Law of Nations or the Principles of Natural Law]. Translated by Charles G. Fenwick. Washington: Carnegie Institute, 1916.

Dudden, F. Homes. *The Life and Times of St. Ambrose*. Oxford: Clarendon Press, 1935.

Gentili, Alberico. *De Jure Belli Libri Tres* (1612) [The Three Books on the Law of War]. Edited by John C. Rolfe. Oxford: Clarendon Press, 1933.

Grotius, Hugo. *De Jure Praedae Commentarius* (1604) [Commentaries on the Law of Prize and Booty]. Translated by G. L. Williams. Oxford: Clarendon Press, 1950.

————. *Mare Liberum* (1608) [The Freedom of the Seas]. Edited by James B. Scott. New York: Oxford University Press, 1916.

————. *De Jure Belli Ac Pacis Libri Tres* (1625) [The Law of War and Peace]. Translated by F. W. Kelsey. Oxford: Clarendon Press, 1925.

Hasebroek, Johannes. *Trade and Politics in Ancient Greece*. London: G. Bell & Sons, 1933.

Horace. *The Odes and Epodes of Horace*. Translated by J. P. Clancy. Chicago: University of Chicago Press, 1960.

Langholm, Odd. *Economics in the Medieval Schools*. Leiden: E. J. Brill, 1992.

Luther, Martin. "To the Christian Nobility of the German Nation (1520)." In *Luther's Works*, edited by Helmut T. Lehmann, vol. 44. Philadelphia: Fortress Press, 1966.

O'Brien, George. *An Essay on Mediaeval Economic Teaching*. London: Longmans, Green & Co., 1920.

Origen. *Contra Celsum*. Leob Classical Library, 1953.

Plato. *Laws*. Leob Classical Library, 1914.

————. *The Republic*. Leob Classical Library, 1930.

Philo. "On the Cherubim." In *Philo*. Leob Classical Library, 1929.

Pliny. "Panegyricus." In *Letters and Panegyricus*. Leob Classical Library, 1969.

Plutarch. "On Whether Water or Fire is More Useful." In *Plutarch's Moralia*, vol. 12. Loeb Classical Library, 1927.

Pufendorf, Samuel. *De Jure Naturae et Gentium Libri Octo* (1660) [The Law of Nature and Nations]. Translated by C. H. Oldfield and W. A. Oldfield, vol. 2. Oxford: Clarendon Press, 1934.

St. Ambrose. "Creation." In *Hexameron*, translated by J. Savage, *The Fathers of the Church*. New York: The Fathers of the Church, Inc., 1961.

St. Augustine. *Saint Augustine: Exposition on the Book of Psalms*, edited by Philip Schaff, vol. VII, *A Select Library of the Nicene and Post-Nicene Fathers of the Christian Church*. New York: Brown Bros., 1888.

St. Basil. "On Hexameron, Homily 4." In *Exegetic Homilies*, translated by A. Way, *Fathers of the Church*, vol. 46. Washington: Catholic University Press, 1963.

St. John Chrysostom. "Discours sur la Componction (2)." In *Oeuvres Completes de S. Jean Chrysostom*, vol. 1, edited by M. L'abbe J. Bareille. Paris: Libraaire de Louis Vives, 1874.

St. Thomas Aquinas. *De Regno, Ad Regem Cypri* [On Kingship, to the King of Cyprus]. Translated by G. B. Phelan. Toronto: Pontifical Institute of Mediaeval Studies, 1944.

―――. *Summa Theologica*. New York: Benziger Bros., 1947.

Seneca. *Naturale Quaestiones*. Leob Classical Library, 1972.

Suarez, Francisco. *De Legibus, Ac Deo Legislatore* (1612). In *Selections from Three Works of Francisco Suarez, S.J.*, vol. 2. Oxford: Clarendon Press, 1934.

Theodoret. *On Divine Providence*. Translated by T. Halton, *Ancient Christian Writers*, no. 49. New York: Newman Press, 1988.

Viner, Jacob. *The Role of the Providence in the Social Order*. Princeton: Princeton University Press, 1976.

―――. *Religious Thought and Economic Society*. Durham, N.C.: Duke University Press, 1978.

―――. *Essays on the Intellectual History of Economics*. Edited by Douglas A. Irwin. Princeton: Princeton University Press, 1991.

Wheeler, Marcus. "Self-Sufficiency and the Greek City," *Journal of the History of Ideas* 16 (June 1955): 416–20.

Wolff, Christian. *Jus Gentium Methodo Scientifica Pertractatum* (1764) [The Law of Nations Treated According to a Scientific Method]. Translated by Joseph H. Drake. Oxford: Clarendon Press, 1934.

Xenephon. *Cyropaedia*. Leob Classical Library, 1914.

―――. "Oeconomicus." In *Memorabilia and Oeconomicus*. Leob Classical Library, 1918.

CHAPTER TWO
THE ENGLISH MERCANTILIST LITERATURE

Anderson, Gary, and Robert Tollison. "Sir James Stewart as the Apothesis of Mercantilism and His Relation to Adam Smith." *Southern Economic Journal* 50 (October 1984): 456–68.

Appleby, Joyce O. *Economic Thought and Ideology in Seventeenth-Century England*. Princeton: Princeton University Press, 1978.

Asgill, John. *A Brief Answer*. London: J. Roberts, 1719.

[Battie, John]. *Merchant's Remonstration*. London: R. H., 1644.

[Bland, John]. *Trade Revived*. London: T. Holmwood, 1659.

Brewster, Sir Francis. *Essays on Trade and Navigation*. London: T. Cockerill, 1695.

Cantillon, Richard. *Essai sur la Nature du Commerce en Général* (1755) [Essay on the Nature of Trade in General]. Edited by Henry Higgs. London: Macmillan, 1931.

Cary, John. *An Essay on the State of England in Relation to Its Trade*. Bristol: W. Bonny, 1695.

Child, Josiah. *A New Discourse of Trade*. London: J. Everingham, 1693.

Clayton, David. *A Short System of Trade*. London: Tookey, 1719.

Coats, A. W. "Mercantilism: Economic Ideas, History, Policy." In *On the History of Economic Thought*. New York: Routledge, 1992.

Coke, Roger. *A Discourse of Trade*. London: H. Brome, 1670.

Coke, Roger. *England's Improvements.* London: H. Brome, 1675.

Cole, Charles W. *French Mercantilist Doctrines Before Colbert.* New York: Smith, 1931.

Coleman, D. C. "Mercantilism Revisited." *Historical Journal* 23 (December 1980): 773–91.

de Roover, Raymond. "Scholastic Economics: Survival and Lasting Influence from the Sixteenth Century to Adam Smith." *Quarterly Journal of Economics* 69 (May 1955): 161–90.

Defoe, Daniel. *Of Royall Educacion.* Edited by Karl D. Bülbring. London: D. Nutt, 1895.

Fortrey, Samuel. *England's Interest and Improvement.* London: J. Field, 1663.

[Gee, Joshua]. *The Trade and Navigation of Great Britain Considered.* London: Buckley, 1729.

Grampp, William D. "The Liberal Elements of English Mercantilism." *Quarterly Journal of Economics* 66 (November 1952): 465–501.

Graunt, John. *Natural and Political Observations upon the Bills of Mortality,* 5th ed. London: J. Martyn, 1676.

Grice-Hutchinson, Marjorie. *Early Economic Thought in Spain, 1177–1740.* Boston: George Allen & Unwin, 1978.

Hutchison, Terence. *Before Adam Smith: The Emergence of Political Economy, 1662–1776.* Cambridge: Basil Blackwell, 1988.

[Janssen, Theodore]. *General Maxims in Trade.* London: S. Buckley, 1713.

Johnson, E.A.J. "British Mercantilist Doctrines Concerning the 'Exportation of Work' and 'Foreign-Paid Incomes.'" *Journal of Political Economy* 40 (December 1932): 750–70.

King, Charles, ed. *The British Merchant.* London: J. Darby, 1721.

Magnusson, Lars. "Mercantilism and 'Reform' Mercantilism: The Rise of Economic Discourse in Sweden during the Eighteenth Century." *History of Political Economy* 19 (Fall 1987): 415–33.

———. *Mercantilism: The Shaping of an Economic Language.* New York: Routledge, 1994.

Malynes, Gerard. *Treatise of the Canker of England's Commonwealth.* London: W. Johnes, 1601.

———. *The Maintenance of Free Trade.* London: W. Sheffard, 1622.

———. *The Center of the Circle of Commerce.* London: W. Jones, 1623.

[Milles, Thomas]. *The Customer's Apology.* 1599?

Misselden, Edward. *Free Trade. Or the Meanes to Make Trade Florish.* London: J. Legatt, 1622.

———. *The Circle of Commerce.* London: J. Dawson, 1623.

[Mun, Thomas]. *A Discourse of Trade.* London: J. Pyper, 1621.

Mun, Thomas. *England's Treasure by Forraign Trade.* London: T. Clark, 1664.

[Papillon, Thomas]. *The East-India-Trade: A Most Profitable Trade to the Kingdom.* London: n.p., 1680.

Paxton, P. *A Discourse Concerning the Nature, Advantage, and Improvement of Trade.* London: R. Wilkin, 1704.

Petty, William. *Political Arithmetick.* London: R. Clavel, 1690.

[Petyt, William]. *Britannia Languens, or a Discourse of Trade.* London: T. Dring, 1680.

Pollexfen, John. *A Discourse of Trade, Coyn and Paper Credit.* London: B. Aylmer, 1697. (*a*)

————. *England and East-India Inconsistent in their Manufactures.* London: n.p., 1697. (*b*)

Postlethwayt, Malachy. *Britain's Commercial Interest Explained and Improved.* London: P. Brown, 1757.

Price, W. H. "The Origin of the Phrase 'Balance of Trade.'" *Quarterly Journal of Economics* 20 (November 1906): 157–67.

[Reynell, Carew]. *A Necessary Companion or, the English Interest Discovered and Promoted.* London: W. Budden, 1685.

Roberts, Lewes. *The Treasure of Traffike.* London: N. Bourne, 1641.

Robinson, Henry. *England's Safety in Trades Encreases.* London: N. Bourne, 1641.

Skinner, Andrew S. "Sir James Steuart: Author of a System." *Scottish Journal of Political Economy* 28 (February 1981): 20–42.

[Smith, Simon]. *The Golden Fleece: or The trade, interest, and well-being of Great Britain considered.* London: R. Viney, 1736.

[Smith, Sir Thomas]. *A Discourse of the Commonweal of This Realm of England* (1581). Edited by Mary Dewar. Charlottesville: The University Press of Virginia, 1969.

Sperling, J. "The International Payments Mechanism in the Seventeenth and Eighteenth Centuries." *Economic History Review*, 2d ser. 14 (April 1962): 446–68.

Steuart, James. *An Inquiry into the Principles of Political Oeconomy.* London: A. Millar & T. Cadell, 1767. References are made to the Scottish Economics Society edition edited by Andrew S. Skinner. Edinburgh: Oliver & Boyd, 1966.

Suviranta, Bruno. *The Theory of the Balance of Trade in England.* Helsingfors, Finland: privately printed, 1923; New York: A. M. Kelley, 1967.

van Tijn, Th. "Dutch Economic Thought in the Seventeenth Century." In *Economic Thought in the Netherlands: 1650–1950*, edited by J. van Daal, and A. Heertje. Aldershot: Avebury, 1992.

Wilkes, Richard C. "The Development of Mercantilist Economic Thought." In *Pre-Classical Economic Thought*, edited by S. Todd Lowry. Boston: Kluwer, 1987.

Wood, William. *A Survey of Trade.* London: Wilkins, 1718.

Wu, Chi-Yuen. *An Outline of International Price Theories.* London: Routledge, 1939.

CHAPTER THREE
THE EMERGENCE OF FREE TRADE THOUGHT

[Barbon, Nicholas]. *A Discourse of Trade.* London: T. Milbourn, 1690.

[Bland, John]. *Trade Revived.* London: T. Holmwood, 1659.

Brewster, Francis. *Essays on Trade and Navigation.* London: Cockerill, 1695.

Cary, John. *An Essay on the State of England in Relation to its Trade.* Bristol: W. Bonny, 1695.

Child, Josiah. *A New Discourse of Trade*. London: J. Everingham, 1693.

Clayton, David. *A Short System of Trade*. London: Tait, 1719.

Coke, Roger. *A Discourse of Trade*. London: H. Brome, 1670.

Davenant, Charles. *Essay upon Ways and Means of Supplying the War*. London: J. Tonson, 1695.

[Davenant, Charles]. *An Essay on the East-India-Trade*. London: n.p., 1696.

Davenant, Charles. *Discourses on the Public Revenues, and the Trade of England*. Part 1. London: J. Knapton, 1698.

de Roover, Raymond. "Monopoly Theory Prior to Adam Smith: A Revision." *Quarterly Journal of Economics* 65 (November 1951): 492–524.

[Decker, Matthew]. *Serious Considerations on the Several High Duties*. London: Palairet, 1743.

———. *An Essay on the Causes of the Decline of the Foreign Trade*. London: Brotherton, 1744.

Fortrey, Samuel. *England's Interest and Improvement*. London: J. Field, 1663.

[Gardner]. *Some Reflections on a Pamphlet, entitled England and East India Inconsistent in their Manufactures*. London: n.p., 1697.

Gervaise, Issac. *The System or Theory of the Trade of the World*. London: H. Woodfall, 1720.

Great Necessity and Advantage of Preserving our own Manufactures. London: T. Newborough, 1697.

Heckscher, Eli. *Mercantilism*. Translated by M. Shapiro. London: George Allen & Unwin, 1935.

Hume, David. *Political Discourses*. Edinburgh: R. Fleming, 1752.

Johnson, Thomas. *A Plea for Free-mens Liberties*. London: T. Johnson, 1646.

[Kayll, R.]. *The Trades Increase*. London: N. Okes, 1615.

Letwin, William. "The Authorship of Sir Dudley North's *Discourses on Trade*." *Economica* 18 (February 1951): 35–56.

Macleod, Christine. "Henry Martyn and the authorship of 'Considerations upon the East India Trade.'" *Bulletin of the Institute of Historical Research* 56 (November 1983): 222–29.

[Martyn, Henry]. *Considerations upon the East India trade*. London: A. & J. Churchill, 1701.

[Massie, Joseph.] *The Proposal*. London: J. Shuckburgh, 1757.

Misselden, Edward. *Free Trade. Or the Meanes to make Trade Florish*. London: J. Legatt, 1622.

North, Dudley. *Discourses upon Trade*. London: T. Basset, 1691.

Parker, Henry. *Of a Free Trade*. London: R. Bostock, 1648.

Pollexfen, John. *England and East-India Inconsistent in their Manufactures*. London: n.p., 1697.

Roberts, Lewes. *The Treasure of Traffike*. London: N. Bourne, 1641.

Thomas, P. J. *Mercantilism and the East India Trade*. London: P. S. King, 1926.

Tryon, Thomas. *Some General Consideration Offered*. London: J. Harris, 1698.

Vanderlint, Jacob. *Money Answers All Things*. London: T. Cox, 1734.

Violet, Thomas. *The Advancement of Merchandize*. London: W. Du-Gard, 1651.

———. *Mysteries and Secrets of Trade and Mint-affairs*. London: W. Du-Gard, 1653.

Waddell, D. "Charles Davenant (1656–1714)—A Biographical Sketch." *Economic History Review*, 2d ser., 11 (1958): 279–88.

Wheeler, John. *A Treatise of Commerce*. London: J. Harison, 1601.

Young, Arthur. *Political Arithmetic*. London: W. Nicoll, 1774.

CHAPTER FOUR
PHYSIOCRACY AND MORAL PHILOSOPHY

Bloomfield, Arthur I. "The Foreign-Trade Doctrines of the Physiocrats." *American Economic Review* 28 (December 1938): 716–35.

Cumberland, Richard. *De Legibus Naturae* (1672) [A Treatise on the Laws of Nature]. Translated by John Maxwell. London: R. Phillips, 1727.

de Mirabeau, Marquis. *The Oeconomical Table*. London: W. Owen, 1766.

Groenewegen, Peter D. "Turgot and Adam Smith." *Scottish Journal of Political Economy* 16 (November 1969): 271–89.

Hirschman, Albert O. *The Passions and the Interests: Political Arguments for Capitalism before Its Triumph*. Princeton: Princeton University Press, 1977.

Hume, David. *Political Discourses*. Edinburgh: R. Fleming, 1752.

————. *Essays and Treatises on Several Subjects*. London: A. Millar, 1758.

Hutcheson, Francis. *A System of Moral Philosophy*, 2 vols. London: A. Millar, 1755.

Hutchison, Terence. *Before Adam Smith: The Emergence of Political Economy, 1662–1776*. Cambridge: Basil Blackwell, 1988.

Kames, Lord (Henry Home). *Sketches of the History of Man*. Edinburgh: W. Creech, 1774.

Keohane, Nannerl O. *Philosophy and the State in France*. Princeton: Princeton University Press, 1980.

Kirk, Linda. *Richard Cumberland and Natural Law: The Secularisation of Thought in Seventeenth Century England*. Cambridge: J. Clark & Co., 1987.

Mandeville, Bernard. *The Fable of the Bees: or, Private Vices, Publick Benefits*. Edited by F. B. Kaye. Oxford: Clarendon Press, 1924.

Meek, Ronald L. "Physiocracy and Classicism in Britain," *Economic Journal* 26 (March 1951): 26–47.

Meyers, Milton. *The Soul of Modern Economic Man: Ideas about Self-Interest, Thomas Hobbes to Adam Smith*. Chicago: University of Chicago Press, 1983.

Quensay, François. "Corn." In *The Economics of Physiocracy: Essays and Translations*, edited by Ronald L. Meek. Cambridge: Harvard University Press, 1963.

————. *Tableau Économique (1758–59)*. Edited and translated by Marguerite Kuczynski and Ronald L. Meek. London: Macmillan, 1972.

Roberts, Hazel van Dyke. *Boisguilbert: Economist of the Reign of Louis XIV*. New York: Columbia University Press, 1935.

Ross, Ian. "The Physiocrats and Adam Smith." *British Journal for Eighteenth Century Studies* 7 (Spring 1984): 177–89.

Rothkrug, Lionel. *Opposition to Louis XIV: The Political and Social Origins of the French Enlightenment*. Princeton: Princeton University Press, 1965.

Schlereth, Thomas J. *The Cosmopolitan Ideal in Enlightenment Thought*. Notre Dame: University of Notre Dame Press, 1977.

Teichgraeber, Richard F. *"Free Trade" and Moral Philosophy: Rethinking the Sources of Adam Smith's Wealth of Nations.* Durham, N.C.: Duke University Press, 1986.

Tucker, Josiah. *A Brief Essay on the Advantages and Disadvantages with Regard to Trade.* London: T. Trye, 1749.

————. *A Second Letter to a Friend Concerning Naturalizations.* London: T. Trye, 1753.

————. *The Elements of Commerce, and Theory of Taxes.* Bristol?: privately printed, 1755.

————. *Instructions for Travelers.* Dublin: W. Watson, 1758.

Turgot, A.R.J. "Letter to L'Abbe Terray on the 'Marque des Fers' " (1773). In *The Economics of A.R.J. Turgot*, edited by Peter D. Groenewegen. The Hague: M. Nijhoff, 1977.

CHAPTER FIVE
ADAM SMITH'S CASE FOR FREE TRADE

Bloomfield, Arthur I. "Adam Smith and the Theory of International Trade." In *Essays on Adam Smith*, edited by A. S. Skinner and T. Wilson. Oxford: Clarendon Press, 1975.

Myint, Hla. "Adam Smith's Theory of International Trade in the Perspective of Economic Development." *Economica* 44 (August 1977): 231–48.

Rosenberg, Nathan. "Some Institutional Aspects of the *Wealth of Nations.*" *Journal of Political Economy* 68 (December 1960): 557–70.

Skinner, Andrew S. "The Shaping of Political Economy in the Enlightenment." *Scottish Journal of Political Economy* 37 (May 1990): 145–65.

Stigler, George J. "The Successes and Failures of Professor Smith." *Journal of Political Economy* 84 (December 1976): 1199–1213.

Smith, Adam. *The Theory of Moral Sentiments.* Edited by A. L. Macfie and D. D. Raphael. Oxford: Clarendon Press, 1976.

Smith, Adam. *Lectures on Jurisprudence.* Edited by R. L. Meek, D. D. Raphael, and P. G. Stein. Oxford: Clarendon Press, 1978.

Viner, Jacob. "Adam Smith and Laissez-Faire." *Journal of Political Economy* 35 (April 1927): 198–232.

CHAPTER SIX
FREE TRADE IN CLASSICAL ECONOMICS

Butt, Isaac. *Protection to Home Industry: Some Cases of its Advantages.* Dublin: Hodges & Smith, 1846.

Chipman, John S. "A Survey of the Theory of International Trade: Part 1, The Classical Theory," *Econometrica* 33 (July 1965): 477–519.

Cliffe Leslie, T. *Essays in Political Economy*, 2d ed. London: Longmans, Green & Co., 1888.

Considerations on the Effects of Protecting Duties. Dublin: Wilson, 1783.

"Corn Laws." *Edinburgh Review* 24 (February 1815): 491–505.

[Empson, William]. "Life, Writings, and Character of Mr. Malthus." *Edinburgh Review* 64 (January 1837): 469–506.

Hollander, Samuel. "Malthus's Abandonment of Agricultural Protectionism: A Discovery in the History of Economic Thought." *American Economic Review* 82 (June 1992): 650–59.

———. "More on Malthus and Agricultural Protection." *History of Political Economy* 27 (Fall 1995): 531–37.

James, Patricia. *Population Malthus*. London: Routledge & Kegan Paul, 1979.

Malthus, Thomas R. *The Grounds of an Opinion on the Policy of Restricting the Importation of Foreign Corn*. London: J. Murray, 1815.

———. *Principles of Political Economy*. London: J. Murray, 1820.

———. *An Essay on the Principle of Population*, 6th ed. London: J. Murray, 1826.

Mill, James. *Commerce Defended*. London: C. & R. Baldwin, 1808.

———. *Elements of Political Economy*. London: Baldwin, Cradock, & Joy, 1821.

[Mill, James]. "Colonies." In the *Encyclopaedia Britannica*, Supplement to the 4th, 5th, and 6th eds. Edinburgh: A. Constable, 1824.

———. "Corn Laws." *Eclectic Review*. n.s., 2 (July 1814): 1–17.

[Mill, John Stuart]. "The Corn Laws." *Westminster Review* 3 (April 1825): 394–420.

O'Brien, Denis P. *J. R. McCulloch: A Study in Classical Economics*. London: G. Allen & Unwin, 1970.

———. *The Classical Economists*. Oxford: Clarendon Press, 1975.

Pullen, J. M. "Malthus on Agricultural Protection: An Alternative View." *History of Political Economy* 27 (Fall 1995): 517–29.

Rashid, Salim. "Adam Smith's Rise of Fame: A Reexamination of the Evidence." *The Eighteenth Century* 23 (Winter 1982): 64–85.

Ricardo, David. *The Works and Correspondence of David Ricardo*. Edited by Piero Sraffa. Cambridge: Cambridge University Press, 1951–55.

Senior, Nassau. *Three Lectures on the Transmission of the Precious Metals from Country to Country and the Mercantile Theory of Wealth*. London: J. Murray, 1828.

Teichgraeber, Richard F. III. "'Less Abuse Than I Had Reason to Expect': The Reception of the Wealth of Nations in Britain, 1776–90," *Historical Journal* 30 (June 1987): 337–66.

Thweatt, William O. "James Mill and the Early Development of Comparative Advantage." *History of Political Economy* 8 (Summer 1976): 207–34.

Torrens, Robert. *The Economists Refuted*. London: S. A. Oddy, 1808.

———. *Essay on the External Corn Trade*. London: J. Hatchard, 1815.

[Vaughan, Benjamin]. *New and Old Principles of Trade Compared*. London: Johnson, 1788.

Willis, Kirk. "The Role in Parliament of the Economic Ideas of Adam Smith, 1776–1800." *History of Political Economy* 11 (Winter 1979): 505–44.

CHAPTER SEVEN
TORRENS AND THE TERMS OF TRADE ARGUMENT

Bickerdike, Charles F. "The Theory of Incipient Taxes." *Economic Journal* 16 (December 1906): 529–35.

Bickerdike, Charles F. "Review of A. C. Pigou's 'Protective and Preferential Import Duties.'" *Economic Journal* 17 (March 1907): 98–108.

"Colonel Torrens on Free Trade." *Westminster Review* 40 (August 1843): 1–20.

Corry, B. A. "Robert Torrens." In *The New Palgrave: A Dictionary of Economics*, edited by J. Eatwell et al. New York: Stockton Press, 1987.

Edgeworth, F. Y. "The Theory of International Values." *Economic Journal* 4 (March 1894): 35–50; (September 1894): 424–43; (December 1894): 606–38.

————. "Appreciations of Mathematical Theories." *Economic Journal* 18 (September 1908): 424–43; (December 1908): 541–56.

Johnson, Harry G. "Optimum Welfare and Maximum Revenue Tariffs." *Review of Economic Studies* 19 (1950–51): 28–35.

Kahn, Richard F. "Tariffs and the Terms of Trade." *Review of Economic Studies* 15 (1947–48): 14–19.

Kaldor, Nicholas. "A Note on Tariffs and the Terms of Trade." *Economica* 7 (November 1940): 377–80.

Lawson, James Anthony. *Five Lectures on Political Economy*. London: Parker, 1843.

Longfield, Montiford. *Three Lectures on Commerce and One on Absenteeism*. Dublin: W. Curry, Jun, & Co., 1835.

Marshall, Alfred. *Money, Credit and Commerce*. London: Macmillan, 1923.

————. *Memorials of Alfred Marshall*. Edited by A. C. Pigou. London: Macmillan, 1925.

McCulloch, J. R. *Principles of Political Economy*, 4th ed. London: Longman, Brown, Green, and Longmans, 1849.

Merivale, Herman. *Lectures on Colonization and Colonies*. London: Longman, Brown, Green, and Longmans, 1842.

[Mill, J. S.]. "Torrens's Letter to Sir Robert Peel," *Spectator*, January 28, 1843, pp. 85–86. Reprinted in *Collected Works of John Stuart Mill*, vol. 24. Toronto: University of Toronto Press, 1986.

Mill, John Stuart. *Essays on Some Unsettled Questions of Political Economy*. London: Parker, 1844.

Nicholson, J. S. "Tariffs and International Commerce." *Scottish Geographical Magazine* 7 (September 1891): 457–71.

————. *Principles of Political Economy*, vol. 3. London: Macmillan, 1901.

Norman, George Warde. *Remarks on the Incidence of Import Duties*. London: privately printed by Boone, 1860.

O'Brien, Denis P., ed. *The Correspondence of Lord Overstone*. Cambridge: Cambridge University Press, 1971.

Palgrave, R.H.I., ed., *Dictionary of Political Economy*. London: Macmillan, 1913.

Political Economy Club. *Centenary Volume*. London: Macmillan, 1921.

"Professor Lawson's Lectures on Political Economy." *Dublin University Magazine* 24 (December 1844): 721–24.

"Reciprocal Free Trade." *Foreign and Colonial Quarterly Review* 2 (October 1843): 526–51.

Ricardo, David. *The Works and Correspondence of David Ricardo*. Edited by Piero Sraffa. Cambridge: Cambridge University Press, 1951–55.

Robbins, Lionel. *Robert Torrens and the Evolution of Classical Economics*. London: Macmillan, 1958.

Rodriguez, Carlos Alfredo. "The Non-Equivalence of Tariffs and Quotas Under Retaliation." *Journal of International Economics* 4 (August 1974): 295–98.

[Senior, Nassau]. "Free Trade and Retaliation." *Edinburgh Review* 78 (July 1843): 1–47.

Sidgwick, Henry. *Principles of Political Economy.* London: Macmillan, 1883.

[Thompson, Perronet]. "Col. Torrens's Letters on Commercial Policy." *Westminster Review* 8 (January 1833): 168–76. (*a*)

————. "Colonel Torrens's Additional Letters on Commercial Policy." *Westminster Review* 8 (April 1833): 421–27. (*b*)

Thweatt, William O. "James and John Mill on Comparative Advantage: Sraffa's Account Corrected." In *Trade in Transit,* edited by H. Visser and E. Schorl. Dordrecht: M. Nijhoff, 1987.

Torrens, Robert. *An Essay on the Production of Wealth.* London: Longman, Hurst, Rees, Orme, and Brown, 1821.

————. *Letters on Commercial Policy.* London: Longman, 1833.

————. *The Budget: On Commercial and Colonial Policy.* London: Smith, Elder, 1844.

CHAPTER EIGHT
MILL AND THE INFANT INDUSTRY ARGUMENT

Armitage-Smith, George. *The Free Trade Movement and Its Results.* London: Blackie, 1898.

Baldwin, Robert E. "The Case Against Infant Industry Protection." *Journal of Political Economy* 77 (May/June 1969): 295–305.

Bastable, Charles F. *The Theory of International Trade.* Dublin: Hodges, Figgis, 1887.

Bentham, Jeremy. "Observations on the Restrictive and Prohibitory Commercial System (1821)." In *The Works of Jeremy Bentham,* edited by John Bowring, vol. 3. Edinburgh: Tait, 1843.

Bourne, E. G. "Alexander Hamilton and Adam Smith." *Quarterly Journal of Economics* 8 (April 1894): 328–44.

Brewer, Anthony. "Economic Growth and Technical Change: John Rae's Critique of Adam Smith." *History of Political Economy* 11 (Spring 1991): 1–11.

Cairnes, John E. *Some Leading Principles of Political Economy, Newly Expounded.* London: Macmillan, 1874.

Carey, Henry. *Principles of Social Science.* Philadelphia: Lippincott, 1858.

Deane, Phyllis. "Marshall on Free Trade." In *Alfred Marshall in Retrospect,* edited by R. M. Tullberg. New York: Elgar, 1990.

Dobbs, Arthur. *An Essay on the Trade and Improvement of Ireland.* Dublin: Rhames, 1729.

Fauveau, P.-G. "Conclusion du Calcul Algébrique au Sujet des droits Protecteurs." *Journal des Économistes* 64 (August 1873): 283–86, and 64 (September 1873): 464.

Fawcett, Henry. *Free Trade and Protection.* London: Macmillan, 1878.

Hamilton, Alexander. "Report on the Subject of Manufactures [1791]." In *The Papers of Alexander Hamilton,* edited by Harold C. Syrett, vol. X, December 1791– January 1792. New York: Columbia University Press, 1966.

Hutcheson, Francis. *Introduction to Moral Philosophy.* 2d ed. Glasgow: R. & A. Foulis, 1753.

Johnson, Harry. "Optimal Trade Intervention in the Presence of Domestic Distortions." In Robert E. Baldwin et al., *Trade, Growth and the Balance of Payments.* Chicago: Rand McNally & Co., 1965.

List, Friedrich. *The National System of Political Economy.* Translated by G. A. Matile. Philadelphia: J. B. Lippincott, 1854.

———. *The National System of Political Economy.* Translated by Sampson S. Lloyd. London: Longman, Green & Co., 1885.

Marshall, Alfred. "Some Aspects of Competition (1890)." In *Memorials of Alfred Marshall,* edited by A.C. Pigou. London: Macmillan, 1925.

———. "Memorandum on Fiscal Policy of International Trade (1903)." In *Official Papers by Alfred Marshall,* edited by J. M. Keynes. London: Macmillan, 1926.

Meade, James. *Trade and Welfare.* London: Oxford University Press, 1955.

Melitz, Jacques. "Sidgwick's Theory of International Values." *Economic Journal* 73 (September 1963): 431–41.

Mill, John Stuart. *Principles of Political Economy.* London: Longmans, Green, 1909.

Nicholson, J. S. *Principles of Political Economy.* London: Macmillan, 1901.

O'Brien, Denis P. *J. R. McCulloch: A Study in Classical Economics.* New York: Barnes and Noble, 1970.

Pigou, A. C. *Protective and Preferential Import Duties.* London: Macmillan, 1906.

Postlethwayt, Malachy. *Britain's Commercial Interest Explained and Improved.* London: D. Brown, 1757.

Rae, John. *Statement of Some New Principles of Political Economy.* Boston: Hilliard, Gray, 1834.

Say, Jean-Baptiste. *A Treatise on Political Economy.* Philadelphia: Grigg & Elliot, 1834.

Scrope, George Poulett. *Principles of Political Economy.* London: Longmans, Rees, Orme, Brown, and Green, 1833.

Simonde de Sismondi, Jean-Charles-Léonard. *Political Economy* (1815). Fairfield, N.J.: A. M. Kelley, 1991.

———. *New Principles of Political Economy* (1826). Translated by Richard Hyse. New Brunswick, N.J.: Transaction Publishers, 1990.

Steuart, James. *An Inquiry into the Principles of Political Oeconomy* (1767). Edited by A. S. Skinner. Edinburgh: Oliver & Boyd, 1966.

Sumner, William Graham. *Protectionism.* New York: Holt, 1885.

Taussig, Frank W. *Protection to Young Industries as Applied in the United States.* Cambridge: Harvard University Press, 1883.

Tucker, Josiah. *Instructions for Travelers.* Dublin: W. Watson, 1758.

Wood, William. *A Survey of Trade.* London: W. Wilkins, 1718.

Yarranton, Andrew. *England's Improvement by Sea and Land.* London: Everingham, 1677.

CHAPTER NINE
GRAHAM AND THE INCREASING RETURNS ARGUMENT

Anderson, Karl. "Tariff Protection and Increasing Returns." In *Explorations in Economics: Notes and Essays Contributed in Honor of F. W. Taussig.* New York: McGraw-Hill, 1936.

Carver, Thomas. "Some Theoretical Possibilities of a Protective Tariff." *Publications of the American Economic Association*. 3d. ser., vol. 3, no. 1 (1902): 167–82.

Chipman, John S. "A Survey of the Theory of International Trade: Part 2, The Neo-Classical Theory," *Econometrica* 33 (October 1965): 685–760.

Edgeworth, F. Y. "Review of Henry Cunynghame's 'A Geometrical Political Economy.'" *Economic Journal* 15 (March 1905): 62–71.

Ethier, Wilfred J. "National and International Returns to Scale in the Modern Theory of International Trade." *American Economic Review* 72 (June 1982): 389–405. (*a*)

——. "Decreasing Costs in International Trade and Frank Graham's Argument for Protection." *Econometrica* 50 (September 1982): 1243–68. (*b*)

Graham, Frank D. "Some Aspects of Protection Further Considered." *Quarterly Journal of Economics* 37 (February 1923): 199–227.

——. "Some Fallacies in the Interpretation of Social Cost: A Reply." *Quarterly Journal of Economics* 39 (February 1925): 324–30.

——. *Protective Tariffs*. New York: Harper & Bros., 1934.

Knight, Frank H. "Some Fallacies in the Interpretation of Social Cost." *Quarterly Journal of Economics* 38 (August 1924): 582–606.

——. "On Decreasing and Comparative Cost: A Rejoinder." *Quarterly Journal of Economics* 39 (February 1925): 331–33.

Markusen, James R. "The Microfoundations of External Economies," *Canadian Journal of Economics* 23 (August 1990): 495–508.

Marshall, Alfred. *Principles of Economics*, 8th ed. London: Macmillan, 1920.

——. "Some Aspects of Competition (1890)." In *Memorials of Alfred Marshall*, edited by A.C. Pigou. London: Macmillan, 1925.

Matthews, R.C.O. "Reciprocal Demand and Increasing Returns." *Review of Economic Studies* 17 (1949–50): 149–58.

Nicholson, J. S. *Principles of Political Economy*, vol. 2. New York: Macmillan, 1897.

Panagariya, Arvind. "Variable Returns to Scale in Production and Patterns of Specialization," *American Economic Review* 71 (March 1981): 221–30.

Prendergast, Renee. "Increasing Returns and Competitive Equilibrium—The Content and Development of Marshall's Theory." *Cambridge Journal of Economics* 16 (December 1992): 447–62.

Price, L. L. "Review of J. S. Nicholson's 'Principles of Political Economy.'" *Economic Journal* 8 (March 1898): 60–64.

Robertson, Dennis H. "Those Empty Boxes." *Economic Journal* 34 (March 1924): 16–30.

Robinson, E.A.G. *The Structure of Competitive Industry*. Cambridge: Cambridge University Press, 1931.

Scitovsky, Tibor. "Two Concepts of External Economies," *Journal of Political Economy* 17 (April 1954): 143–51.

Senior, Nassau. *An Outline of the Science of Political Economy*. London: W. Clowes & Sons, 1836.

Taussig, Frank. *International Trade*. New York: Macmillan, 1927.

Tinbergen, Jan. "Professor Graham's Case for Protection." Appendix 1 in *International Economic Cooperation*. Amsterdam: Elsevier, 1945.

Viner, Jacob. "Cost Curves and Supply Curves," *Zeitschrift für Nationalökonomie* 3 (1931): 23–46.

Walker, Francis. "Increasing and Diminishing Costs in International Trade." *Yale Review* 12 (May 1903): 32–59.

[West, Edward]. *Essay on the Application of Capital to Land.* London: T. Underwood, 1815.

Chapter Ten
Manoïlescu and the Wage Differential Argument

Balogh, Thomas. "The Concept of a Dollar Shortage." *The Manchester School of Economic and Social Studies* 17 (May 1949): 186–201.

Bastable, Charles F. *The Theory of International Trade*, 3d ed. London: Macmillan, 1900.

Bhagwati, Jagdish. "The Generalized Theory of Distortions and Welfare." In Jagdish Bhagwati et al., *Trade, Balance of Payments, and Growth.* Amsterdam: North Holland, 1971.

Bhagwati, Jagdish, and V. K. Ramaswami. "Domestic Distortions, Tariffs, and the Theory of Optimum Subsidy." *Journal of Political Economy* 71 (February 1963): 44–50.

Cairnes, John E. *Some Leading Principles of Political Economy, Newly Expounded.* London: Macmillan, 1874.

Coats, A. W. "Changing Attitudes to Labor in the Mid-Eighteenth Century." *Economic History Review* 11 (August 1958): 35–51.

Corden, W. M. "Tariffs, Subsidies, and the Terms of Trade." *Economica* 24 (August 1957): 235–42.

The Grand Concern of England Explained. London: n.p., 1673.

Haberler, Gottfried. "Some Problems in the Pure Theory of International Trade," *Economic Journal* 60 (June 1950): 223–40.

Hagen, Everett E. "An Economic Justification of Protectionism," *Quarterly Journal of Economics* 72 (November 1958): 496–514.

Harris, John R., and Michael P. Todaro. "Migration, Unemployment, and Development: A Two-Sector Analysis." *American Economic Review* 60 (March 1970): 126–42.

Hont, Istvan. "The 'Rich Country-Poor Country' Debate in Scottish Classical Political Economy." In *Wealth and Virtue: The Shaping of Political Economy in the Scottish Enlightenment*, edited by Istvan Hont and Michael Ignatieff. New York: Cambridge University Press, 1983.

Hume, David. *Essays and Treatises on Several Subjects.* London: A. Millar, 1758.

———. *Writings on Economics.* Edited by Eugene Rotwein. Madison: University of Wisconsin Press, 1955.

Johnson, Harry. "Optimal Trade Intervention in the Presence of Domestic Distortions." In Robert E. Baldwin et al., *Trade, Growth and the Balance of Payments.* Chicago: Rand McNally & Co., 1965.

Longfield, Montiford. *Three Lectures on Commerce and One on Absenteeism.* Dublin: Milliken & Son, 1835.

Low, J. M. "An Eighteenth Century Controversy in the Theory of Economic Progress." *Manchester School of Economics and Social Science* 20 (September 1952): 311–30.

Magee, Stephen P. "Factor Market Distortions, Production, and Trade: A Survey." *Oxford Economic Papers* 25 (March 1973): 1–43.

Maitland, James (Earl of Lauderdale). *An Inquiry into the Nature and Origin of Public Wealth.* Edinburgh: Archibald Constable & Co., 1804.

Manly, Thomas. *Usury at Six Percent Examined.* London: T. Radcliffe and T. Daniel, 1669.

Manoïlescu, Mihaïl. *The Theory of Protection and International Trade.* London: P. S. King, 1931.

———. "Arbeitsproduktivität und Auaenhandel." *Weltwirtschaftliches Archiv* 42 (1935): 13–43.

Meade, James E. *Trade and Welfare.* London: Oxford University Press, 1955.

Myint, Hla. "The 'Classical Theory' of International Trade and Underdeveloped Countries." *Economic Journal* 68 (June 1958): 317–37.

Nicholson, J. S. *Principles of Political Economy.* Vol. 2. London: Macmillan, 1897.

Ohlin, Bertil. "Protection and Non-Competing Groups." *Weltwirtschaftliches Archiv* 33 (1931): 30–45.

[Powell, John]. *View of Real Grievances.* London: n. p., 1772.

Propositions for Improving the Manufactures, Agriculture, and Commerce of Great Britain. London: W. Sandby, 1763.

Semmel, Bernard. "The Hume-Tucker Debate and Pitt's Trade Proposals." *Economic Journal* 75 (December 1965): 759–70.

Senior, Nassau. *Three Lectures on the Cost of Obtaining Money.* London: John Murray, 1830.

Taussig, Frank. "Wages and Prices in Relation to International Trade." *Quarterly Journal of Economics* 20 (August 1906): 497–522.

———. *International Trade.* New York: Macmillan, 1927.

Tucker, Josiah. *Four Tracts Together with Two Sermons, On Political and Commercial Subjects.* Gloucester: R. Raikes, 1774.

Viner, Jacob. "Review of Mihaïl Manoïlescu's 'The Theory of Protection and International Trade.'" *Journal of Political Economy* 40 (February 1932): 121–25.

Wallace, Robert. *Characteristics of the Present Political State of Great Britain.* London: A. Millar, 1758.

CHAPTER ELEVEN

THE AUSTRALIAN CASE FOR PROTECTION

Anderson, Karl L. "Protection and the Historical Situation: Australia." *Quarterly Journal of Economics* 53 (November 1938): 86–104.

Bastable, Charles F. *The Theory of International Trade.* Dublin: Hodges and Figgis, 1887; 3d ed. London: Macmillan, 1903.

———. "Economic Notes." *Hermathena* 7 (1890): 109–25.

———. "On Some Disputed Points in the Theory of International Trade," *Economic Journal* 11 (July 1901): 226–29.

Brigden, J. B. "The Australian Tariff and the Standard of Living." *Economic Record* 1 (November 1925): 29–46.

Brigden, J. B. et al. *The Australian Tariff: An Economic Inquiry*. Melbourne: Melbourne University Press, 1929.

Copland, D. B. "A Neglected Phase of Tariff Controversy." *Quarterly Journal of Economics* 45 (February 1931): 289–308.

Edgeworth, F. Y. "The Theory of International Values, III." *Economic Journal* 4 (December 1894): 606–38.

———. "Review of Charles Bastable's 'The Theory of International Trade, 2nd ed.'" *Economic Journal* 7 (September 1897): 397–403.

———. "Review of Charles Bastable's 'The Theory of International Trade, 3rd ed.'" *Economic Journal* 10 (September 1900): 389–93.

———. "Disputed Points in the Theory of International Trade." *Economic Journal* 11 (December 1901): 582–95.

Loria, Achille. "Notes on the Theory of International Trade." *Economic Journal* 11 (March 1901): 85–89.

Manger, Gary. "The Australian Case for Protection Reconsidered." *Australian Economic Papers* 20 (December 1981): 193–204.

Metzler, Lloyd. "Tariffs, the Terms of Trade, and the Distribution of National Income." *Journal of Political Economy* 62 (February 1949): 1–29.

Nicholson, J. S. *Principles of Political Economy*, vol. 2. London: Macmillan, 1897.

Patten, Simon N. *The Economic Basis of Protection*. Philadelphia: Lippincott, 1890.

Ruffin, Roy J., and Ronald W. Jones. "Protection and Real Wages: The Neoclassical Ambiguity." *Journal of Economic Theory* 14 (April 1977): 337–48.

Samuelson, Marion Crawford. "The Australian Case for Protection Reexamined." *Quarterly Journal of Economics* 54 (November 1939): 143–49.

Samuelson, Paul A. "Summing Up on the Australian Case for Protection." *Quarterly Journal of Economics* 96 (February 1981): 147–60.

Sidgwick, Henry. *Principles of Political Economy*. London: Macmillan, 1883; 3d ed., 1901.

Stolper, Wolfgang F., and Paul A. Samuelson. "Protection and Real Wages." *Review of Economic Studies* 9 (November 1941): 58–73.

Taussig, Frank W. "Recent Literature on Protection." *Quarterly Journal of Economics* 7 (January 1893): 162–76.

Torrens, Robert. *An Essay on the Production of Wealth*. London: Longman, Hurst, Rees, Orme, and Brown, 1821.

Viner, Jacob. "The Australian Tariff: A Review Article." *Economic Record* 5 (November 1929): 306–15.

CHAPTER TWELVE

THE WELFARE ECONOMICS OF FREE TRADE

Chipman, John S. "The Paretian Heritage." *Revue Européenne des Sciences Sociales et Cahiers Vilfredo Pareto*. 14 (1976): 65–171.

———. "Compensation Principle." In *The New Palgrave: A Dictionary of Economics*, edited by J. Eatwell et al. New York: Stockton Press, 1987.

Chipman, John S., and James C. Moore. "The New Welfare Economics, 1939–1974." *International Economic Review* 19 (October 1978): 547–84.

Graaf, J. de V. "On Optimum Tariff Structures." *Review of Economic Studies* 17 (1949–50): 47–59.

Grandmont, Jean M., and Daniel McFadden. "A Technical Note on Classical Gains from Trade." *Journal of International Economics* 2 (May 1972): 109–25.

Harrod, Roy. "Scope and Method of Economics." *Economic Journal* 48 (September 1938): 383–412.

Hicks, John R. "The Foundations of Welfare Economics." *Economic Journal* 49 (December 1939): 696–712.

———. "The Valuation of Social Income." *Economica* n.s. 7 (May 1940): 105–24.

Kaldor, Nicholas. "Welfare Propositions of Economics and Interpersonal Comparisons of Utility." *Economic Journal* 49 (September 1939): 549–52.

Kemp, Murray C. "The Gain from International Trade." *Economic Journal* 82 (December 1962): 803–19.

Maneschi, Andrea. "Pareto on International Trade Theory and Policy." *Journal of the History of Economic Thought* 15 (Fall 1993): 210–28.

Maneschi, Andrea, and William O. Thweatt. "Barone's 1908 Representation of an Economy's Trade Equilibrium and the Gains from Trade." *Journal of International Economics* 22 (May 1987): 375–82.

[Mill, John Stuart]. "The Corn Laws." *Westminster Review* 3 (April 1825): 394–420.

Mill, John Stuart. "On the Definition of Political Economy; and on the Method of Investigation Proper to It." *London and Westminster Review* 26 (October 1836): 1–29. Reprinted in *Essays on Some Unsettled Questions of Political Economy*. London: Parker, 1844.

Pareto, Vilfredo. "Il Massimo di Utilità dato dalla Libera Concorrenza," *Giornale degli Economisti* 9 (July 1894): 48–66.

———. "Teoria Matematica del Commercio Internazionale," *Giornale degli Economisti* 10 (April 1895): 476–98.

Robbins, Lionel. *An Essay on the Nature and Significance of Economic Science.* London: Macmillan, 1932.

———. "Interpersonal Comparisons of Utility: A Comment." *Economic Journal* 48 (December 1938): 635–41.

Samuelson, Paul A. "The Gains from International Trade." *Canadian Journal of Economics and Political Science* 5 (May 1939): 195–205.

———. "The Gains from International Trade Once Again." *Economic Journal* 82 (December 1962): 820–29.

Scitovsky, Tibor. "A Note on Welfare Propositions in Economics." *Review of Economic Studies* 9 (November 1941): 77–88.

Sen, A. K. "The Welfare Basis of Real Income Comparisons." *Journal of Economic Literature* 17 (March 1979): 1–45.

Senior, Nassau. *Outline of the Science of Political Economy.* London: W. Clowes & Sons, 1836.

———. "Presidential Address to Section F of the British Association for the Advancement of Science." *Report of the British Association for the Advancement of Science.* London, 1860.

CHAPTER THIRTEEN
KEYNES AND THE MACROECONOMICS OF PROTECTION

Alexander, Sidney S. "Devaluation versus Import Restrictions as an Instrument for Improving the Foreign Trade Balance." *IMF Staff Papers* 1 (April 1951): 379–96.

Beveridge, William, ed. *Tariffs: The Case Examined*. London: Longmans Green, 1931.

Bickerdike, C. F. "Review of Richard Schüller's 'Schutzzoll und Freihandel.'" *Economic Journal* 15 (September 1905): 413–15.

Clark, Peter. *The Keynesian Revolution in the Making, 1924–1936*. Oxford: Oxford University Press, 1988.

Collyns, Charles. *Can Protection Cure Unemployment?* Thames Essay No. 31. London: Trade Policy Research Centre, 1982.

Corden, W. M. "Real Wage Rigidity, Devaluation, and Import Restriction." In *Protection, Growth, and Trade*. New York: Basil Blackwell, 1985.

Corden, W. M., I.M.D. Little, and M. FG. Scott. "Import Controls versus Devaluation and Britain's Economic Prospects." Guest Paper No. 2, London: Trade Policy Research Centre, March 1975.

Department of Applied Economics. University of Cambridge. *Economic Policy Review*. February 1975, March 1976.

Eichengreen, Barry. "A Dynamic Model of Tariffs, Output, and Employment under Flexible Exchange Rates." *Journal of International Economics* 11 (August 1981): 341–59.

———. "Protection, Real Wage Resistance, and Employment." *Weltwirtschaftliches Archiv* 119 (1983): 429–51.

———. "Keynes and Protection." *Journal of Economic History* 44 (June 1984): 363–73.

Friedman, Milton. "The Case for Flexible Exchange Rates." In *Essays on Positive Economics*. Chicago: University of Chicago Press, 1953.

———. "The Role of Monetary Policy." *American Economic Review* 58 (March 1968): 1–17.

Godley, Wynne, and Robert M. May. "The Macroeconomic Implications of Devaluation and Import Restrictions." *Economic Policy Review*, March 1977.

Haberler, Gottfried. "Currency Depreciation and the Terms of Trade (1952)." In *Selected Essays of Gottfried Haberler*, edited by A.Y.C. Koo. Cambridge: MIT Press, 1985.

Hawtrey, R. G. *Trade Depression and the Way Out*. London: Longmans Green, 1931.

Hicks, J. R. "Free Trade and Modern Economics." In *Essays in World Economics*. Oxford: Clarendon Press, 1959.

Hinshaw, Randall. "Keynesian Commercial Policy." In *The New Economics: Keynes' Influence on Theory and Public Policy*, edited by Seymour E. Harris. New York: A. A. Knopf, 1947.

Howson, Susan, and Donald Winch. *The Economic Advisory Council, 1930–39*. Cambridge: Cambridge University Press, 1977.

Keynes, John Maynard. *The Collected Writings of John Maynard Keynes*. Edited by Elizabeth Johnson and Donald Moggridge. London: Macmillan for the Royal Economics Society, 1971–89.

Meade, James. "The Case for Variable Exchange Rates." *Three Banks Review*, September 1955.

Moggridge, D. E. *Maynard Keynes: An Economist's Biography*. New York: Routledge, 1992.

Mundell, Robert A. "Flexible Exchange Rates and Employment Policy." *Canadian Journal of Economics and Political Science* 27 (November 1961): 509–17.

Radice, Hugo. "Keynes and the Policy of Practical Protectionism." In *J. M. Keynes in Retrospect: The Legacy of the Keynesian Revolution*, edited by John Hillard. Aldershot, England: Edward Elgar Pub., 1988.

Robbins, Lionel. "Economic Notes on Some Arguments for Protection." *Economica* 11 (February 1931): 45–62.

———. *Autobiography of an Economist*. London: Macmillan, 1971.

Robinson, Joan. "Beggar-my-Neighbour Remedies for Unemployment." In *Essays in the Theory of Employment*. New York: Macmillan, 1937.

———. "The Pure Theory of International Trade." *Review of Economic Studies* 14 (1946–47): 112.

Taussig, Frank W., ed. *Selected Readings in International Trade and Tariff Problems*. Boston: Ginn & Co., 1921.

Wolf, Bernard M., and Nicholas P. Smook. "Keynes and the Question of Tariffs," In *Keynes and Public Policy After Fifty Years*, edited by O. F. Hamouda and J. N. Smithin, vol. 2. New York: New York University Press, 1988.

CHAPTER FOURTEEN
STRATEGIC TRADE POLICY

Anderson, Gary M., and Robert D. Tollison. "Adam Smith's Analysis of Joint-Stock Companies." *Journal of Political Economy* 90 (December 1982): 1237–56.

Baldwin, Robert E. "Are Economists' Traditional Trade Policy Views Still Valid?" *Journal of Economic Literature* 30 (June 1992): 804–29.

Bhagwati, Jagdish. "Is Free Trade Passé After All?" *Weltwirtschaftliches Archiv* 125 (1989): 17–44.

Brander, James A. "Rationales for Strategic Trade and Industrial Policy." In *Strategic Trade Policy and the New International Economics*, edited by Paul R. Krugman. Cambridge: MIT Press, 1986.

———. "Strategic Trade Policy." In *The Handbook of International Economics*, vol. 3, edited by Gene M. Grossman and Kenneth Rogoff. Amsterdam: North-Holland, 1995.

Brander, James A., and Barbara J. Spencer. "Tariffs and the Extraction of Foreign Monopoly Rents under Potential Entry." *Canadian Journal of Economics* 14 (August 1981): 371–89.

———. "Export Subsidies and International Market Share Rivalry." *Journal of International Economics* 18 (February 1985): 83–100.

Carmichael, Calum M., "The Control of Export Credit Subsidies and its Welfare Consequences." *Journal of International Economics* 23 (August 1987): 1–19.

Cournot, Augustin. *Researches into the Mathematical Principles of the Theory of Wealth* (1838). Translated by Nathaniel T. Bacon. New York: Macmillan, 1927.

Dixit, Avinash. "International Trade Policy for Oligopolistic Industries." *Economic Journal* (Supplement) 94 (1984): 1–16.

Dixit, Avinash, and Gene M. Grossman. "Targeted Export Promotion with Several Oligopolistic Industries." *Journal of International Economics* 21 (November 1986): 233–49.

Dixit, Avinash, and Albert S. Kyle. "The Use of Protection and Subsidies for Entry Promotion and Deterrence." *American Economic Review* 75 (March 1985): 139–52.

Eaton, Jonathan, and Gene M. Grossman. "Optimal Trade and Industrial Policy Under Oligopoly." *Quarterly Journal of Economics* 101 (May 1986): 383–406.

Ekelund, Jr., Robert B., and Robert F. Hébert. "Cournot and His Contemporaries: Is an Obituary the Only Bad Review?" *Southern Economic Journal* 57 (July 1990): 139–49.

Enke, Stephen. "A Monopsony Case for Tariffs." *Quarterly Journal of Economics* 58 (February 1944): 229–45.

Grossman, Gene M. "Strategic Export Promotion: A Critique." In *Strategic Trade Policy and the New International Economics*, edited by Paul R. Krugman. Cambridge: MIT Press, 1986.

Horstmann, Ignatius J., and James R. Markusen. "Up the Average Cost Curve: Inefficient Entry and the New Protectionism." *Journal of International Economics* 20 (May 1986): 225–47.

Irwin, Douglas A. "Mercantilism as Strategic Trade Policy: The Anglo-Dutch Rivalry for the East India Trade." *Journal of Political Economy* 99 (December 1991): 1296–1314.

―――. "Mercantilist Trade Rivalries and Strategic Trade Policy." *American Economic Review* (Papers and Proceedings) 82 (May 1992): 134–39.

Krugman, Paul R. "Is Free Trade Passé?" *Journal of Economic Perspectives* 1 (Fall 1987): 131–41.

―――. "Does the New Trade Theory Require a New Trade Policy?" *The World Economy* 15 (July 1992): 423–41.

Lee, Sanghack. "International Equity Markets and Trade Policy." *Journal of International Economics* 29 (August 1990): 173–84.

Magnan de Bornier, Jean. "The 'Cournot-Bertrand Debate': A Historical Perspective.' *History of Political Economy* 24 (Fall 1992): 623–56.

Schneider, Erich. "Vilfredo Pareto: The Economist in Light of His Letters to Maffeo Pantaleoni." *Banca Nazionale del Lavoro Quarterly Review* 14 (September 1961): 247–95.

Spencer, Barbara J., and James A. Brander. "International R&D Rivalry and Industrial Strategy." *Review of Economic Studies* 50 (October 1983): 707–22.

Conclusion

Athukorala, Premachandra, and James Riedel. "The Small Country Assumption: A Reassessment with Evidence from Korea." *Weltwirtschaftliches Archiv* 127 (1991): 138–51.

Bhagwati, Jagdish. "The Generalized Theory of Distortions and Welfare." *Trade, Balance of Payments and Growth: Papers in International Economics in Honor of Charles P. Kindleberger*. Edited by J. N. Bhagwati, R. A. Mundell, R. W. Jones, and J. Vanek. Amsterdam: North-Holland, 1971.

Brown, Drusilla K. "Tariffs, the Terms of Trade and National Product Differentiation." *Journal of Policy Modeling* 9 (Fall 1987): 503–26.

Edgeworth, F. Y. "The Pure Theory of International Values." *Economic Journal* 4 (March 1894): 35–50.

Farrer, Thomas H. *Free Trade versus Fair Trade*, 3d ed. London: Cassell & Co., 1886.

Graham, Frank D. *Protective Tariffs*. New York: Harper & Bros., 1934.

Hicks, John R. "Free Trade and Modern Economics." In *Essays in World Economics*. Oxford: Clarendon Press, 1959.

Jevons, William Stanley. *Methods of Social Reform*. London: Macmillan, 1883.

Johnson, Harry. "Optimum Tariffs and Retaliation." *Review of Economic Studies* 21 (1953–54): 142–53.

———. "Implications of the International Corporation." In *Studies in International Economics*, edited by I. A. McDougall and R. H. Snape. Amsterdam: North-Holland, 1970.

Krugman, Paul R. "Is Free Trade Passé?" *Journal of Economic Perspectives* 1 (Fall 1987): 131–44.

Laudan, Larry. *Progress and Its Problems: Towards a Theory of Scientific Growth*. Berkeley: University of California Press, 1977.

Little, Ian, Tibor Scitovsky, and Maurice Scott. *Industry and Trade in Some Developing Countries*. London: Oxford University Press, 1970.

Marshall, Alfred. "Memorandum on Fiscal Policy of International Trade (1903)." In *Official Papers by Alfred Marshall*, edited by J. M. Keynes. London: Macmillan, 1926.

Riedel, James. "The Demand for LDC Exports of Manufactures: Estimates from Hong Kong." *Economic Journal* 98 (March 1988): 138–48.

Sidgwick, Henry. *The Scope and Method of Economic Science*. London: Macmillan, 1885.

———. *Principles of Political Economy*, 2d ed. London: Macmillan, 1887.

Taussig, Frank W. "The Present Position of the Doctrine of Free Trade." *Publications of the American Economic Association*, 3d ser. 6 (February 1905): 29–65. Reprinted in Frank W. Taussig, *Free Trade, the Tariff, and Reciprocity*. New York: Macmillan, 1920.

Whalley, John. *Trade Liberalization among Major World Trading Areas*. Cambridge: MIT Press, 1985.

World Bank. *The World Development Report, 1987*. New York: Oxford University Press for the World Bank, 1987.

INDEX

Italicized numbers indicate illustrations.

DOUGLAS A. IRWIN is Associate Professor of Business Economics, Graduate School of Business, University of Chicago.